PRAISE FOR STATISTICS FOR PEOPLE WHO (THINK THEY) HATE STATISTICS, SECOND EDITION, BY NEIL J. SALKIND

Your statistics book is several orders of magnitude better than any other I have seen, knowledgeable and professional, but approachable by the mathematically-challenged student. Again, you should be very proud of your statistics book. It is a towering pedagogical achievement.

—John Evans, Professor
Nova Southeastern University
Assistant Vice President at the Educational Testing Service

I just finished reading *Statistics for People* . . . and I loved it. I only wish I would have known about the existence of it when I was struggling through my first two statistics courses in graduate school. My understanding of the basics of statistics was quite limited and your book has clarified things considerably.

—Jared A. Farley
Department of Political Science
Miami University

As an English Professor forced by default into being the statistician for a grant report, I was delighted to find *Statistics for People*. . . . In just a few weeks it helped me to provide convincing data, in the proper form, in order to show that our experiment worked with a high degree of significance.

—Roger Connor
Emeritus Professor of English
Wilbur Wright College

I put off returning to complete my PhD due to fear of statistics courses. Your book helped build a solid foundation of understanding for me and I have since completed multivariate statistics and regression analysis classes; I still returned to your book to clarify the concepts. Your book truly took the fear out of statistics for me and obviously gave me a solid foundation.

—Jane Fink
The University of Akron
Medina, Ohio

(Continued)

I just want to say that I love your book. As an undergrad, statistics classes were the bane of my academic existence. Now, while taking a research methods class for my master's degree in education, my class is using your book as a guide for developing a practical understanding of the statistics found in educational research, and I wish I'd had it ten years ago as an undergrad as well! Thanks for writing about a dry subject with a sense of humor; it makes all the difference in the world.

—Sarah Stack
Graduate Student
Northeastern Illinois University

I enjoyed *Statistics for People Who (Think They) Hate Statistics* and I appreciate your work. It serves very well, even for someone like me who took statistics before and would like to have a quick review.

—Ashley Lanting, PhD
Formative Evaluation Research Associates
Kalamazoo, MI

I am using the text you authored in order to assist me in my statistics class. I just want to say that it is extremely helpful and I can't thank you enough for putting it together. Although I have yet to begin on my assignments, your book is exposing me to the language of statistics, which our textbook does not do.

—Saima R. Khalil

I just finished a statistics course in which we used your book, *Statistics for People Who (Think They) Hate Statistics,* and I want to thank you! I have *never* been a numbers person (however, I did marry a math major), but your book made my lessons for this class so interesting and *easy*! I actually enjoyed the fact that I didn't have to run and ask my husband about anything; I could just find it in your book. I very much enjoyed your humor and found everything about the book enjoyable and easy to understand.

—Mary Courtney Wilson
Guidance Counselor
Winona Elementary School

TESTS & MEASUREMENT for People Who *(Think They)* HATE TESTS & MEASUREMENT

TESTS & MEASUREMENT for People Who (Think They) HATE TESTS & MEASUREMENT

NEIL J. SALKIND
University of Kansas

SAGE Publications
Thousand Oaks ■ London ■ New Delhi

For information:

Sage Publications, Inc.
2455 Teller Road
Thousand Oaks, California 91320
E-mail: order@sagepub.com

Sage Publications Ltd.
1 Oliver's Yard
55 City Road
London EC1Y 1SP
United Kingdom

Sage Publications India Pvt. Ltd.
B-42, Panchsheel Enclave
Post Box 4109
New Delhi 110 017 India

Printed in the United States of America

Library of Congress Cataloging-in-Publication Data

Salkind, Neil J.
Tests & measurement for people who (think they) hate tests & measurement / Neil J. Salkind.
     p. cm.
Includes bibliographical references and index.
ISBN 1-4129-1363-2 (cloth)—ISBN 1-4129-1364-0 (pbk.)
    1. Educational tests and measurements. I. Title.
LB3051.S243 2006
371.26—dc22

                                        2005008155

This book is printed on acid-free paper.

05   06   07   08   09   10   9   8   7   6   5   4   3   2   1

Acquisitions Editor:	Lisa Cuevas Shaw
Associate Editor:	Margo Beth Crouppen
Editorial Assistant:	Karen Gia Wong
Production Editor:	Melanie Birdsall
Copy Editor:	Liann Lech
Typesetter:	C&M Digitals (P) Ltd.
Proofreader:	Mary Meagher
Indexer:	Kathy Paparchontis
Cover Designer:	Michelle Kenny

In memory of Nona Tollefson, Esther Thalen, and Flip Kissam
"Seventy-five percent of success is passing the baton."
—with thanks to Carl Boyd

BRIEF CONTENTS

PART IV

PART V

DETAILED CONTENTS

PART III

PART IV

PART V

A NOTE TO THE STUDENT: WHY I WROTE THIS BOOK

Some of you might know that I have received a special amount of pleasure in having written *Statistics for People Who (Think They) Hate Statistics,* and learning from e-mails and calls how much people have benefited from that straightforward and gentle approach.

Well, it had to happen, and much of what I say in this introduction is the same that I said in the introduction to the statistics book—take things slowly, listen in class, work hard, and you'll do fine.

People were asking about a similar book for the area of tests and measurement, and here it is. Like teaching stats, teaching tests and measurement courses finds students generally anxious, but not very well informed, about what's expected of them. Of course, like any worthwhile topic, learning about tests and measurement takes an investment of time and effort (and there is still the occasional monster for a teacher). But most of what they've heard (and where most of the anxiety comes from)—that tests and measurement is unbearably difficult—is just not true. Thousands of fear-struck students have succeeded where they thought they would fail. They did it by taking one thing at a time, pacing themselves, seeing illustrations of basic principles as they are applied to real-life settings, and even having some fun along the way.

After a great deal of trial and error and some successful and many unsuccessful attempts, I have learned to teach tests and measurement in a way that I (and many of my students) think is unintimidating and informative.

So, what's in store for you in these pages is the information you need to understand what the field and study of basic tests and measurement are about. You'll learn the fundamental ideas about testing and tests, and how different types of tests are created and used.

There's some theory, but most of what we do focuses on the most practical issues facing people who use tests, such as what kinds of tests are available, what kind should I use, how tests are created and evaluated, and what test scores mean. There's a bit of math required but very little. Anxious about math? Get over it—no kidding.

The more advanced tests and measurement material is very important, but you won't find it here. Why? Because at this point in your studies, I want to offer you material at a level I think you can understand and learn with some reasonable amount of effort, while at the same time not be scared off from taking future courses.

So, if you are looking for the most recent controversy about item response theory or the newest approach to establishing reliability, go find another good book from Sage Publications (I'll be glad to refer you to one). But, if you want to learn why and how tests and measurement can work, and then to understand the material you read in journal articles and what it means to you as a test taker and a test user, this is exactly the place.

Good luck, and let me know how I can improve this book to even better meet the needs of the beginning tests and measurement student.

—*Neil J. Salkind*
The University of Kansas
Lawrence, KS 66045
njs@ku.edu

ACKNOWLEDGMENTS

C. Deborah Laughton got me started thinking about this kind of a book, and Lisa Cuevas Shaw very competently took over when C. Deborah left Sage. Lisa and her assistant editor, Margo Beth Crouppen, guided this book along with gentle yet firm hands and an understanding and helpful spirit. If the book does see any measure of success, it is to a large extent due to them. My sincerest thanks to them both.

Thanks also to others at Sage, including Melanie Birdsall, Liann Lech, Helen Salmon, and Michelle Kenny, who still think that authors deserve to be treated fairly and with respect. Thanks to Jason Love for providing the book's illustrations. And megagigantic thanks to Vicki Schmidt for her stellar work on the materials that will appear on the Instructor's Resources CD. Finally, special thanks to my colleague Professor Bruce Frey for his ideas, critiques, and willingness to help.

Sage Publications gratefully acknowledges the following reviewers for their contributions: John Q. Hodges, University of Missouri-Columbia; Denise von Herrmann, The University of Southern Mississippi; Joseph Matthews, Brigham Young University; Christopher P. Bettinger, San Francisco State University; Eve Brank, University of Florida; Derek C. Briggs, University of Colorado at Boulder; and Laikwoon The, Ministry of Education, Singapore.

PART I

In the
Beginning . . .

Snapshots

(Sounds of Thunder and Lightning)

Ａnd in the beginning, there was . . . tests and measurement.
Not really, but you will be surprised to learn shortly how early
this measurement thing started. That's what the first part of *Tests
& Measurement for People Who (Think They) Hate Tests &
Measurement* is all about—a little history, an introduction to what
kinds of tests there are and what they are used for, and then something about how to use this book.

You're probably new to this, and I'm sure you couldn't wait for
this course to begin ☺. Well, it's here now, and, believe it or not,
there's a lot to learn that can be instructive and even fun—and
immeasurably valuable. Let's get to it.

1

Why Me-asurement?

An Introduction

Difficulty Index ☺☺☺☺☺ (the easiest one in the book)

I t's been happening to you, and you've been doing it since you were very young—being tested and taking tests.

When you were born, the doctor administered the APGAR to assess your *Appearance* (or color), *Pulse* (or heart rate), *Grimace* (or response to stimulation), *Activity* (or muscle tone), and *Respiration* (or respiration). You were also screened (and it's the law) for certain types of metabolic disorders (such as PKU or phenylketonuria)—and that may have been tests number one and two.

Then there may have been preschool tests, spelling tests, the ACT (American College Testing) or the SAT (which actually is not an acronym—see Chapter 15 for more on this), maybe even the GRE (Graduate Record Exam). Along the way, you might have received some career counseling using the SVIB (Strong Vocational Interest Blank) and perhaps a personality test or two such as the MMPI (Minnesota Multiphasic Personal Inventory) or the Myers-Briggs Type Inventory. My, that's a lot of testing, and you're nowhere near done.

You've still probably got a test or two to complete once you graduate from school, perhaps as part of a job application, for additional studies, or for screening for a highly sensitive job as a secret agent.

Testing is ubiquitous in our society, and you can't pick up a copy of the *New York Times,* the *Chicago Tribune,* or the *Los Angeles Times* without finding an article about testing and some associated controversy.

The purpose of *Tests & Measurement for People Who (Think They) Hate Tests & Measurement* is to provide an overview of the many different facets of testing, including the design of tests; the use of tests; and some of the basic social, political, and legal issues that the process of testing involves.

This first part of *Tests & Measurement for People Who (Think They) Hate Tests & Measurement* will familiarize you with a basic history of testing and what the major topics are that we as teachers, nurses, social workers, psychologists, parents, and human resource managers need to understand to best negotiate our way through the maze of assessment that is a personal and professional part of our lives.

Let's start at the beginning and take a brief look at what we know about the practice of testing and how we got to where we are.

A FIVE-MINUTE HISTORY OF TESTING

First, you can follow all of this history stuff by using the cool time line shown below and throughout this chapter for what happened when. Here's a written summary.

Imagine this. It's about 2200 years B.C.E. (Before the Common Era), and you're a young citizen living in a large city in China looking for work. You get up, have some breakfast, walk over to the local "testing bureau," and sit down and take a test for what we now know as a civil service position (such as a mail carrier). And at that time, you had to be proficient in such things as writing, arithmetic, horsemanship, and even archery to be considered for such a position. Must have been an interesting mail route.

Yep—testing in one form or another started that long ago, and for almost 3,000 years in China, this open (anyone could participate), competitive (only the best got the job) system proved to be the model for later systems of evaluating and placing individuals (such as the American and British civil service systems that started around 1889 and 1830, respectively).

Interestingly, this system of selection was abandoned in China around the turn of the 20th century, but we know from our own experience that the use of testing for all different purposes has grown rapidly.

Way back (around 2200 B.C.E.)

Public officials tested in China

How Much to Take That Test?

Testing is on the increase by leaps and bounds (see Chapter 19) and it's not getting any cheaper. Eduventures, a consulting company in Boston (you can find out more about them at www.eduventures.com) estimates that $1.8 billion was spent on assessment for only the K–12 crowd—no college-level testing included. That's a ton of money, and the entire endeavor is expected to get even more expensive as the federal government moves toward expanding standardized testing to more grades in the near future.

Not much of a formal or recorded nature occurred before the middle of the 19th century, and by about the end of the 19th century along comes our friend Charles Darwin, who you may know from some of your other classes as the author of the *Origin of Species*. This book (of which only 11 copies of the first edition have survived) is a groundbreaking work that stressed the importance of what he called "descent with modification" (which we now call evolution). His thesis was that through the process of variation, certain traits and attributes are selected (that is, they survive while others die out), and these traits or attributes are passed on from generation to generation as organisms adapt.

So why are we talking about Charles Darwin and biology in a tests and measurement book? Two reasons. First, Darwin's work led to an increased interest and emphasis on individual differences—and that's what most tests examine. And second, Darwin's cousin (how's that for a transition?), Francis Galton, was the first person to devise a set of tools for assessing individual differences in his anthropometric lab, where one could have all kinds of variables measured such as height, weight, strength, and even how steady you can hold your hands. His motto was "Wherever you can, count" (and by the way, Sherlock Holmes's motto was "Data! Data! Data!"). They must have been *very* busy guys.

1644

"If something exists, it exists in some amount. If it exists in some amount, then it is capable of being measured."
Rene Descartes, *Principles of Philosophy*

Once physical measurements were being made regularly, it was not long before such noted psychologists as James Cattell were working on the first "mental test." Cattell was a founder of the Psychological Corporation in the early 1920s, now known as one of the leading publishers of tests throughout the world.

When we get to the 20th century, testing and measurement activity really picks up. There was a huge increase in interest devoted to mental testing, which shortly became known as intelligence testing and also included the testing of cognitive abilities such as memory and comprehension. More about this in Chapter 16.

A major event in the history of testing occurred around 1905 when Alfred Binet (who was then the Minister of Public Instruction in Paris) started applying some of these new tools to the assessment of Parisian schoolchildren who were not performing as well as expected. Along with his partner, Theodore Simon, Binet used tests of intelligence in a variety of settings—and for different purposes—beyond just evaluating schoolchildren's abilities. Their work came to America about 1916 and was extended by Lewis Terman at Stanford University, which is probably why one of the most commonly used, modern intelligence tests is named the Stanford-Binet.

As always, necessity is the mother and father of invention, and come World War II, there was a huge increase in the need to test and classify accurately those thousands of (primarily) men who were to join the armed services. This occurred around World War I as well, but with nowhere near the scientific deliberation or extent.

And as always, intense efforts at development within the government usually spill over to civilian life, and after the war (World War II, that is), hundreds of different types of tests were available for use in the civilian sector and made their way into hospitals, schools, and businesses. Indeed, we have come a long way from spelling tests.

While all of these mental and ability tests were being developed, increased attention was also being paid to other dimensions of psychological functioning, such as personality development (see Chapter 14). People might be smart (or not smart), but psychologists also wanted to know how well

1850	1869
"Whenever you can, count." Frances Galton	Frances Galton publishes his work on correlation

adjusted they were and whether they were emotionally mature enough to assume certain important responsibilities. Hence, the field of personality testing (around World War I) got started in earnest and certainly is now a major component of the whole field of tests and measurement.

But our brief history of testing does not stop with intelligence or personality testing. As education became more important, so did evaluating achievement (see Chapter 13). For example, in 1937, the then-called Stanford Achievement Tests (or SATs) became required for admission to Ivy League schools (places such as Brown, Yale, and Princeton)—with more than 2,000 high school seniors taking the exam. Another example? In 1948, the Educational Testing Service (known as ETS) opened, almost solely to emphasize the assessment of areas other than intelligence. They are the folks that bring you today's SAT, Graduate Record Exam (or GRE), and the always popular and loveable Test of English as a Foreign Language (or TOEFL)—all taken by hundreds of thousands of students each year.

Now, thousands upon thousands of high school students take standardized tests at the beginning of their senior year, and so do college seniors, trying to gain admission to medical, law, and other graduate programs.

It's no wonder that services offering (and sometimes guaranteeing) success began to proliferate around 1945 with Stanley Kaplan. A very smart New Yorker (who was denied admission to medical school), he started tutoring students in the basement of his home for $0.25 per hour. His success (and it's still a hotly debated issue whether you can indeed raise people's scores through instruction) led him to create an empire of test centers (sold off for a bunch of millions to a big test company) that is still successful today.

Today, thousands and thousands of tests (and hundreds of test publishers—see Appendix B) measure everything from Advanced Placement Examination in Studio Art, which is designed to measure college-level achievements in studio arts, to the Health Problems Checklist, which is used to assess the health status and potential health problems of clients in psychotherapy settings.

1890

James Cattell coins the
phrase "mental test"

1900

College Entrance Examination
Board created

SO, WHY TESTS AND MEASUREMENT?

This question has a pretty simple answer, but simple does not mean lacking in complexity or implications.

No matter what profession we enter, be it teaching, social work, nursing, or any one of thousands, we are required to make judgments every day, every hour, and, in some cases, every few minutes about our work. We do it so often that it becomes second nature. We even do it automatically.

In the most straightforward of terms, we use a test (be it formal or informal) to measure an outcome and make sense of that judgment. And because we are smart, we want to be able to communicate that information to others. So, if we find that Russ got 100% on a spelling test or a 34 on his ACTs, we want everyone who looks at that score to know exactly what that score means.

For example, consider the teacher who records a child's poor grade in math and sends home some remedial work that same evening; the nurse who sees a patient shivering and takes his or her temperature; or the licensed clinical social worker who recognizes that her client has significant difficulties concentrating and administers a test to evaluate that client's ability to stay on task and, based on the score, designs an intervention—these people all recognize a symptom of something that has to be looked into further, and they take appropriate action.

What all these professionals have in common is that in order for them to take action to help the people with whom they work, they need to first assess a particular behavior or set of behaviors. And to make that assessment, they use some kind of formal test (such as a standardized test in the case of the nurse) or informal test (such as in the teacher's case) to complete an assessment. Then, based on training and experience, a decision as to what course of action to take is made.

For our purposes here, we are going to define a **test** as a (pick any of the following) tool, procedure, test, device, examination, investigation, assessment, or measure of an outcome (which is usually some kind of behavior). A test can take the form of a 50-question, multiple-choice history exam or a 30-minute interview of a parent's relationships with his or her children. It can be a set

1905	1916
Alfred Binet and Theodore Simon create the first test of intelligence	The Stanford revision of the Binet-Simon scale is published

of tasks that examines how good someone is at fitting together blocks into particular designs, or whether they prefer multigrain Cheerios® to plain Cheerios®. We use tests that come in many different forms to measure many different things.

What We Test

We test many, many different things, and the thousands of tests that are available today cover a wide range of areas. Here's a quick review of some of the content areas that tests cover. We'll go into greater detail in each of these in Part IV of *Tests & Measurement for People Who (Think They) Hate Tests & Measurement.*

We'll define these different general areas here, and in Table 1.1 you can see a summary along with some real word examples.

Achievement tests assess an individual's level of knowledge in a particular domain. For example, your midterm in history was an achievement test.

Personality tests (covered in Chapter 14) assess an individual's unique and stable set of characteristics, traits, or attitudes. You may have taken an inventory that determined your level of introversion or extraversion.

Aptitude tests (covered in Chapter 15) measure an individual's potential to succeed in an activity requiring a particular skill or set of skills. For example, you may take an aptitude test that assesses your potential for being a successful salesperson.

Ability or intelligence tests (covered in Chapter 16) assess one's level of skill or competence in a wide variety of areas. For example, intelligence tests are viewed as measures of ability (but don't be fooled by the name of a test—there are plenty of intelligence tests that are also seen as being aptitude tests as well—see the following lightbulb!).

Finally, **vocational or career tests** (covered in Chapter 17) assess an individual's interests and help classify those interests as they relate to particular jobs and careers. For example, you may have taken a vocational test that evaluates your level of interest in the culinary arts or the health care professions.

Table 1.1 summarizes what these different types of tests measure and gives you a few real word examples.

1926

The College Board publishes the Scholastic Aptitude Test

1927

Carl Spearman's notion of a general and specific factor theory of intelligence

TABLE 1.1   An Overview of What We Test and Some Examples of Such Tests

Type of Test	What It Measures	Some Examples
Achievement	Level of knowledge in a particular domain	• Closed High School Placement Test • Early School Assessment • Norris Educational Achievement Tests • Test of Basic Adult Education
Personality	Unique and stable set of characteristics, traits, or attitudes	• Achievement/Motivation Profile • Aggression Questionnaire • Basic Living Skills Scale • Dissociative Features Profile • Inventory of Positive Thinking Traits
Aptitude	Potential to succeed	• Differential aptitude tests • Scholastic Aptitude Scale • Aptitude Interest Category • Evaluation Aptitude Test • Wilson Driver Selection Test
Ability or Intelligence	Skill or competence	• Wechsler Intelligence Scale for Children • Stanford-Binet Intelligence Test • Cognitive Abilities Test • General clerical ability tests • School of Readiness test
Performance	Basic performance of particular tasks	• Achenbach System of Empirically Based Assessment • Assessment in Nursery Education • Functional Communication Profile • The Egan Bus Puzzle Test
Vocational or Career	Job-related interests	• Adaptive Functioning Index • Career Interest Inventory • Prevocational Assessment Screen • Rothwell-Miller Interest Blank • Vocational Adaptation Rating Scales

NOTE: You can find out more about each and every one of these tests by going to the Buros Center for testing at http://www.unl.edu/buros/index.html.

1938	1939
Mental Measurements Yearbook first published	Wechsler-Bellevue Intelligence Scale developed

> **Just What Test Is That?**
>
> There is always a great deal of overlap in the way people categorize particular types of tests and what they assess. For example, some people consider intelligence to be an ability (and would place it under ability tests), whereas others think of it as an achievement test because it tests one's knowledge about a particular area of information. Or, aptitude tests can end up as ability tests as well as personality tests, or they can stand all on their own.
>
> So, what's right? They are all right. The way in which we classify tests is strictly a matter of organization and convenience, and even a matter of how they are used. I think that the definitions and examples I gave best reflect the current thinking about tests and measurement. Others feel differently. Welcome to the real world.

Why We Test

Now you know that there are different forms of tests and that there are many different areas of human performance and behavior that are tested regularly. But for what purpose? Here's a summary of the five main purposes (and there are surely more) for which tests can be used.

Tests are used for *selection*. Not everyone can be a jet pilot, so only those men or women who score at a certain level of performance on physical and psychological assessments will be selected for training.

Tests are used for *placement*. Upon entering college, not everyone should be in the most advanced math class or in the most basic. A placement test will determine where the individual belongs.

Tests are used for *diagnosis*. An adult might seek out psychological counseling, and the psychologist may administer a test or group of tests that helps diagnose any one of many different mental disorders. Diagnostic tests are also used to identify individual strengths and weaknesses.

1940	1941
Development of the Minnesota Multiphasic Personality Inventory	Raymond Catell theory of fluid and crystallized intelligence

Tests are used for *hypothesis testing*. A hypothesis is simply an "if . . . then" statement. For example, if children get extra reading help throughout the week, then they will score better on a reading test of comprehension than will children who do not get extra help. One important part of testing this question is using a test that measures reading comprehension accurately.

Finally, tests are used to *classify*. Want to know what profession might suit you best? One of several different tests can provide you with an idea of your aptitude (or future potential) for a career in the culinary arts, auto mechanics, medicine, or child care.

THINGS TO REMEMBER

Tests are used widely for a variety of purposes; among them selection, placement, diagnosis, hypothesis testing, and classification.

SOME IMPORTANT REMINDERS

You'll learn many different things throughout *Tests & Measurement for People Who (Think They) Hate Tests & Measurement* (at least I sure hope you will). And with any vibrant and changing discipline, there are always discussions both pro and con about different aspects of the subject. But there are some constants as well, and I want to bring you a few of those now.

1. *Some behaviors can be observed more closely and more precisely than others.* It's pretty easy to measure one's ability to add single

1941	1942
Invention of M&Ms, used in countless tests and measurement classroom demonstrations	Beginning of General Education Development

digits (such as 6 + 5 = ?), but to understand *how* one solves (not *if* one can solve) a quadratic equation is a different story. The less obvious behaviors take a bit more ingenuity to measure, but that's part of the challenge (and delight) of doing this.

2. *Our understanding of behavior is only as good as the tools we use to measure it.* There are all kinds of ways that we try to measure outcomes, and sometimes we use the very best instruments available—and at other times, we may just use what's convenient. The best takes more time, work, and money, but it gives us accurate and reliable results. Anything short of the best forces us to compromise, and what you see may, indeed, not be what you get.

THINGS TO REMEMBER

No matter how interesting your theory or approach to a problem, what you learn about behavior is only as accurate and as worthwhile as the integrity and usefulness of the tools you use to measure that behavior.

3. *Tests and measurement tools can take make different forms.* A test can be paper and pencil, self-report, observation, or performance and often gives us very similar information on some outcome in which we are interested. The lesson here is to select the form of test that best fits the question you are asking.

4. *The results of any test should always be interpreted within the context in which they were collected.* In many communities, selected junior high students take a practice Scholastic Assessment Test. Although some of these students do very, very well, others perform far below what you would expect a high school junior or senior to do—these younger children simply have not yet had the coursework. To interpret the results of the younger children using the

1947	1957
Educational Testing Service created	Donald Super's theory of career development

same metric and scoring standards as for the older children would surely not do either group any justice. The point is to keep test scores in perspective—and, of course, to understand them within the initial purpose for the testing.

5. *Test results often can be misused.* It doesn't take a rocket scientist to know that there have been significant controversies over how tests are used. You'll learn more about this in Part V of *Tests & Measurement for People Who (Think They) Hate Tests & Measurement,* but many of you know how non-English-speaking immigrants who tried to get sanctuary in the United States were turned away in the 1930s based on their test scores. To use tests fairly and effectively, you need to know the purpose of the test, the quality of the test, how it is administered and used, and how the results are interpreted. We'll do all that in *Tests & Measurement for People Who (Think They) Hate Tests & Measurement.*

6. *Many tests, especially achievement tests, have as their goal distinguishing between those who know the material and those who do not.* We want the biology student to understand evolution and the sixth grader to know something about American and world history.

WHAT AM I DOING IN A TESTS AND MEASUREMENT CLASS?

There are probably many reasons why you find yourself using this book. You might be enrolled in an introductory tests and measurement class. You might be reviewing for your comprehensive exams. Or, you might even be reading this on summer vacation (horrors!) in preparation and review for a more advanced class.

In any case, you're a tests and measurement student whether you have to take a final exam at the end of a formal course or whether you're just in it of your own accord. But there are plenty of good reasons to be studying this material—some fun, some serious, and some both.

1964	1966
Civil Rights Act	Equality of Education Report from James Coleman

Here's a list of some of the things that my students hear at the beginning of our introductory tests and measurement course.

1. Tests and Measurement 101 or Introduction to Testing or whatever it's called at your school looks great listed on your transcript. Kidding aside, this may be a required course for you to complete your major. But even if it is not, having these skills is definitely a big plus when it comes time to apply for a job or for further schooling. And with more advanced courses, your résumé will be even more impressive.

2. If this is not a required course, taking a basic tests and measurement course sets you apart from those who do not. It shows that you are willing to undertake a course that is above average in regard to difficulty and commitment.

3. Basic information about tests and measurement is an intellectual challenge of a kind that you might not be used to. A good deal of thinking is required, as well as some integration of ideas and application. The bottom line is that all this activity adds up to what can be an invigorating intellectual experience because you learn about a whole new area or discipline.

4. There's no question that having some background in tests and measurement makes you a better student in the social or behavioral sciences. Once you have mastered this material, you will have a better understanding of what you read in journals and also what your professors and colleagues may be discussing and doing in and out of class. You will be amazed the first time you say to yourself, "Wow, I actually understand what they're talking about." And it will happen over and over again because you will have the basic tools necessary to understand exactly how scientists reach the conclusions they do.

5. If you plan to pursue a graduate degree in education, anthropology, economics, nursing, sociology, or any one of many other social, behavioral, and biological pursuits, this course will give you the foundation you need to move further.

6. Finally, you can brag that you completed a course that everyone thinks is the equivalent of building and running a nuclear reactor.

1970	**1974**
National Assessment of Educational Progress	Family Educational Rights and Privacy Act

TEN WAYS TO USE THIS BOOK (AND LEARN ABOUT TESTS AND MEASUREMENT AT THE SAME TIME!)

Yep. Just what the world needs—another tests and measurement book. But this one is different. It's directed at the student, is not condescending, is informative, and is as basic as possible in its presentation. It assumes only the most basic information at the start, and, if you don't have that, you can go to Appendix A and get it.

However, there has always been a general aura surrounding the study of tests and measurement that it's a difficult subject to master. And I don't say otherwise, because parts of it are challenging. On the other hand, millions and millions of students have mastered this topic, and you can, too. Here are a few hints to close this introductory chapter before we move on to our first topic.

• *You're not dumb.* That's true. If you were, you would not have gotten this far in school. So, treat tests and measurement like any other new course. Attend the lectures, study the material, and do the exercises in the book and from class, and you'll do fine. Rocket scientists know how to use this stuff, but you don't have to be a rocket scientist to succeed.

• *How do you know tests and measurement is hard?* Is this topic difficult? Yes and no. If you listen to friends who have taken the course and didn't work hard and didn't do well, they'll surely volunteer to tell you how hard it was and how much of a disaster it made of their entire semester, if not their lives. And let's not forget—we always tend to hear from complainers. So, I suggest that you start this course with the attitude that you'll wait and see how it is and judge the experience for yourself. Better yet, talk to several people who have had the class and get a good general idea of what they think. Just don't base your opinion on one spoilsport's experience.

1975	1975
John Holland's classification system of careers	Education for All Handicapped Children Act (Public Law 94-142)

- *Form a study group.* This is one of the most basic ways to ensure some success in this course. Early in the semester, arrange to study with friends. If you don't have any who are in the same class as you, then make some new ones or offer to study with someone who looks to be as happy about being there as you are. Studying with others allows you to help them if you know the material better, or to benefit from others who know the material better than you. Set a specific time each week to get together for an hour and go over the exercises at the end of the chapter or ask questions of one another. Take as much time as you need. Studying with others is an invaluable way to help you understand and master the material in this course.

> **Stay on Task and Take One Thing at a Time**
>
> Material about testing and measurement can be tough to understand, especially if you have never heard any of these terms before or thought about any of these ideas. Follow the guidelines mentioned here and talk with your teacher as soon as you find yourself not understanding something or falling behind.

- *Ask your teacher questions, and then ask a friend.* If you do not understand what you are being taught in class, ask your professor to clarify it. Have no doubt—if you don't understand the material, then you can be sure that others do not as well. More often than not, instructors welcome questions. And especially because you've read the material before class, your questions should be well informed and help everyone in class to better understand the material.

- *Do the exercises at the end of a chapter.* The exercises are based on the material and the examples in the chapter they follow. They are there to help you apply the concepts that were taught in the chapter and build your confidence at the same time. How do the

1979	2001
Truth in Testing legislation	No Child Left Behind Act

exercises do that? An explanation for how each exercise is solved accompanies the problem. If you can answer these end-of-chapter exercises, then you are well on your way to mastering the content of the chapter.

- *Practice, practice, practice.* Yes, it's a very old joke:

  Q. How do you get to Carnegie Hall?

  A. Practice, practice, practice.

Well, it's no different with basic statistics. You have to use what you learn and use it frequently to master the different ideas and techniques. This means doing the exercises in the back of the chapter as well as taking advantage of any other opportunities you have to understand what you have learned.

- *Look for applications to make it more real.* In your other classes, you probably have occasion to read journal articles, talk about the results of research, and generally discuss the importance of the scientific method in your own area of study. These are all opportunities to look and see how your study of tests and measurement can help you better understand the topics under class discussion as well as the area of beginning statistics. The more you apply these new ideas, the better and more full your understanding will be.

- *Browse.* Read the assigned chapter first, then go back and read it with more intention. Take a nice leisurely tour of *Tests & Measurement for People* . . . to see what's contained in the various chapters. Don't rush yourself. It's always good to know what topics lie ahead as well as to familiarize yourself with the content that will be covered in your current statistics class.

- *Have fun.* This indeed might seem like a strange thing for you to read, but it all boils down to you mastering this topic rather than letting the course and its demands master you. Set up a study schedule and follow it, ask questions in class, and consider this intellectual exercise to be one of growth. Mastering new material is always exciting and satisfying—it's part of the human spirit. You can experience the same satisfaction here—just keep your eye on the ball and make the necessary commitment to stay current with the assignments and work hard.

• *Finally, be easy on yourself.* This is not material that any introductory student masters in a matter of hours or days. It takes some thinking and some hard work, and your expectations should be realistic. Expect to succeed in the course and you will.

About Those Icons

An **icon** is a symbol. Throughout *Tests & Measurement for People Who (Think They) Hate Tests & Measurement,* you'll see a variety of different icons.

Here's what each one is and what each represents:

 This icon represents information that goes beyond the regular text. It might be necessary to elaborate on a particular point, and that can be done more easily outside of the flow of the usual material.

 In TechTalk, I select some more technical ideas and tips to discuss and to inform you about what's beyond the scope of this course. You might find these interesting and useful.

 Every now and then, but not often, you'll find a small stepladder icon like the one you see here. This indicates that there is a set of steps coming up that will direct you through a particular process. These steps have been tested and approved by whatever federal agency approves these things.

 That finger with the bow is a cute icon, but its primary purpose is to help reinforce important points about the topic that you just read about. Try to emphasize these points in your studying because they are usually central to the topic.

The Famous Difficulty Index

For want of a better way to give you some upfront idea about the difficulty of the chapter you are about to read, I have developed a highly secret difficulty index using smileys. This lets you know what to expect as you begin reading.

How Hard Is This Chapter?	Look at Mr. Smiley!
very hard	☺
hard	☺☺
not too hard, but not easy either	☺☺☺
easy	☺☺☺☺
very easy	☺☺☺☺☺

GLOSSARY

Bolded terms in the text are included in the glossary at the back of the book.

SUMMARY

Now you have some idea about what a test is and what it does, what areas of human behavior are tested, and even the names of a few tests you can throw around at tonight's dinner table. But most of all, I introduced you to a few of the major content areas we will be focusing on throughout *Tests & Measurement for People Who (Think They) Hate Tests & Measurement.*

TIME TO PRACTICE

1. What are some of your memories of being tested? Be sure to include (if you can) the nature of the test itself, the settings under which the test took place, how prepared or unprepared you felt, and your response upon finding out your score.

2. Go to the library (not to the Internet) and identify five journal articles in your area of specialization, such as teaching math or nursing or social work. Now, create a chart like this for each set of five.

Journal Name	Title of Article	What Was Tested	What Test Was Used to Test It?
1.			
2.			
3.			
4.			
5.			

   a. Were most of the tests used developed commercially, or were they developed just for this study?
   b. Which test do you think is the most interesting, and why?
   c. Which test do you think got the closest to the behavior that the authors wanted to measure?

3. Using any search engine you choose, search the Internet for the words "intelligence testing" and then do a separate search for "personality testing" (include the quotes). Try and classify the hits and reach some conclusion as to what the content of these different areas is and how they might differ.

4. One of the things we did in this opening chapter was to identify five different purposes of tests (see page 11). Think of at least two other ways that tests might be used, and give a real-world example.

5. Interview someone who teaches in your department (personally or through e-mail). Try to get an idea of the importance he or she places on being knowledgeable about testing and what role it plays in his or her research and everyday professional career. Is he or she convinced that tests assess behavior fairly? Does he or she use alternatives to traditional testing? Does he or she find the results of tests useful for helping students further?

PART II

The Psychology of Psychometrics

Snapshots

"Well, all of your morals check out. Now we just need you to take this two-part exam…"

I n this part of *Tests & Measurement for People Who (Think They) Hate Tests & Measurement,* we discuss some of the most important and fundamental ideas that provide the foundation for developing and using tests.

In Chapter 2, we review levels of measurement—what they are and how they are used. Here, you'll learn how different levels of measurement coincide with different amounts of information that a particular measure conveys.

Our study of reliability, in Chapter 3, takes us on a tour of the idea of how consistent a test is. This chapter brings us information on the conceptual nature of what reliability is, the many different types of reliability and how they are used, when each is appropriate to use, and how each is established in practice.

Probably the most important construct in the study of tests and measurement is validity—reliability's first cousin—or whether a test does what it is supposed to. What validity is, the different types of validity, and how validity is established are all covered in Chapter 4.

Finally, Chapter 5 provides us with a review of test scores and how to best understand them.

2

One Potato, Two Potatoes . . . Levels of Measurement and Their Importance

Difficulty Index ☺☺☺ (a bit harder than Chapter 1, but easily understood)

How things are measured is very important to our study of tests and measurement. And, how *precisely* they are measured is just as important. In one study, self-efficacy and other beliefs were compared among 168 female Korean college students. The method involved measuring self-efficacy at varying levels of measurement (the big topic for this chapter). The results showed that different measures of self-efficacy were positively related to one another, and they were also related to a task-value factor that was measured. Most important for our purposes was the fact that as the measurement became more precise (that is, as the level of measurement increased), scores on self-efficacy factors tended to decrease.

Want to know more? Take a look at Bong, M. (2001). Role of self-efficacy and task-value in predicting college students' course performance and future enrollment intentions. *Contemporary Educational Psychology, 26*(4), 553–570.

FIRST THINGS FIRST

Before we start talking about levels of measurement, let's spend a moment defining a few important terms; specifically, variable and measurement.

A **variable** is anything (such as a test score) that can take on more than one value. For example, a score on the SAT can take on more than one value (such as 750), as can what category of color your hair falls into (such as red). Age is another variable (someone can be 2 months old or 87 years old), as is gender (someone can be male or female). Notice that the labels we apply to outcomes can be quantitative (such as 87 years) or qualitative (such as male or female). Good, that's out of the way.

Now, the term **measurement** means the assignment of labels to (you guessed it) a variable or an outcome. So, when we apply the label "male" to a particular outcome, we are measuring that outcome. We can measure the number of windows in a house, the color of a car, score on a test of memory, and how fast someone can run 100 yards. In every case, we are assigning a label to an outcome.

As the world turns, about 60 years ago in 1946, S. S. Stevens, the famous experimental psychologist (not the steamship), started to wonder about how different types of variables are measured and whether the level of precision at which those variables are measured might be classified so that they can be more easily understood. Even better, he asked the question of whether a system could be developed so that the outcomes that result from the measurement process can be classified based on the *characteristics* of the variable itself, rather than the actual score on the variable.

And, coming in at about 10 lbs., 11 ounces—the idea of levels of measurement was born.

THINGS TO REMEMBER

Variables can be measured in different ways, and the way a variable is being measured determines the level of measurement being used. For example, we can measure the variable height in several different ways. If we say that Group 1 is taller than Group 2, then we have chosen to measure this variable at a level that distinguishes one group from another only in rank or magnitude. On the other hand, if we chose to measure this variable at a level that distinguishes groups by a certain number of inches, that is much more precise, and therefore much more informative.

THE FOUR HORSEMEN (OR LEVELS) OF MEASUREMENT

A **level of measurement** represents how much information is being provided by the outcome measure. There are four levels of measurement—nominal, ordinal, interval, and ratio—each of which we will talk about in the following paragraphs.

The Nominal Level of Measurement

The **nominal level of measurement** describes a measurement system where there are differences in quality rather than quantity. These are variables that are *categorical* or *discrete* in nature. Here, outcome scores can be placed into one (and only one) category. These "labels" are qualitative in nature, and scores can be placed in one and only one category, which is why such scores are mutually exclusive. You just can't be in one spelling group (the Guppies) and another spelling group (the Sharks) at the same time.

For example, Max is in the Guppies and Russ is in the Sharks. Knowing that much information tells us only that Max and Russ are in two different spelling groups—not how the groups differ, nor who is better, nor how many words Max or Russ can spell—just that they are in two different groups.

It's called the nominal level of measurement (after the word *nomin* in Latin, meaning name) because the only distinction we can make is that variables differ in the category in which they are placed. Measuring a variable such as spelling by group assignment (and nothing more) is similar to distinctions between Republicans and Democrats; white, black, yellow, and red folks; Chevy and Volvo drivers, and shoppers at HyVee and Dillons— they differ from one another by the nature of the group to which they belong.

Want to know more about these differences? Well, you can't just by knowing what group they are in, and that's a significant limitation to the nominal level of measurement. If you want more information, then you have to dig more or define the variable in a more precise way, which we will do shortly.

An example of a study that uses a nominal-level variable is the following: Rik Verhaeghe and his colleagues, in a 2003 article that appeared in *Stress and Health: Journal of the International Society for the Investigation of Stress,* examined job stress among middle-aged health care workers and its relation to absences due to sickness. One assessment that had to be made was based on the assignment of people to one of two groups—nurses or non-nurses—and that variable is being measured at the nominal level. As you can see, a participant can be in only one group at a time (they are mutually exclusive), and at this level of measurement, you can assign only a label (nurse or non-nurse).

Want to know more? Take a look at Verhaeghe, R., Mak, R., VanMaele, G., Kornitzer, M., & De Backer, G. (2003). Job stress among middle aged health care workers and its relation to sickness absence. *Stress and Health: Journal of the International Society for the Investigation of Stress, 19*(5), 265–274.

THINGS TO REMEMBER

1. The categories in which measures can be placed on the nominal scale are always mutually exclusive. You can't be in the red preschool room and the blue preschool room at the same time.

2. Nominal-level measures are always qualitative (the values have no inherent meaning). Being in the red room is neither here nor there, as to being in the blue room. You're a preschooler in both rooms and that's it—the room assignment says nothing about anything other than that—just which room you are in.

The Ordinal Level of Measurement

Next, we have the **ordinal level of measurement**, which describes how variables can be ordered along some type of continuum (Get it? Ordinal as in ordering a set of things). So, outcomes are placed in categories (like the nominal scale), but they have an order or rank to them as well, like stronger and weaker, taller and shorter, faster and slower, and so on.

For example, let's take Max and Russ again. As it turns out, Max is a better speller than Russ. Right there is the one and only necessary criterion for a measure to be at the ordinal level of measurement. It's the "better than" or "worse than" thing.

From better or worse, we cannot tell anything about how good of a speller either Max or Russ is, because ordinal levels of measurement do not include this information. Max might get only 3 words out of 10 correct, whereas Russ might get only 2. That makes Max better, but not very good, right?

But you can say that Max is a better speller than Russ and is better than Avi (another classmate), and Avi is a better speller than Sheldon—all relative statements.

Our real-world example is a study by Kathe Burkhardt and her colleagues that appeared in the journal *Behavior Change* in 2003. They examined common childhood fears in 9- to 13-year-old South African children, and one of the ways that they assessed fears was by having children rank them. In fact, the researchers found that the children's rankings of fears differed from rankings derived using a scale that attached an actual value to the fear.

Want to know more? Take a look at Burkhardt, K., Loxton, H., & Muris, P. (2003). Fears and fearfulness in South African children. *Behaviour Change, 20*(2), 94–102.

The Interval Level of Measurement

That's two levels of measurement down and two to go.

The **interval level of measurement** gives us a nice jump in the amount of information we obtain from a new level of measurement. You already know that we can assign names (nominal level) and rank (ordinal level), but it is with the interval level of measurement that we can assign a value to an outcome that is based on some underlying continuum that has equal intervals. And if there is an underlying continuum, then we can make very definite statements about someone's position (his or her score) along that continuum and his or her position relative to another person's position, including statements about such things as differences. Wow, that's a lot more complex than the earlier two levels of measurement, and provides a lot more information as well.

For example, not only do we know that Max and Russ fall into two different categories of spellers (nominal) and that Max is better than Russ (interval), but we can now know how much better Max actually is. In fact, Max got 8 out of 10 correct and Russ got 4 out of 10 correct. Because one of the assumptions of this level of measurement is that it is based on a scale that has equally appearing intervals (1 correct, 2 correct, 3 correct, etc.), we can say that Max got four more correct than Russ. Or, if Max got six correct and Russ got five correct, then Max would have gotten one more correct than Russ.

TECH TALK

Although an interval-level scale provides much more information than an ordinal- or nominal-level scale, you have to be careful in how you interpret these scores. For example, scoring 50% more on a history test does not mean that that score represents 50% more knowledge (unless the test is a perfect, perfect, perfect representative of all the questions that could be asked). Rather, it means only that 50% more of the questions were answered correctly. We can conclude that the more questions correct, the better one is in history, but don't carry it too far and overgeneralize from a test score to an entire area of knowledge or a construct such as intelligence.

What's the big advantage of the interval level of measurement over the ordinal and nominal besides increased precision? In one word, *information*—there's much more of it when we know what a score actually means. Remember, Max could be ranked #1 in his class, but get only 50% of the words correct on Friday's test. On the other hand, knowing what his exact score is relative to some type of underlying continuum provides us with an abundance of information when it comes time to make a judgment about his performance.

Jennifer Hill and her colleagues used an interval level of measurement when they used the Wechsler Intelligence Scale for Children to determine the effects of high participation in an infant early intervention program that targeted low-birthweight premature infants. They found that infants who participated had higher scores on the Wechsler when they were 8 years old than did those who did not participate. Scores on the Wechsler are based on an underlying continuum such that a score of 100 represents two points less than a score of 102.

Want to know more? Take a look at Hill, J., Brooks Gunn, J., & Waldfogel, J. (2003). Sustained effects of high participation in an early intervention for low-birth-weight premature infants. *Developmental Psychology, 39*(4), 730–744.

The Ratio Level of Measurement

By far the most interesting measurement, yet the one that is least likely to be seen in the social or behavioral sciences. Why? Because the **ratio level of measurement** is characteristic of all the other scales we have already talked about, but it also includes a very important assumption—an *absolute zero* corresponding to an absence of the trait or characteristic being measured.

For example, it is possible for receive a score of zero on a spelling test, right? You just need not spell any words correctly. But here's the big question. Does getting such a score indicate that one has no spelling ability? Of course not. It means only that on this test, no words were spelled correctly.

That's the challenge here. Is there any trait or characteristic in the behavioral or social sciences that an individual can have a complete absence of? If there is not, then a ratio level of measurement is impossible. In fact, this is one reason why, when this material is taught, the interval and ratio levels often are combined into one. We're not doing that here because we think they are important enough to keep separated.

Now, in the physical and biological sciences, it's no problem. Consider temperature. Absolute zero is defined as –459 degrees Fahrenheit and –273 degrees Celsius (for all you metric fans) and indicates no molecular activity. That is truly a true zero. But even if someone scores zero on an intelligence test (perhaps one taken in Russian), does that mean he or she has no intelligence? Or, if someone receives a zero on a spelling test, does that mean he or she cannot spell? Of course not.

So, for us social and behavioral scientists (like most of you), you will rarely (if ever) see a ratio-level scale in the journal articles that you review and read.

A SUMMARY: HOW LEVELS OF MEASUREMENT DIFFER

We just discussed four different levels of measurement and what some of their characteristics are. You also know by now that a more precise level of measurement has all the characteristics of an earlier level and provides more information as well.

In Table 2.1, you can see a summary table that addresses the following questions:

1. Are you measuring most of the available information?

2. Can you assign a name to the variable being measured?

3. Can you assign an order to the variable being measured?

4. Can you assign an underlying quantitative scale to the variable being measured?

Remember, the more precise you can be, the more information is conveyed.

TABLE 2.1	**A Summary of Levels of Measurement and the Characteristics That Define Them**				
Level of Measurement	*Are You Measuring Most of the Available Information?*	*Can You Assign Names to the Variable Being Measured?*	*Can You Assign an Order to the Variable Being Measured?*	*Can You Assign an Underlying Quantitative Scale to the Variable Being Measured?*	*Can You Assign an Absolute Zero to the Variable Being Measured?*
Ratio	Most	☺	☺	☺	☺
Interval	More	☺	☺	☺	☹
Ordinal	Less	☺	☺	☹	☹
Nominal	Least	☺	☹	☹	☹

This table shows us that the ratio level of measurement allows us to answer yes (☺) to these four questions, whereas the nominal level of measurement allows us to answer yes to only one.

OK, SO WHAT'S THE LESSON HERE?

The lesson here is that, when you can, try to select a technique for measuring a variable that allows you to use the highest level of measurement possible (most likely the interval level).

For example, when testing the effectiveness of strength training in senior citizens, don't classify them as weak or strong after the intervention is over and after they have been tested. Rather, try to get a ranking of how strong they are, and, even better, try to get an actual number associated with the amount of weight they can lift. That provides much more information and makes your entire quest for knowledge a more powerful one.

But the real world sometimes demands that certain outcomes be measured in certain ways, and that limits us as to the amount of information that is available. For example, what if you wanted to study prejudice? You may not be able to ascertain anything more than placing participants into ordinal levels called *very prejudiced,* *somewhat prejudiced,* and *not at all prejudiced.* Not as much information as we might like, but not bad either. It is what it is.

THE FINAL WORD(S)

OK, so we have the four levels (three of which are very commonly used)—what can we say about all of them? Here are at least three things:

1. What we measure—be it a score on a test of intelligence, the number right on a chemistry final exam, or whether you prefer peanut or plain M&Ms—belongs to one of these three levels of measurement. The key, of course, is how finely and precisely the variable is being measured.

2. The qualities of one level of measurement (such as nominal) are characteristic of the next level up as well. In other words, variables measured at the ordinal level also contain the qualities of variables measured at the nominal level. Likewise, variables measured at the interval level contain the qualities of variables measured at both the nominal and ordinal level. For example, if you know that Dave swims faster than Laurie, that's great information (and it's ordinal in nature). But if you know that Dave swims 7.6 seconds faster than Laurie (and that's interval-level information), that's more informative and even better.

3. The more precise (and higher) the level of measurement (with ratio being highest, but in our discussion, interval is),

the more accurate the measurement process will be and the closer you'll get to measuring the true outcome of interest.

4. How you choose to measure an outcome defines the outcome's level of measurement.

5. Finally, most researchers take some liberty in treating ordinal variables (such as scores on a personality test) as interval-level variables, and that is fine as long as they remember that the intervals may not be (and probably are not) equal. Their interpretation of the data needs to consider that inequality.

TECH TALK

These four levels of measurement are not carved in stone. We might contend that most measures in the social and behavioral sciences fall at the ordinal or interval level; in practice, however, we surely *act* as if most (if not all) occur at the interval level when they actually probably occur at the ordinal level. We are very quick to say with some degree of confidence that Jim (who has an IQ of 120) is smarter than Bill (who has an IQ of 115), when we know that "smart" is relative and not very well represented by a number.

To make matters even more complicated, even if scales (such as those of intelligence) are interval-level measures, does one assume that the five-point difference between a score of 100 and a score of 105 is equivalent to a five-point difference between a score of 125 and 130? An interval-level scale would lead us to believe that, but nope—that's just not the case. Moving from a score of 100 to 105 is not anywhere near the change that is represented by going from a score of 125 to 130. The lower set indicates movement with the average range, whereas the higher set indicates movement from the top of the average range to the superior range. There is a real qualitative meaning associated with these scores, regardless of the underlying continuum.

SUMMARY

Oodles of good work. Now that we understand what levels of measurement are and how they work, we will turn our attention to the first of two very important topics in the study of tests and measurement—reliability. And that discussion comes in the next chapter.

TIME TO PRACTICE

1. Why are levels of measurement useful?

2. For the following variables, define at what level of measurement each one occurs and *tell why.*
   a. Hair color—for example, red, brown, and blonde.
   b. IQ score—for example, 110 or 143.
   c. Average number of Volvos owned by each family in Great Neck, NY—for example, 2 or 3.
   d. The number correct on a third-grade math test out of 20 possible correct—for example, 17, 19, or 20.
   e. Speed of running 10 yards—for example, 15 seconds or 12.5 seconds.

3. Go the library and select three journal articles that include an empirical study. Be sure that you select these articles from your own discipline. Now, for each one, answer the following questions.
   a. What is the primary variable of interest, or what variable is being studied?
   b. How is it being measured?
   c. At what level of measurement is it being measured?

4. How does the interval level of measurement provide more information than the nominal level of measurement, and why would you want to use the interval level of measurement if you have a choice?

5. Select five things that are important to measure in your area of expertise, and identify how they can be measured at the nominal, ordinal, or interval level of measurement.

ANSWERS TO PRACTICE QUESTIONS

1. Levels of measurement are useful because they allow us to specify the precision with which a variable is being measured and to select or design instruments that assess that variable accurately.

2. Here you are . . .
   a. Nominal—These are categories to which you can belong only one at a time.
   b. Interval—This is the interval level of measurement because you assume that the points along the underlying continuum are equally spaced, but some people would argue that it is not that precise.
   c. Ratio—Those folks can have no Volvos, right?—nothing, is nothing, is nothing.
   d. Interval—Equally spaced points once again.
   e. Interval—You might think this is ratio in nature, but it's hard to see how someone can run any distance in no time (which would make it ratio).

3. You're on your own for this one. If you can't find an article that you can understand, don't try and complete the assignment using that article. Hunt for articles

that you can first understand—otherwise, you'll have hard time answering the main part of the question.

4. It provides more information because it is more precise. You want to use it because the more precise a level of measurement is, the more information you have available and the more accurate your assessment (all other things being equal).

5. Let's say you're a reading teacher:
   a. Ratio—number of books in a child's house
   b. Ratio—number of minutes a child is read to by his or her parents
   c. Nominal—the group of readers in which a child belongs
   d. Interval—score on a comprehension test of reading
   e. Ordinal—rankings according to the number of books read over the summer

WANT TO KNOW MORE?

Further Readings

- Laird, S. P., Snyder, C. R., Rapoff, M. A., & Green, S. (2004). Measuring private prayer: Development, validation, and clinical application of the Multidimensional Prayer Inventory. *International Journal for the Psychology of Religion, 14*(4), 251–272.

What an interesting variable to measure, and at what measurement level? Quantitative and qualitative aspects of prayer are measured, and results revealed five distinct types of prayer. Very interesting use of measurement.

- McHugh, M. L., & Hudson-Barr, D. (Ed.). (2003). Descriptive statistics, Part II: Most commonly used descriptive statistics. *Journal for Specialists in Pediatric Nursing, 8,* 111–116.

These authors support what you already read here—that data of different levels of measurement require different statistics measures. And to use descriptive statistics in the best manner, it is important to know what measurement levels should be used with the statistic and what information the statistic can provide.

And on the Internet

- Learn all about counting systems (also a kind of level of measurement) at http://galileoandeinstein.physics.virginia.edu/lectures/babylon.html.

3

Getting It Right Every Time

Reliability and Its Importance

Difficulty Index ☺☺ (tougher than most)

R eliability is pretty easy to figure out. It's simply whether a test, or whatever you use as a measurement tool, measures something consistently. It's all about the consistency of scores for the same set of people. If you administer a test of personality before a special treatment occurs, will the administration of that same test 4 months later be reliable? Or, if you have two forms of the same test, will the results be comparable relative to the two different testings? Those, my friend, are some of the questions.

Cindy Woods, in her dissertation work, demonstrated the importance of interrater reliability (one of several kinds we will discuss in this chapter). She performed an analysis of 18 studies where she examined parent-child coercive interactions that involved parenting practices and punishment and the impact of those interactions on the development of boys' aggression. Aggression, the primary variable of interest, was studied directly and indirectly, and interrater reliability was established using indirect or secondhand occurrences. She found that unskilled parenting had the most significant effect on the later development of aggression in boys.

Want to know more? Take a look at Woods, C. (2004). Unskilled parenting practices and their effect on the development of aggression in boys: A meta-analysis of coercion theory based studies. *Dissertation Abstracts International: Section B: The Sciences and Engineering, 64*(11B), 5808.

We'll get to the various forms of reliability and how they are computed, but first a bit about how reliability works and why it is such a cool idea.

TEST SCORES: TRUTH OR DARE

What really is so cool about the whole notion of reliability is that it is based on the separation of the different components of what makes up any test score. When you take a test in this class, you may get a score such as 89 (good for you) or 65 (back to the books!). That test score consists of several different elements: the **observed score** (or what you actually get on the test, such as 89 or 65); a **true score** (the true, 100% accurate reflection of what you *really* know); and an **error score,** or that which accounts for day-to-day differences between the true and error score. We can't directly measure true score because it is a theoretical reflection of the actual amount of the trait or characteristic possessed by the individual. But it's a terrific idea nonetheless and the cornerstone of understanding reliability.

TECH TALK

Nothing about this tests and measurement stuff is clear cut, and this true score stuff surely qualifies. Here's why. We just defined true score as an accurate reflection of whatever is being measured, independent of any error. So far, so good. But there's another point of view as well. Some psychometricians (the people who do tests and measurement for a living) believe that true score has nothing to do with whether the construct of interest is really being reflected. Rather, true score is the average score an individual would get if he or she took a test an infinite number of times, and it represents the theoretical typical level of performance on a given test. Now, one would hope that the typical level of performance would reflect the construct of interest, but that's another question (one about validity, at that). The distinction here is that a test is reliable if it consistently produces whatever score a person would get on average, regardless of whatever it is the test is measuring. In fact, a perfectly reliable test might not produce a score that has anything to do with the construct of interest, such "what you really know."

Why aren't true and observed scores equal to one another? Well, they would be if the test (and the resulting observed score) is a perfect (and we mean absolutely perfect) reflection of what's being measured, time after time after time.

But the Yankees don't always win, the bread mostly falls on the buttered side, and Murphy's Law tells us that the world is not yet perfect. So, what you see as an observed score may come close to the true score, but rarely (almost never) are they the same. Rather, the difference as you see here is in the amount of error that is introduced.

Error? Yes—in all its glory. For example, let's suppose for a moment that someone gets an 89 on his or her tests and measurement test, but their true score (which we never really know) is 80. That means that the 9-point difference (the amount of error) is due to error, or the reason why individual test scores vary from being a 100% true reflection of that individual's understanding or knowledge of what he or she is being tested on.

THINGS TO REMEMBER

Error is the difference between one's observed score and one's theoretical true score.

What might be the source of such error? Well, perhaps the room in which the test is taken is so warm that it's easy for you to fall asleep. That would certainly have an impact on your test score. Or, perhaps you didn't study for the test as much as you should have. Ditto. How about the test instructions being unclear? Or, your attitude just isn't right that day to undertake a 4-hour final.

These are all sources of error that can contribute to the unreliability of an instrument because these sources mask the true performance or true score, which would be measured if the sources of error were not present.

GETTING CONCEPTUAL

The less error, the more reliability—it's that simple.

So, what we know up to this point is that the score we observe (the results of, let's say, a spelling test) are composed of an individual's actual score (true score) and something we call error score. The formula shown here gives you an idea as to how these two relate to one another:

Observed score = true score + error score

Now, let's take a moment and go one step further.

The error part of this simple equation consists of two types of errors, one called *trait error* and one called *method error*—both of which (once again) contribute to differences between the true and observed score, right?

Trait errors are those sources of errors that reside within the individual taking the test (such as, I didn't study enough, I felt bad about that missed blind date, I forgot to set the alarm, excuses, excuses). **Method errors** are those sources of error that reside in the testing situation (such as lousy test instructions, too-warm room, or missing pages).

If we expand the earlier simple equation and show you what you just read, we get this equation.

$$\text{Observed score} = \text{true score} + \text{error score} \begin{cases} \text{trait error} \\ \text{method error} \end{cases}$$

And, we only have one more equation and one more simple step to understand how error and reliability fit together.

Take a look at this equation:

$$\text{Reliability} = \frac{\text{True Score}}{\text{True Score} + \text{Error Score}}$$

That's the deal. As the error component (Error Score) gets smaller, what happens to the reliability value? It gets larger. And in the most perfect of all worlds, what happens if there is no error score at all? Voila! Reliability is perfect because it is equal to an individual's true score.

Our job is to reduce those sources of error as much as possible by, for example, having good test-taking conditions and making sure you are encouraged to get enough sleep. Reduce the error and you increase the reliability, because the observed score more closely matches the true score.

TECH TALK

In more technical terms, reliability goes something like this. Scores on repeated testings tend to vary. What the concept of reliability allows us to do is to understand which proportion of the variation in test scores is due to actual changes in performance or behavior and which is due to error variance. It's reducing that error variance that makes a test more reliable.

IF YOU KNOW ABOUT r_{xy}, SKIP THIS SECTION . . .

But if you don't know about r_{xy}, then read on a bit.

As we said earlier, reliability reflects the consistency of test performance upon additional testings—and those testings can take place at different times, as different forms of the same test, or some combination.

The way that reliability is measured is through the computation of a correlation coefficient. You can learn a lot more about correlation coefficients in Appendix A, but we'll give you a bit of a review here.

A short review will tell us that a correlation coefficient is a numerical index that tells us how closely two variables (such as two administrations of the *same* test) are related to one another—more accurately, how much the variables share or have in common. For reliability purposes, correlation coefficients tend to range between .00 and +1.00. The higher the number, the more reliable the test.

For example, let's look at the following set of two scores on a 10-item achievement test that is given to 15 adults in September and given again in December to the same 15 adults. We have two scores for each adult. We *always* have at least two scores per individual—perhaps on two separate testings or perhaps using two different forms of the same test—but always two scores. If this test is reliable, we expect that these two sets of scores have a lot in common with one another—and that there will be a high correlation between them.

Well, it turns out that, using the formula shown on page 335, the correlation between the score from testing in September and the score from testing in December is .90, certainly high enough for

ID	September Testing	December Testing
1	78	79
2	65	78
3	65	66
4	78	80
5	89	78
6	99	94
7	93	95
8	75	78
9	69	72
10	87	82
11	45	49
12	66	68
13	87	81
14	85	87
15	78	69

us to conclude that this test is reliable. We'll get more into interpreting reliability coefficients later in this chapter, but this is enough information for you to continue to learn about the different types of reliability and how their respective coefficients are computed.

DIFFERENT FLAVORS OF RELIABILITY

Reliability can be computed in many different ways, and we'll cover the four most important and most often used in this section. They are all summarized in Table 3.1.

Test-Retest Reliability

Here's the first kind of reliability we'll talk about. **Test-retest reliability** is used when you want to examine whether a test is reliable over time.

TABLE 3.1 Different Types of Reliability, When They Are Used, How They Are Computed, and What They Mean

Type of Reliability	When You Use It	How Do You Do It?	What Can You Say When You're Done?
Test-retest reliability	When you want to know whether a test is reliable over time	Correlate the scores from a test given in Time 1 with the same test given in Time 2.	The Bonzo test of identity formation for adolescents is reliable over time.
Parallel forms reliability	When you want to know if several different forms of a test are reliable or equivalent	Correlate the scores from one form of the test with scores from a second form of the same test of the same content (but not the exact same test).	The two forms of the Regular Guy test are equivalent to one another and have shown parallel forms reliability.
Internal consistency reliability	When you want to know if the items on a test assess one, and only one, dimension	Correlate each individual item score with the total score.	All of the items on the SMART Test of Creativity assess the same construct.
Interrater reliability	When you want to know whether there is consistency in the rating of some outcome	Examine the percentage of agreement between raters.	The interrater reliability for the best dressed Foosball player judging was .91, indicating a high degree of agreement between judges.

There are always different names used for the same topic or procedure in science, and it's not any different with tests and measurement. You may see test-retest reliability called *time sampling* because the samples of scores are taken at more than one point in time.

For example, let's say that you want to evaluate the reliability of a test that will examine preferences for different types of vocational programs. You may administer the test in September and then readminster the same test (and it's important that it be the same test) again in June. Then, the two sets of scores (remember, the same people took it twice) are correlated, and you have a measure of reliability.

Test-retest reliability is a must when you are examining differences or changes over time. You must be very confident that what you are measuring is being measured in a reliable way such that the results you are getting come as close as possible to the individual's true score each and every time.

Here are some scores from tests at Time 1 and Time 2 for the MVE (Mastering Vocational Education Test) under development. Our goal is to compute the Pearson correlation coefficient as a measure of the test-retest reliability of the instrument.

ID	Score From Test 1	Score From Test 2
1	54	56
2	67	77
3	67	87
4	83	89
5	87	89
6	89	90
7	84	87
8	90	92
9	98	99
10	65	76

The first and last step in this process is to compute the **Pearson product moment correlation** (see Chapter 5 for a refresher on this), which is equal to

$$r_{\text{Time1·Time2}} = .89$$

The subscript to the r in the above (Test 1·Test 2) indicates that we are looking at the reliability of a test using scores from both Test 1 and Test 2. We'll get to the interpretation of this value later in this chapter.

Oops! The Problem With Test-Retest Reliability

You might have thought about these shortcomings already. The biggest critique of test-retest reliability is that when you administer the same test in succession, you run the risk of practice effects (also called carryover effects). This occurs when the first testing influences the second—in other words, on the first testing, the test takers may remember the questions, ideas, concepts, and so on, and that may have an impact on the second testing and their score.

Another problem might be with the interaction between the amount of time between tests and the nature of the sample being tested. For example, suppose you are working with an instrument that assesses some aspect of growth and development in young children. Because individual differences at young ages are so profound, waiting 3 or 6 months to retest motor skills might result in an inaccurate correlation, not because the test is unreliable, but because dramatic changes in behavior occur at that age over that period of time. It's like trying to hit a moving target, and, indeed, if the change is that rapid (and if there is that much variability among those being tested), there may be no way to establish test-retest reliability.

Parallel Forms Reliability

Parallel forms reliability is used when you want to examine the equivalence or similarity between two different forms of the same test.

> You already have seen how test-retest reliability can appear under a different name (time sampling); well, it's the same with parallel forms reliability. You may see parallel forms reliability be called *item sampling* because the samples of scores are taken using different sets of items.

For example, let's say that you are doing a study on memory, and part of the Remember Everything Test (RET) task is to look at 10 different words, memorize them as best as you can, and then recite them back after 20 seconds of study and 10 seconds of rest. As with any good scientist, you want to be sure the reliability of the RET is tested and reported as part of your research.

Because this study takes place over a 2-day period and involves some training of memory skills, you want to have another set of items that is exactly similar in task demands, but obviously cannot be the same as far as content (too easy to remember, right?). So, you create another list of words that is similar to the first. In this example, you want the consistency to be high across forms—the same ideas are being tested, just using a different form.

Here are some scores from the IRMT (I Remember Memory Test) in both Form A and Form B. Our goal is to compute the Pearson correlation coefficient as a measure of the parallel forms reliability of the instrument.

ID	Scores From Form A of the RET	Scores From Form B of the RET
1	4	5
2	5	6
3	3	5
4	6	6
5	7	7
6	5	6
7	6	7
8	4	8
9	3	7
10	3	7

The first and last step in this process is to compute the Pearson product moment correlation, which, in this example, is equal to

$$r_{FormA \cdot FormB} = .12$$

The subscript to the r in the above (Form A·Form B) indicates that we are looking at the reliability of a test using different forms. We'll get to the interpretation of this value shortly.

Internal Consistency Reliability

Internal consistency reliability is quite a bit different from the two previous types of reliability that we have explored. Internal consistency is used when you want to know whether the items on a test are consistent with one another in that they represent one, and only one, dimension, construct, or area of interest throughout the test.

Let's say that you are developing the Attitude Toward Health Care Test (the ATHCT), and you want to make sure that the set of 20 items (with individuals responding on a scale from 1 = *strongly agree* to 5 = *strongly disagree*) measures just that, and nothing else. You would look at the score for each item (for a group of test takers) and see if individual scores correlate with the total score. You would expect that people who scored high on certain items (e.g., "I like my HMO") would have scored low on others (e.g., "I don't like anything other than private health insurance") and that this would be consistent across all the people who took the test.

Split Half Reliability

The first and most simple way to establish internal consistency of a test is by "splitting" the test into two halves and computing what is affectionately called **split half reliability**. Here, the scores on one half of the test are compared with scores on the second half of the test to see if there is a strong relationship between the two. If so, then we can conclude that the test has internal consistency.

THINGS TO REMEMBER

An easy way to estimate internal consistency of a test is through the use of split half reliability. But remember to apply the Spearman-Brown correction (sometimes called the Spearman-Brown correlation or prophecy formula).

But like King Solomon, we have a decision to make here. How do you split the test? If it's a 20-item test, do we take the first 10 items and correlate them with the last 10 items in the group? Or, do we take every other item to form an odd group (such as Items 1, 3, 5, and 7) and an even grouping (such as Items 2, 4, 6, and 8)? It's easier to do the first half-second half method, but dangerous.

Why? Because if items tend to be grouped (inadvertently by subject matter or by difficulty), it is less likely that the groups of items will be deemed equal to one another. Potential trouble in paradise.

So, for our purposes here (and maybe for your purposes there), it's best to select all the odd items for one grouping and all the evens for another, and then turn to computing the correlation coefficient. Fifty such scores appear on page 49. We can see

- ID for each participant

- Total score on each test

- Total score on only the odd items

- Total score on only the even items

To compute the split half reliability coefficient as an indicator of how well integrated or how internally consistent the test is, we simple correlate the score of each person on the odd half of his or her test with the score on the even half. The result? $r_{odd \cdot even}$ = .2428. Internally consistent? We'll get there soon.

King Solomon Might Have Been Off by Half, or Correct Me If I Am Wrong

The big "Oops!" of computing split half reliabilities is that, in effect, you cut the test in half, and, because shorter tests are less reliable, the real degree of reliability is constrained. Spearman Brown to the rescue!

The **Spearman-Brown formula** makes that correction. It's simple and straightforward:

$$r_t = \frac{2r_h}{1 + r_h}$$

where

r_t = equals the simple Pearson product moment correlation (see Appendix A)

r_h = equals the half correlation

ID	Total	Score on Odd Items	Score on Even Items	ID	Total	Score on Odd Items	Score on Even Items	ID	Total	Score on Odd Items	Score on Even Items	ID	Total	Score on Odd Items	Score on Even Items	ID	Total	Score on Odd Items	Score on Even Items
1	43	21	22	11	48	25	23	21	43	18	25	31	47	23	24	41	44	22	22
2	45	18	27	12	42	27	15	22	42	15	27	32	46	21	25	42	41	23	18
3	43	21	22	13	31	17	14	23	31	15	16	33	37	19	18	43	23	11	12
4	46	23	23	14	33	16	17	24	44	15	29	34	32	12	20	44	26	11	15
5	32	15	17	15	31	15	16	25	50	27	23	35	38	14	24	45	28	11	17
6	34	15	19	16	45	23	22	26	14	6	8	36	48	25	23	46	32	14	18
7	21	10	11	17	41	22	19	27	36	18	18	37	41	33	8	47	31	15	16
8	27	13	14	18	43	31	12	28	43	25	18	38	21	13	8	48	45	17	28
9	43	23	20	19	46	15	31	29	23	12	11	39	46	21	25	49	50	29	21
10	36	18	18	20	31	16	15	30	44	22	22	40	43	15	22	50	12	7	5

Here are the steps we take to compute the corrected split half reliability estimate:

1. Compute the split half correlation by either selecting every other item and calculating a score for each half, or selecting the first and second halves of the test and calculating a score for each half.

2. Enter the values in the equation you see above and compute r_t the corrected correlation coefficient.

For example, if you computed the split half reliability coefficient as r = .73, then the corrected split half coefficient would be

$$r_t = \frac{2(.73)}{1 + .73} = .84$$

That's a pretty substantial increase. Take a look at this simple chart of split half correlations before and after they are corrected.

Original Split Half Reliability	Corrected Split Half Reliability	Difference in Reliability Coefficients
0.1	.18	.15 (15%)
0.2	.33	.13 (13%)
0.3	.46	.11 (11%)
0.4	.57	.10 (10%)
0.5	.67	.08 (8%)
0.6	.75	.07 (7%)
0.7	.82	.07 (7%)
0.8	.89	.06 (6%)
0.9	.95	.05 (5%)

Let's first understand what we have here (look at the bolded entries in the table). To begin with, if you have a split half reliability coefficient of 0.5, after correction it is 0.67. And if the corrected split half reliability coefficients increase from 0.67 to 0.75, you have an increase of 0.08. Got all that?

Now, here's what's really, really interesting. If you look at the table, you can see that the amount of increase for corrected split half reliability coefficients *decreases* as the original split half reliability coefficient *increases*, right? Why? Simple—the more reliable the original estimate (the first column), the less room for improvement when corrected. In other words, as a test is more reliable, the less room it has for change.

King Solomon was wise in his decision, but splitting a test in half means half as long a test, and that can create a problem. Why? Shorter tests are less reliable than longer ones in general because shorter tests are less representative than longer ones of the universe of all possible items. For example, if you are preparing a history achievement test on the American Civil War, 20 items would surely cover some information, but 100 would cover much more—a much more representative sample of what could be tested that greatly increases chances that the test is consistent.

Cronbach's Alpha (or α)

Now here's our second way of computing internal consistency estimates for a test: (Lee) **Cronbach's Alpha** (also referred to as **coefficient alpha**) symbolized by the cool little Greek letter alpha, which looks like this: α.

Page 52 lists some sample data for 10 people on a five-item attitude test (the I♥HMO test), where scores are between 1 (*strongly disagree*) and 5 (*strongly agree*) on each item. Cronbach's Alpha is especially useful when you are looking at the reliability of a test that doesn't have right or wrong answers, such as a personality or attitude test. It is used to evaluate the reliability of tests with right answers as well.

TECH TALK

When you compute Cronbach's Alpha (named after Lee Cronbach), you are actually correlating the score for each item with the total score for each individual and then comparing that to the variability present for all individual item scores. The logic is that any individual test taker with a high(er) total test score should have a high(er) score on each item (such as 5, 5, 3, 5, 3, 4, 4, 2, 4, 5) for a total score of 40, and that any individual test taker with a low(er) total test score should have a low(er) score on each individual item (such as 5, 1, 5, 1, 5, 5, 1, 5, 5, 1, 5, 1) for a total score of 40 as well.

ID	Item 1	Item 2	Item 3	Item 4	Item 5
1	3	5	1	4	1
2	4	4	3	5	3
3	3	4	4	4	4
4	3	3	5	2	1
5	3	4	5	4	3
6	4	5	5	3	2
7	2	5	5	3	4
8	3	4	4	2	4
9	3	5	4	4	3
10	3	3	2	3	2

Here's the formula to compute Cronbach's Alpha:

$$\alpha = \left(\frac{k}{k-1}\right)\left(\frac{s_y^2 - \sum s_i^2}{s_y^2}\right)$$

where

k = the number of items

s_y^2 = the variance associated with the observed score

$\sum s_i^2$ = the sum of all the variances for each item

Page 53 shows the same set of data with the values (the variance associated with the observed score, or s_y^2, and the sum of all the variances for each item) needed to complete the above equation, or $\sum s_i^2$.

When you plug all these figures into the equation and get the following equation,

$$\alpha = \left(\frac{5}{5-1}\right)\left(\frac{6.40 - 5.18}{6.4}\right) = .24$$

you find that coefficient alpha is .24 and you're done (except for the interpretation that comes later!).

ID	Item 1	Item 2	Item 3	Item 4	Item 5	Total Score
1	3	5	1	4	1	14
2	4	4	3	5	3	19
3	3	4	4	4	4	19
4	3	3	5	2	1	14
5	3	4	5	4	3	19
6	4	5	5	3	2	19
7	2	5	5	3	4	19
8	3	4	4	2	4	17
9	3	5	4	4	3	19
10	3	3	2	3	2	13
					$s_y^2 = 6.4$	
Item Variance	0.32	0.62	1.96	0.93	1.34	$\sum s_i^2 = 5.18$

The Last One: Internal Consistency
When You're Right or Wrong, and Kuder-Richardson

We've gone through several different ways of estimating internal consistency, and this is the last one. The Kuder-Richardson formulas (there's one called 20 and one called 21) are used when answers are right or wrong, such as true-false tests.

Here are some data for us to work with on another 10-item test, this one containing true and false items.

ID	Item 1	Item 2	Item 3	Item 4	Item 5	Number Correct
1	1	1	1	1	1	5
2	1	1	1	1	1	5
3	1	1	1	1	1	5
4	1	1	1	0	1	4
5	1	1	1	1	1	5
6	1	1	1	0	0	3
7	1	1	1	1	0	4
8	1	1	0	1	0	3
9	1	1	1	0	1	4
10	0	0	0	1	1	2
% Correct (P)	0.90	0.90	0.80	0.70	0.70	
% Incorrect (Q)	0.10	0.10	0.20	0.30	0.30	
P*Q	0.09	0.09	0.16	0.21	0.21	
Sum of P*Q	0.76					
Variance of Number Correct	1.11					
Number of Items	5					
Number of Test Takers	10					

where

ID = the test taker's ID number

Item 1, Item 2, etc. = whether or not the item was correct (1) or not (0)

Number Correct = the total number of correct items

P = the percentage of individuals who got an item correct

Q = the percentage of individuals who got an item incorrect

P*Q = the product of P and Q

Variance = the variance of the number correct on the test across individuals

And the magic formula is

$$KR_{20} = \left(\frac{n}{n-1} \right) \left(\frac{s^2 - \Sigma PQ}{s^2} \right)$$

where

n = the number of items on the test

s^2 = the variance of total test scores

ΣPQ = the sum of the product of the percentage of correct times and the percentage of incorrect on each item

When we plug in the data you see above into the KR_{20} formula, the grand total (and drum roll, please) is

$$KR_{20} = \left(\frac{5}{5-1} \right) \left(\frac{1.11 - .76}{s} \right) = .40$$

A KR_{20} of .40—good, bad, or indifferent? Hang on for more soon.

Interrater Reliability

We've covered pretty extensively a variety of different types of reliability, but all of these had to do with the reliability of the instrument. Now let's tackle the reliability of those *administering* the instrument. We measure **interrater reliability** when we want to know how much two raters agree on their judgments of some outcome.

For example, let's say you are interested in a particular type of social interaction during a transaction between a banker and a potential checking account customer. You observe both people in real time (you're observing behind a one-way mirror) to see if the new and improved customer relations course that the banker took resulted in increased smiling and pleasant types of behavior toward the potential customer. Your job is to note every 10 seconds if the banker is demonstrating one of the three different behaviors she has been taught—smiling, leaning forward in her chair, or using her hands to make a point. Each time you see any one of those behaviors, you mark it on your scoring sheet as a slash (/). If you observe nothing, you record a dash like this: —.

As part of this process, and to be sure that what you are recording is a reliable measure, you will want to find out what the level of agreement is between different observers as to the occurrence of these behaviors. The more similar the ratings are, the higher the level of interrater agreement and interrater reliability.

In this example, the really important variable here is whether or not any one of the three customer-friendly acts occurred within a set of 10-second time frames across 2 minutes (or twelve 10-second periods). So, what we are looking at is the rating consistency across a 2-minute time period broken down into twelve 10-second periods. A slash on the scoring sheet means that the behavior occurred, and a dash means it did not.

Time period →	1	2	3	4	5	6	7	8	9	10	11	12
Rater 1 Dave	/	—	/	/	/	—	/	/	—	—	/	/
Rater 2 Anne	/	—	/	/	/	—	/	/	—	/	—	/

For a total of 12 periods (and 12 possible agreements), there are 7 where both Dave and Anne agreed that the banker did do the customer-friendly thing (Periods 1, 3, 4, 5, 7, 8, and 12), and 3 where they agreed it did not (Periods 2, 6, and 9), for a total of 10 agreements and 2 disagreements.

Interrater reliability is computed using the following simple formula.

$$\text{Interrater reliability} = \frac{\text{Number of agreements}}{\text{Number of disagreements}}$$

and when we plug in the numbers as you see here,

$$\text{Interrater reliability} = \frac{10}{12} = .833$$

the resulting interrater reliability coefficient is .83.

TECH TALK   Notice in the case of interrater reliability, the coefficient that we use is an actual proportion. This is not the case with the correlations used to describe other types of reliability. Even though they may look like proportions, they are not.

HOW BIG IS BIG? INTERPRETING RELIABILITY COEFFICIENTS

OK—now we get down to the business of better understanding just how big a reliability coefficient, regardless of its flavor (test-retest, etc.), has to be in order to be "acceptable."

We want only two things here:

- We want reliability coefficients to be positive.
- We want reliability coefficients that are as large as possible (between +.00 and +1.00).

For example, let's look at the reliability coefficients we computed for the four types of reliability discussed in this section of the chapter and make some judgments.

Type of Reliability	Sample Value	Interpretation	What's Next?
Test-retest reliability	.89	The test is reasonably consistent over time. A reasonable goal is for the coefficient to be above .70, and, better, to be in the .80s or .90s.	Not much. This is a pretty reliable test, and you can move forward using it with confidence.
Parallel forms reliability	.12	The test does not seem to be very consistent over different forms. The value .12 is a very low reliability coefficient.	Work on the development of a new and better alternative form of the test.
Internal consistency reliability	.24	The test does not seem to be one-dimensional in that these items are not consistently measuring the same thing.	Be sure that the items on the test measure what they are supposed to (which, by the way, is as much a validity issue as a reliability issue—stay tuned for the next chapter).

In general, an acceptable reliability coefficient is .70 or above, but much more acceptable is .8 and above. It's rare to see values much larger than that. However, when it comes to interrater reliability, we should really expect nothing less than 90%. It's so easily raised (just have the judges do more training, given that the terms on the test are good ones) that there is no reason why this higher level should not be reached.

THINGS TO REMEMBER

OK, here's the big warning. If you're reading along in a journal article and realize, "Hey—there's nothing here about the reliability of the instruments they used," then a little flag should go up. There are usually two reasons for this. The first is that the test being used is so well known and so popular that it is common knowledge in the field. That would be true for such tests as the Wechsler Intelligence Scale for Children, the Stanford Achievement Tests, or the Minnesota Multiphasic Personality Inventory. The second reason would be that the original designers of the test never collected the kind of data they needed to make a judgment about the reliability of the test—a very dangerous and unproductive situation. If someone is going to go to the effort of establishing the reliability of a test, and not use it unless it is reliable, they are surely going to brag about it a bit. If the information isn't there, and it is not because of reason #1 above, look for trouble in River City beginning with a U (for unreliable).

AND IF YOU CAN'T ESTABLISH RELIABILITY . . . THEN WHAT?

The road to establishing the reliability of a test is not a smooth one at all, and not one that does not take a good deal of work. What if the test is not reliable?

Here are a few things to keep in mind. Remember that reliability is a function of how much error contributes to the observed score. Lower that error and you increase the reliability.

- Make sure that the instructions are standardized across all settings when the test is administered.

- Increase the number of items or observations, because the larger the sample from the universe of behaviors you are investigating, the more likely the sample is representative and reliable. This is especially true for achievement tests.

- Delete unclear items, because some people will respond in one way and others will respond in a different fashion, regardless of their knowledge, ability level, or individual traits.

- For achievement tests especially (such as spelling or history tests), moderate the easiness and difficulty of tests, because any test that is too difficult or too easy does not reflect an accurate picture of one's performance.

- Minimize the effects of external events and standardize directions. If a particularly important event—such as Mardi Gras or graduation—occurs near the time of testing, postpone any assessment.

JUST ONE MORE THING (AND IT'S A BIG ONE)

The first step in creating or using an instrument that has sound psychometric (how's that for a big word?) properties is to establish its reliability (and we just spent some good time on that).

Why? Well, if a test or measurement instrument is not reliable, is not consistent, and does not do the same thing time after time after time, it does not matter what it measures (and that's the mother of all validity questions), right?

But the real reasoning is as follows.

Let's say you are looking at the effects of X on Y and you create some test to measure Y. If the test that you create is not reliable, how can you ever know that X actually caused any change you see in Y? Perhaps the change was just due to random variation and error and nothing related to X. And, if there is no change in Y, how do you know it's not due to a poorly constructed and developed test rather than the fact that X has no effect?

This is not easy stuff and takes thoughtfulness on the part of the practitioner as well as the consumer. Know whether or not your test is unreliable, what kind of reliability is important given the purpose of the test, and how to increase it if necessary.

SUMMARY

Reliability of test instruments is essential to good science no matter what you are studying. You've learned about several ways that reliability can be established. Now it's time to move on and look at reliability's first cousin, validity, and discuss what validity is essential and how it is established.

TIME TO PRACTICE

1. Go the library and find five articles from journals in your field or discipline that do empirical research where data are collected and hypotheses are stated. Now answer these questions:
   a. What types of reliability coefficients are appropriate for each of the five articles?
   b. How many of these articles discuss the reliability of the measures that are being used?
   c. If information about the reliability of the measures is not discussed, why do you think this is the case?

2. Dr. Stu has already created an ability personality test that he finds to be highly unreliable, and he knows that unreliability is usually due to method or trait error. Name three potential sources of each of these kinds of error and speculate on how they might be eliminated or decreased.

3. Here are some data on the same test that was administered at the beginning of a treatment program (for balance training in the elderly) given in October and given again in May after 7 months of programs.
   a. What kind of reliability coefficient would you establish and why?
   b. What's your interpretation of the reliability coefficient?

October Score	May Score
5	8
4	7
3	5
6	7
7	8
8	9
7	8
5	5
5	6
8	9

4. What does it mean to say that a test is internally consistent, and when might that not be important?

5. What's the primary danger in using a test that's not reliable?

ANSWERS TO PRACTICE QUESTIONS

1. You're on your own on this one, but be sure to find articles in your own discipline and those you find of interest.

2. For method error, we might
   a. have a poorly reproduced test (change the toner in the copy machine)
   b. be in a room that's too cold (raise the thermostat)
   c. be trying to work on a computer that won't boot (use a different computer)

   For trait error, we might
   a. party too late for too long (don't)
   b. fail to study (don't)
   c. study with the wrong study group (duh!)

3. a. Test-retest reliability
   b. The resulting coefficient is .82, pretty high and certainly indicating that there is a significant and strong correlation between the two testings and, hence, test-retest reliability.

4. A test is internally consistent when it "speaks with one voice." That is, the items tend to measure the same construct, idea, or information. It is important when the goal of the test is to measure one, and only one, idea, construct, or thing.

5. If the test that you use is unreliable, you'll never know if it's valid (how can something do what it is supposed to do if it cannot do it consistently?). And, your hypothesis is never fairly tested. You never know if the hypothesis is supported because the instrument you use is unreliable and the results are untrustworthy.

WANT TO KNOW MORE?

Further Readings

- Winstanley, M. R. (2004). The relationship between intimacy and later parenting behaviors in adolescent fathers. *Dissertation Abstracts International: Section B: The Sciences and Engineering,* 64(11B), 5822.

   This study demonstrates how the lack of reliability threatens the value of a study's results.

- Eckstein, D., & Cohen, L. (1998). The Couple's Relationship Satisfaction Inventory (CR51): 21 points to help enhance and build a winning relationship. *Family Journal of Counseling and Therapy for Couples and Families, 6*(2), 155–158.

  A hands-on example of using an instrument with established reliability.

And on the Internet

- You can find a discussion of the reliability, validity, and fairness of classroom testing at http://www.ncrel.org/sdrs/areas/issues/methods/assment/as5relia.htm.

- And as a construct, reliability is very important as well when applied to different areas, such as the reliability of child witnesses. Read more at http://abcnews.go.com/Technology/story?id=97726&page=1.

The Truth, the Whole Truth, and Nothing But the Truth

Validity and Its Importance

Difficulty Index ☺☺ (right there with
Chapter 3—a bit tough)

Validity is simply the property of an assessment tool that indicates that the tool does what it says it does. And if it does that (that is, a test has validity), then test scores have meaning. After all, if a test is not valid, then what meaning can we attach to outcomes produced by it? For example, if an achievement test is supposed to measure knowledge of history, and it is a valid test, then that's what it does—it measures knowledge of history. If an intelligence test is supposed to measure intelligence as defined by the test's creators, and it is a valid test, then it does just that.

Our hands-on, real-life examples come from John Govern and Lisa Marsh, who developed and validated the Situational Self-Awareness Scale (or SSAS—test folks love acronyms), which is a measure of self-awareness. The authors conducted five studies to assess the reliability and validity of the scale using 849 undergraduates as participants and found that the scale detected differences in public and private self-awareness. In other words, it does what it says it does!

Want to know more? Govern, J., & Marsh, L. (2001). Development and validation of the Situational Self-Awareness Scale. *Consciousness and Cognition: An International Journal, 10*(3), 366–378.

A BIT MORE ABOUT THE TRUTH

Establishing the validity of a test is a whole different ball game from establishing its reliability. The primary reason for this is that when we discussed reliability as we did in Chapter 3, we specified objective measures that you could use to quantify the degree of reliability (using correlation coefficients). With validity, this is just not the case.

There are some quantitative measures of validity, but we'll leave those for the next tests and measurement course you'll be taking. What we need to be concerned about here is what kind of *external evidence* (be that a judge or results from another study) we can bring to our understanding of a test so that we can conclude that the test is valid. And because we can't attach a number to the notion of validity very easily, we talk about the degree of validity along a continuum from weak to strong.

TECH TALK Let's get more technical about a definition of validity. The several governing bodies that have guidelines about the development of tests (such as the American Psychological Association and the National Council on Measurement in Education) have this as the general definition of validity—*the extent to which inferences made from it are appropriate, meaningful, and useful*. A bit more wordy, but it conveys the general message that a valid test does what it's supposed to.

For example, if you design a physics test that covers the laws of thermodynamics (are we having fun yet?), you could claim that this test has validity by providing the following kinds of evidence:

- Several physicists who are recognized as leaders in their field identify the questions you created as ones that accurately reflect the content in the field.

- You can show that other tests that cover the same material (and have already been validated) are very closely related to this test.

- Your activities used to plan this unit in the course are well reflected by the number and types of items on the test.

Here's another example, this time for a test of aggression. What can you do to provide evidence that this test is valid?

- You have observed previously identified aggressive people, and they score higher on the test (meaning they are more aggressive) than those who are not aggressive.

- You correlate your findings with a set of other criteria that, in theory, supports your definition and ideas of what aggression is.

We'll attach formal names to these procedures and the type of validity that they describe later on in this chapter, but for now remember this. A test is valid when it does what it was designed to do—nothing more and nothing less.

Reliability and Validity: Very Close Cousins

Now that you have some idea of what validity is, it's a good time to mention the very special relationship between reliability and validity.

THINGS TO REMEMBER

Always remember that validity wants to know what's being tested and reliability how consistently.

Most simply put, a test cannot be valid before it is reliable. Think about it—reliability is the quality of a test being consistent, right? And validity, of a test doing what it is designed to do. How can anything do what it is supposed to (validity) if it cannot do what it is supposed to consistently (reliability)? It can't. End of story.

DIFFERENT TYPES OF VALIDITY

Just as there are different types of reliability, so are there different types of validity, and we'll cover the three most important types in this section. They are all summarized in Table 4.1.

TABLE 4.1	Different Types of Validity and How They Work		
Type of Validity	When You Use It	How You Do It	An Example of What You Can Say When You're Done
Content validity	When you want to know whether a sample of items truly reflects an entire universe of items in a certain topic.	Examine the content very closely and be sure that it is an accurate sample of what you want to test.	My weekly quiz in my stat class fairly assesses the chapter's content.
Criterion validity	When you want to know if test scores are systematically related to other criteria that indicate the test taker is competent in a certain area.	Correlate the scores from the test with some other measure that is already valid and assesses the same set of abilities.	The EATS test (of culinary skills) has been shown to be correlated with being a fine chef 2 years after culinary school (an example of predictive validity).
Construct validity	When you want to know if a test measures some underlying psychological construct.	Correlate the set of test scores with some theorized outcome that reflects the construct for which the test is being designed.	It's true – men who participate in body contact and physically dangerous sports score higher on the TEST(osterone) test of aggression.

Content Validity

Content validity is the property of a test such that the test items sample the universe of items for which the test is designed. Content validity is most often used for achievement tests (like everything from your first-grade spelling test to the SAT).

Establishing Content Validity

Establishing content validity is really a matter of answering the following question: Does the collection of items on the test fairly represent all the possible questions that could be asked?

Some tests and measurement specialists think that content validity is nothing other than a sampling issue. How well do you select items for the test that are representative of all the possible items? Let's use that physics test we mentioned earlier as an example.

Let's say you are creating a final exam for a Physics I class and you want the exam to have content validity. One thing you can do is map out and then define the amount of time you spend on each topic (such as the experimental method or the laws of thermodynamics, and so on). The number of items on the test should reflect the amount of time spent teaching each topic. In theory, you will be creating a test that accurately reflects the universe of knowledge from which these items can be drawn.

TECH TALK

Want to get fancy? Remember that as good scientists, we are very interested in providing data that support our conclusions and such. So, wouldn't it be grand to have some quantifiable measure of content validity? It would, and here it is.

C. H. Lawshe, the vocational psychologist, invented one such measure called the *content validity ratio*. A set of judges decides whether each question on a test is essential, useful but not essential, or not necessary to the performance of the job or skill under examination. Then, the data are entered into this equation:

$$CVR = \frac{n_e - \frac{N}{2}}{\frac{N}{2}}$$

where

CVR = the content validity ratio

n_e = the number of judges who selected the essential questions

N = the total number of judges

So, for each item, the CVR is computed. For example, if there were 10 judges and 5 of them judge an item as essential (perhaps the criterion you want to use), then CVR would equal

$$CVR = \frac{5 - \frac{10}{2}}{\frac{10}{2}} = 0$$

So, any value less than 0 means that there is less than adequate agreement that the item is essential to the job or skill for which it is intended. This ratio really pertains to item performance (not test), but you can certainly get a good idea as to which items seem to have the level of content validity you need to proceed.

Content validity is used most often for achievement tests and certification or licensing.

> Appearances can be misleading. Sometimes, you'll see the phrase "face validity" used synonymously with the phrase "content validity." Nope—not the same. Face validity is claimed to be present if the items on a test appear to adequately cover the content or if a test expert thinks they do. Kind of like, "Hey Albert (or Alberta), do you think this set of 100 multiple-choice items accurately reflects all the possible topics and ideas that I would expect the students in my introductory class to understand?" In this context, face validity is more like "approval" validity—it's the general impression that the test does what one thinks it should. The important distinction is that face validity is more or less a social judgment rendered by some outside person (even if an expert) without the application of any external criterion such as the type we discussed about content validity.

Criterion Validity

Criterion validity assesses whether a test reflects a set of abilities in a current or future setting as measured by some other test. If the criterion is taking place in the here and now (around the same time or simultaneously), we talk about concurrent criterion validity or just **concurrent validity**. Criterion validity is used most often for achievement tests and certification or licensing.

If the criterion is taking place in the future, we talk about predictive concurrent validity or just **predictive validity**. Predictive validity is most often used in entrance examinations (such as the Graduate Record Exam) and for employment (such as the ACER Test of Employment Entry Mathematics published by the Australian Council for Educational Research Ltd.).

For criterion validity to be present, one need not establish both concurrent and predictive validity—only the one that works for the purposes of the test.

Establishing Concurrent Validity

You've been hired by the Universal Culinary Institute to design an instrument that measures culinary skills, perhaps for certification or licensing by a national board. Some part of culinary training has to do with basic knowledge, such as "What's a roux?" That's left to the achievement test side of things.

So, you develop a test that you think does a good job of measuring culinary skills (such as knife technique, pasty crust creation, and so on—hungry yet?), and now you want to establish the level of concurrent validity of the test. To do this, you design the COOK scale, a set of 5-point items across a set of criteria (presentation, cleanliness, etc.) that each judge will use. So, the COOK scale is the assessment tool for which you want to establish criterion validity. Now we need a criterion against which to judge COOK performance.

As a criterion (and that's the key here), you have a set of judges rank each student from 1 to 10 on overall ability as the school has been doing it for years. So, the average judge's grade is the criterion. Then, you simply correlate the COOK scores with the judge's rankings. If the validity coefficient (a simple correlation) is high, you're in business—if not, it's back to the drawing board. In this example, you have established construct validity by the very nature of the criterion being closely related to what you want your test to measure.

There's More to Validity Than Meets the Eye

In some ways, validity is a pretty straightforward concept—if a test does what it should, then it's valid. But the threats to validity go way, way beyond this simple idea.

The presence of validity can also be thought of as a very general criterion affected by a host of variables such as bias, ethics, and the wide-ranging social and legal implications that surround testing and the testing establishment (those folks who design, manufacture, and sell tests). Each one of these topics deserves a book in itself, but we'll provide a brief overview in Part V of *Tests & Measurement . . .* Stay tuned.

Establishing Predictive Validity

Let's say that the cooking school has been percolating (heh heh) along just fine for 10 years, and you are interested not only in how well people cook (and that's the concurrent validity part of this exercise that you just established) but also in the *predictive validity* of the COOK scale. In other words, how well does the COOK scale predict cooking success later on? Now the criterion changes from a here-and-now score (the one that judges give) to one that looks to the future.

We are interested in how well scores on the COOK test predict success as a chef 10 years down the line. Now, to do that, of course (because we are exploring the predictive nature of the COOK test), we need to locate graduates of the program who have been out cooking for 10 years and look at their previously taken COOK scores.

The criterion being used here is whether the graduates own their own restaurant and whether it has been in business for more than 1 year (given that the failure rate for new restaurants is more than 70% within the first year). The rationale here is that if a restaurant is in business for more than 1 year, then the chef must be doing something right.

To complete this exercise, you correlate the COOK score with a value of 1 (if the restaurant is in business for more than a year and owned by the graduate) or 0 (if the graduate is now selling fries at a local fast food place) with the COOK score from 10 years earlier. A high coefficient indicates predictive validity, and a low correlation indicates the lack thereof.

Hmmm . . . About That Criterion

It's probably obvious to you by now that the key to establishing either concurrent or predictive validity (criterion validity of any kind) is the *quality of the criterion*. If the criterion is not an accurate reflection of what it is that you want to be sure you are measuring, then the correlations mean nothing, right? For example, if you wanted to test the concurrent validity of the COOK scale, you would not use income as the criterion because it has no clearly established relationship to the skill learned in culinary school.

So, what makes a good criterion, and how do you find one?

First, as usual and as Ben Franklin surely said at one point, common sense doesn't hurt. Criterion validity is often used to establish the validity of aptitude and performance tests, and it does not take a rocket scientist to determine what set of skills might be related to those being tested. If you're interested in looking at the concurrent validity for a test of secretarial skills, criteria such as personality, organizing skills, and efficiency (all defined in one way or another) would seem to fit fine. Or, if you are interested in the predictive validity of an aptitude test for teaching, then teacher ratings would work just fine as well.

Second, there's always the massive amount of literature on a particular ability or trait or performance skill that you can find in the library in your discipline's journals. If an article discusses how important spatial skills are to mechanical engineering, then you might move toward an established test of spatial skills (such as the Minnesota Spatial Relations Test published by American Guidance Service, Inc.). Here's where having a good understanding of your subject matter comes in very handy.

Third, any criterion that you select should (of course) be reliable (in the same sense as we use the term in Chapter 3) and should not be too close to what you are validating (called **criterion contamination**—a big oops!). For example, if you are looking for the predictive validity of real estate selling, don't use as a criterion sales figures in another area, such as cars or appliances—just too close to what you are trying to accomplish. Or, if you have judges rating people on some external criterion, be sure that the judges know nothing about the student's previous performance, study habits, attitudes, and so forth.

Construct Validity

Construct validity is the most interesting, ambitious, and difficult of all the validities to establish. This is because constructs are not easily defined concepts, and, hence, the tests that measure them are difficult to construct and validate.

You may remember from your extensive studies in Psych 1 that a construct is a group of interrelated variables. For example, aggression is a construct (consisting perhaps of such variables as inappropriate touching, physical violence, lack of successful social interaction, etc.), as is intelligence, mother-infant attachment, and hope—all constructs. And keep in mind that constructs are always generated from some theoretical position that the researcher assumes—that's really important.

For example, one's theoretical model of aggression might propose that aggressive men are more often in trouble with the authorities than nonaggressive men. This is important because such predictions or hypotheses then can be translated into real-world tests of these relationships and tests of the instrument's construct validity as well.

Establishing Construct Validity

So, you have the FIGHT test (of aggression), which is a self-report, paper-and-pencil tool that consists of a series of items that is an outgrowth of your theoretical view about what the construct of aggression consists of. You know from your extensive review of the criminology literature that males who are aggressive do certain types of things more than males who are not aggressive—for example, they get into more arguments, they are more physically aggressive (pushing and such), they commit more crimes of violence against others, and they have fewer successful interpersonal relationships.

The FIGHT scale includes different types of items, some of them related to these behaviors (and the underlying theory) and others that are not. Once the FIGHT scale is completed, you examine the results to see if "positive" scores on the FIGHT correlate with the presence of the kinds of behaviors you would predict (level of involvement in crime, quality of personal relationships, etc.) and don't correlate with the kinds of behaviors that should not be related (such as lack of domestic violence, completion of high school, steady employment, etc.). If the correlation is high for the items that you predict should correlate and low for the items that should not, then you can conclude that there is something about the FIGHT scale (and it is probably the items you designed) that does accurately assess aggression. Congratulations, you've established construct validity.

But wait (with thanks to Ron Popeil)—there's more!

The Tough (But Cool) One: The Multitrait-Multimethod Way of Establishing Construct Validity

Our previous description is a simple and elegant way of establishing construct validity, but there are others as well. One ingenious way that you'll read about in your studies and deserves a bit of time here is the **multitrait-multimethod matrix** developed by Julian Campbell and Donald Fisk in 1959. Warning—this is not terribly easy stuff, but just spend some time thinking about the following explanation as you work through Figure 4.1. This technique is the Rolls-Royce of establishing construct validity, so taking a little extra time to understand it will be well worth it.

		Observation			Self-Report			Teacher Ratings		
		Aggression	Intelligence	Emotional Stability	Aggression	Intelligence	Emotional Stability	Aggression	Intelligence	Emotional Stability
Observation	Aggression	(Very High)								
	Intelligence	Moderate	(Very High)							
	Emotional Stability	Moderate	Moderate	(Very High)						
Self-Report	Aggression	**High**	Low	Low	(Very High)					
	Intelligence	Low	**High**	Low	Moderate	(Very High)				
	Emotional Stability	Low	Low	**High**	Moderate	Moderate	(Very High)			
Teacher Ratings	Aggression	**High**	Low	Low	**High**	Low	Low	(Very High)		
	Intelligence	Low	**High**	Low	Low	**High**	Low	Moderate	(Very High)	
	Emotional Stability	Low	Low	**High**	Low	Low	**High**	Moderate	Moderate	(Very High)

Figure 4.1   Here's How a Multitrait-Multimethod Matrix Would Look if Construct Validity Is Present

73

THINGS TO REMEMBER

The multitrait-multimethod matrix is the top-of-the-mountain way of establishing construct validity, but it takes a good deal of time and resources to see it through to completion.

In the multitrait-multimethod technique, you measure more than one trait using more than one method and then look for certain relationships (between methods and traits that support your ideas). For example, let's say that you wanted to establish the construct validity of the FIGHT test and you use the following methods:

1. An observational tool

2. A self-report tool (the FIGHT method)

3. Teacher ratings

to measure the following three traits:

1. Aggression (the FIGHT trait)

2. Intelligence

3. Emotional stability

As you can see in Figure 4.1, you have a bunch of correlations between all traits and all methods, and if the FIGHT scale really works (that is, it has construct validity) as a measure of aggression, here's what you would expect:

1. The lows (the plain type in Figure 4.1) represent different methods being used to measure different traits. You'd expect these to be very low because they share nothing in common—no trait or method similarities.

2. The *moderates* (in the shaded cells in Figure 4.1) represent the same methods being used to measure different traits. You'd expect these to be moderate because they have the same method in common.

3. The *highs* (appearing in bold and italic in Figure 4.1) represent correlations between different methods measuring the same trait—and these are all very important validity coefficients. Here's where a high value validates the use of a new method (such as the FIGHT test) with an existing one that has already been validated through different means.

4. The (very high)s (appearing in parentheses in Figure 4.1 along the diagonal of the set of correlation coefficients) represent correlations between the same method measuring the same trait—you know these already as reliability coefficients.

The whole logic behind this technique is based on the fundamental assumption that the correlations between two methods being used to measure the same trait are higher than the correlations where the same method is used to measure different traits (the moderates in Figure 4.1).

In other words, regardless of the method being used (the FIGHT scale or an observational tool, for example), the results are similar. And that, coupled with the correlations between different methods measuring the same trait (the bolded validity coefficients in Figure 4.1) being high, gives you strong evidence that the FIGHT test has construct validity.

And If You Can't Establish Validity . . . Then What?

Well, this is a tough one.

In general, if you don't have the validity evidence you want, it's because your test is not doing what it should (but there's more). If it's an achievement test, and a satisfactory level of content validity is what you seek, you probably have to redo the questions on your test to make sure they are more consistent with what they should be according to that expert.

If you are concerned with criterion validity, then you probably need to reexamine the nature of the items on the test and answer the question of how well you would expect these responses to these questions to relate to the criterion you selected. And, of course, you have to examine the reliability and usefulness or relevance of the criterion.

And finally, if it is construct validity that you are seeking and can't seem to find, better take a close look at the theoretical rationale that underlies the test you developed and the items you created to reflect that rationale. Perhaps your definition and theoretical model are underdeveloped (a euphemism for wrong!), or perhaps they just need some critical rethinking.

A LAST FRIENDLY WORD

Now that we are at the end of our discussion on reliability and validity, here are some friendly words of advice.

There's a great temptation for undergraduate students working on their honors thesis or semester project, or graduate students working on their thesis or dissertation, to design an instrument for their final project. *Danger, Will Robinson!* This may not be such a good idea, for the simple reason that the process of establishing the reliability and validity of any instrument can take years of intensive work (which is reason enough to leave it alone). And, what can make matters even worse is when the naïve or unsuspecting individual wants to create a new instrument to test a new hypothesis. On top of everything else that comes with testing a new hypothesis, there is also the work of making sure the instrument works.

THINGS TO REMEMBER

It is a Herculean task to design anything other than the most simple of tests for use in your research. So, if you propose to do such, get ready for lots of questions as to why you don't want to use an existing test.

If you are doing original research of your own—such as for your thesis or dissertation requirement—be sure and try to find a measure that has already had reliability and validity evidence well established. That way, you can get on with the main task of testing your hypotheses and not fooling with the huge task of instrument development—a career in and of itself.

TECH TALK

More Reliability-Validity Goings-on

You've read about the relationship between reliability and validity several places in this chapter, but there's a very cool one lurking out there that you may read about later in your coursework that you should know about now. This relationship says that the maximum level of validity (such as that measured by one of the coefficients we talked about) is equal to the square root of the reliability coefficient. For example, if the reliability coefficient for establishing the test-retest validity for a test of mechanical aptitude is .87, the validity coefficient (the correlation of a test with some other test) can be no larger than .93 (which is the square root of .87). What this means in tech talk is that the validity of a test is constrained by how reliable it is. And that makes perfect sense if we stop to think that a test must do what it does consistently before we are sure it does what it says it does.

SUMMARY

This has been an interesting tour through the world of validity (after just having discussed reliability), so you now have a good idea regarding the value of both consistency and truthfulness when it comes to understanding tests and how they are constructed and used. Our next task takes us to understanding test scores, the focus of Chapter 5.

TIME TO PRACTICE

1. Go to the library and find five journal articles in your area of interest where reliability and validity data are reported, as well as the outcomes measures that are used. Identify the type of reliability that was established, the type of validity, and comment whether you think that the levels are acceptable. If not, how can they be improved?

2. Provide an example of how you establish the construct validity of a test of shyness.

3. When testing any experimental hypothesis, why is it important that the test you use to measure the outcome be both reliable and valid?

4. You're smart, right? Why not spend your dissertation or thesis time developing a test?

5. Why pay so much attention to the selection of the criterion when criterion validity is under discussion?

ANSWERS TO PRACTICE QUESTIONS

1. Do this one on your own, but keep in mind that long-established and -used tests often do not have any reports of these indexes because they have been established and are common knowledge in the field.

2. Here's one way:
   a. Develop your test based on some theory that relates to the construct of shyness.
   b. Using some other well-established criterion, find people who are shy and those who are not and administer your test.
   c. Now, find out how the people in both of these groups scored on your test of shyness. Those who were in the shy group should be differentiated on the test by those in the nonshy group.
   d. If so, you're done! Congratulations. If not, take the next course.

3. You need to use a test that is both reliable and valid because if you get a null result, you will never be sure that the instrument is not measuring what it is supposed to rather than the hypothesis being faulty.

4. It's just a matter of time (and money). If you have 5 or 10 years to finish school, then this is fine because it can take a very long time to develop almost any test, especially one that deals with complex social or psychological topics. Instead, why not use an already established tool?

5. Because the criterion is it! The criterion, in theory anyway, should relate to whatever outcome you are trying to validate through the use of the test you are creating.

WANT TO KNOW MORE?

Further Readings

- Edwards, W. R., & Schleicher, D. J. (2004). On selecting psychology graduate students: Validity evidence for a test of tacit knowledge. *Journal of Educational Psychology, 96*(3), 592–602.

  These researchers looked for evidence for the criterion-related validity of tacit knowledge (TK) as another measure for selecting graduate students for advanced study in psychology.

- Supple, A. J., Peterson, G. W., & Bush, K. R. (2004). Assessing the validity of parenting measures in a sample of Chinese adolescents. *Journal of Family Psychology, 18*(3), 539–544.

  These investigators found that measures of negative parenting that included physical or psychological manipulations may be relevant for understanding the development of Chinese adolescents.

And on the Internet

- Lots more on the very cool multitrait-multimethod matrix, brought to you by William M. K. Trochim at http://www.social researchmethods.net/kb/mtmmmat.htm.

- A detailed discussion by William C. Burns on content, face, and quantitative validity awaits you at http://www.burns.com/ wcbcontval.htm.

5 Welcome to Lake Woebegone, Where All the Children Are Above Average

Norms and Percentiles

Difficulty Index ☺☺☺ (a bit of math)

I t seems to be part of the testing thing. Almost all of us get very anxious about our test scores. We can't wait to get that paper back, check the listing of grades posted on the professor's door (not by name or student number—see Chapter 19), or check the class Web site and find out if we got the grade we wanted.

But test scores and grades and assessment results come in all shapes and sizes. A score of 5 is not that great on a 50-question, multiple-choice history test, but it's the best you can get on an Advanced Placement Writing Test offered by the Educational Testing Service. So, a 5 is not always a 5 is not always a 5.

And, being in the 90th percentile is a pretty high *relative* score (and you'll learn about percentiles, or relative scores, in this chapter) and sounds acceptable, unless the skill you're trying to master is so important (like properly filling a syringe) that anything short of the 99th percentile is not acceptable.

THINGS TO REMEMBER

A raw score is a raw score is a raw score. Not always. Raw scores are one thing, but scores can take on many different appearances and be used in different ways as well.

So, we have all these different types of test scores, and we need to know what they mean and how we can use them. That's what this chapter is all about.

Throughout this chapter, we'll use the data set that you see in Table 5.1, which is the number correct on a 20-item test for 50 different people.

TABLE 5.1   Number Correct on a 20-Item Test for 50 Different People

ID	Name	Raw Score	ID	Name	Raw Score
1	Bruce	12	26	Sabey	17
2	Chandler	20	27	David	11
3	Susan	17	28	Maria	14
4	Zachary	8	29	Maureen	19
5	Danae	15	30	Keith	13
6	Talya	6	31	Mark	6
7	Michael	15	32	Pam	9
8	Noah	5	33	Kim	16
9	Jerry	15	34	Burce	12
10	Faith	8	35	Adam	19
11	David	19	36	Stu	18
12	Leni	15	37	Nancy	17
13	Sara	8	38	David	8
14	Micah	11	39	Suzie	16
15	Pepper	14	40	Jan	12
16	Lew	16	41	Kent	5
17	Linda	7	42	Annette	5
18	Rachael	20	43	Lisa	9
19	Gregory	17	44	Jim	6
20	Russ	11	45	Deborah	5
21	Sue	19	46	Sam	16
22	Max	16	47	Seth	19
23	Sophie	14	48	George	9
24	Dave	19	49	Ann Marie	9
25	Lori	7	50	John	5

THE BASICS: RAW (SCORES) TO THE BONE!

Let's start with the basics. A **raw score** is the score you observe or the observed score (we talked about this in Chapter 3). It is the original and *untransformed* score before any operation is performed on it or anything is done to it. It is, what it is, what it is. It's the list of scores you see in Table 5.1.

But because raw scores do have an important use (we'll get there in a moment), they do need to be collected and reported accurately. What's important about them? Raw scores form the basis for other scores, such as percentiles, standard scores, and so on—and those scores are very important for interpreting performance.

So, raw scores, by themselves, are relatively meaningless. Even if we know that someone got 18 out of 20 questions correct, we have no idea how difficult the questions are, what type of questions were used, whether the test was timed or not, and a wealth of other factors that provide us with the kind of information we need to make decisions about performance.

For example, in Table 5.1, you can see that Stu (ID #36) got a raw score of 18 and Lori (ID #25) got a raw score of 7. We know that there were 20 items on the test, but we don't know much more. In some instances (such as reaction time for an airline pilot), a lower score is better, whereas in others (number of correct responses), a higher score is. Let's move on and distinguish between two general classes of scores and then discuss them in depth.

The first class of scores is **norm-referenced scores**, where we use norms to evaluate one's relative performance. Within that general category, we'll discuss such scores as percentiles, standard scores, and normalized scores. For example, Stu scored much better than the majority of the other 49 test takers.

Then, we'll move on to criterion-referenced scores, where we compare scores to a certain absolute criterion. For example, Stu did not meet the criterion of 95% correct (which, let's say, is required as a condition of being certified as a CPR instructor).

Norms are a set of scores that represents a collection of individual performances and is developed by administering a test to a large group of test takers. Then, this complete set of scores is the measure by which the individual scores of other test takers are compared.

THINGS TO REMEMBER

Norms are valuable for lots of reasons, but perhaps most important, they allow us to compare outcomes with others in the same test-taker group.

For example, the Emotional or Behavior Disorder Scale–Revised (authored by Stephen McCarney and Tamara Arthaud) is used in the early identification of students with emotional or behavioral disorders. In this case, 4,308 students, ages 5 through 18 years, were used as a group to develop the norms. To know how excessive behavior might be for any one child within that same age range, the child's score is compared to this set of norms to see how different it is.

The most common way to use norms is to take an individual raw score and convert that into one of several scores that is more easily understood by students, parents, and teachers, and one that is more easily shared in that it has some universal characteristics—all of which we will begin addressing in our discussion of percentiles or percentile ranks.

PERCENTILES OR PERCENTILE RANKS

A very common way of understanding individual raw scores is to examine the score relative to the rest of the scores in the set. For example, we know that Stu got a score of 18, but what does that mean relative to the other scores in the group?

A **percentile** or a **percentile rank** is a point in a distribution of scores below which a given percentage of scores fall. It's a particular point within an entire distribution of scores, and there are 100 of them. For example, the 45th percentile (and it looks like this—P_{45}) is the score below which 45% of the other scores fall. Percentiles and percentile ranks (terms that are often used interchangeably) are probably the most often-used score for reporting test results.

But you may have also noticed that this definition of a percentile tells us nothing about absolute performance. If someone has a percentile rank of 45, it means that he or she could have a raw score of 88 or a raw score of 22—we just don't know. However, the lower the percentile, the lower the person's rank in the group.

> **Percentage or Percentile?**
>
> These are very different animals. A percentile is a location along a continuum from 0 (corresponding to the lowest score) to 99 (corresponding to the highest score). A percentage is just another form of raw score that simply reflects a proportion (such as the percent correct). It's conceivable that someone could get 50% correct on a test and be in the 99th percentile, right? That occurs if everyone except for that one person got fewer than half of the items correct.

Here is the formula for computing the percentile for any raw score in a set of scores.

$$P_r = \frac{B}{N} \times 100$$

where

P_r = the percentile

B = the number of observations with lower values

N = the total number of observations

Let's compute Stu's percentile given that his raw score is 18. Here's how.

---

1. Rank all the scores with the lowest value (that's descending order) at the bottom of the ranking. You can see we did that in Table 5.2.

2. Count the number of occurrences where the score is worse than Stu's (which appears in bold and is 18). So, Susan (who got a score of 17) is the first one to be counted. Counting down, there are 41 scores, or people, worse than Stu.

3. The total number of scores is 50 (which is N).

Once those values are plugged into the formula we showed you above, the percentile for a raw score of 18 in the set of scores shown in Table 5.1 is 82, as shown here:

$$P_r = \frac{41}{50} \times 100 = 82.$$

TABLE 5.2   Scores Ranked by Descending Order

ID	Name	Raw Score	ID	Name	Raw Score
2	Chandler	20	30	Keith	13
18	Rachael	20	34	Burce	12
21	Sue	19	40	Jan	12
29	Maureen	19	1	Bruce	12
47	Seth	19	14	Micah	11
11	David	19	20	Russ	11
24	Dave	19	27	David	11
35	Adam	19	32	Pam	9
36	**Stu**	**18**	43	Lisa	9
3	Susan	17	48	George	9
19	Gregory	17	49	Ann Marie	9
26	Sabey	17	4	Zachary	8
37	Nancy	17	38	David	8
16	Lew	16	10	Faith	8
22	Max	16	13	Sara	8
33	Kim	16	17	Linda	7
39	Suzie	16	25	Lori	7
46	Sam	16	31	Mark	6
5	Danae	15	44	Jim	6
7	Michael	15	6	Talya	6
9	Jerry	15	41	Kent	5
12	Leni	15	8	Noah	5
15	Pepper	14	42	Annette	5
23	Sophie	14	45	Deborah	5
28	Maria	14	50	John	5

In this example, the percentile of 82 corresponds to a raw score of 18. Eighty-two percent of all the scores in the distribution fall below Stu's score of 18.

Some formulas compute the percentile by not counting equal scores. In our set of 50 scores you see in Table 5.2, there are only 15 unique scores (two 20s, six 19s, etc.). So, instead of 41 scores being below Stu's, there are only 12, and the percentile is computed as 12/15 × 100, or .80. It's just another way of computing a percentile.

Ever see a percentile of 100 for a score on a test? Nope—and you never will. The upper limit for a percentile for even the best score on a test is 99. Why? You can be better than everyone (and that would be the other 99%), but you can't be better than everyone including yourself! That's what it would take to be at the 100th percentile.

What's wonderful about percentiles is that they are very easy to compute, are easy to understand, and can be applied across almost any test situation for almost any kind of test. Whether it's a test of culinary skills or internal locus of control, a percentile of 70 always means the individual scored higher than 70% of the rest of the test takers.

TECH TALK What's not so wonderful is that percentile ranks tell us little about qualitative performance. The use of percentile ranks is based on the assumption that the larger sample from which they came is normally distributed, and it's the fact that this curve is bell shaped (see Section 2 in Appendix A) that creates this situation. For example, the difference in performance between percentile ranks of 40 and 50 (which is 10 percentile ranks) is probably quite different from performance between percentile ranks of 10 and 20 (also 10 percentile ranks). This is because the more extreme scores take into account a larger proportion of cases, allowing for a larger difference. Percentile ranks are not equally spaced on whatever underlying scale is being tested. It's not a shortcoming of percentiles or percentile ranks; it's just something that needs to be understood when it comes time to interpret them.

Percentiles: The Sequel

You now know what a percentile or a percentile rank is, but you may not know that different percentiles are also known by other terms.

The 50th percentile, or the score at which 50% of the remaining scores fall below and the remainder above, is also called the **median**. You can learn more about this measure of central tendency in Section 1 of Appendix A.

The 25th percentile is also known as **Q1** or the **first quartile**, and the 75th percentile is also known as **Q3** or the **third quartile**.

And as you already know, a percentile is 1 of 100 "parts" of an entire set of scores, such as the 34th, 56th, or 88th percentile. Likewise, if you took a set of scores and divided it into 10 equal parts, rather than 100, you would have a set of **deciles**. The first decile is the first 10 percentile ranks, the second decile is the second set of 10, and so on. Table 5.3 illustrates the definitions of percentiles, quartiles, and deciles for one raw score—18.

TABLE 5.3	**Definitions of Percentiles, Quartiles, and Deciles for One Raw Score**		
	Percentile	*Quartile*	*Decile*
	1st	1st	1st
	2nd		
	3rd		
	4th		
	5th		
	6th		
	7th		
	8th		
	9th		
	10th		2nd
	11th		
	12th		
	13th		
	14th		
	15th		
	16th		
	17th		
	18th		
	19th		
	20th		3rd
	21st		
	22nd		
	23rd		
	24th		

Percentile	Quartile	Decile
25th	2nd	
26th		
27th		
28th		
29th		↓
30th		4th
31st		
32nd		
33rd		
34th		
35th		
36th		
37th		
38th		
39th		↓
40th		5th
41st		
42nd		
43rd		
44th		
45th		
46th		
47th		
48th		
49th	↓	↓
50th	3rd	6th
51st		
52nd		
53rd		
54th		
55th		
56th		
57th		
58th		
59th		↓
60th		7th
61st		
62nd		
63rd		
64th		
65th		
66th		
67th		
68th		
69th		↓
70th		8th
71st		
72nd		
73rd		
74th	↓	
75th	4th	

(Continued)

TABLE 5.3 (Continued)

	Percentile	Quartile	Decile
	76th		
	77th		
	78th		
	79th		
	80th		9th
	81st		
Raw Score = 18	82nd		
	83rd		
	84th		
	85th		
	86th		
	87th		
	88th		
	89th		
	90th		10th
	91st		
	92nd		
	93rd		
	94th		
	95th		
	96th		
	97th		
	98th		
	99th		
	100th		

So Stu's score of 18 is in the 82nd percentile, the fourth quartile, and the ninth decile.

What's to Love About Percentiles

Here's the quick and dirty about why percentile ranks are useful:

- They are easy to calculate and are easily understood by all parties (test takers, parents, teachers, specialists).

- They are computed based on one's relative position to others in the group—hence, they are norm-referenced.

- You can compare across different areas of performance because a percentile is a percentile is a percentile—and percentiles are independent of raw scores.

What's Not to Love About Percentiles

Similarly, some things about percentiles don't endear us:

- Percentile ranks reflect raw scores but do not accurately reflect differences between raw scores and differences between percentiles.
- Oops—is that a percentage or a percentile, and what's the difference? They are a source of possible confusion.

But love them or not, percentiles are here to stay, and you will see them time and again when you seek out information on what a raw test score actually represents.

STANINES (OR STANINE SCORES)

Stanines are a particularly interesting type of normed score. They are interesting because, as percentiles, they divide a distribution into segments. But unlike percentiles or quartiles or deciles, **stanines** divide a distribution into nine equal segments, numbered from 1 to 9. It's as if you took the normal curve and divided it into nine equal sections. And to make things even more interesting (and useful), each of the nine stanines represents one half of a standard deviation except for Stanines 1 and 9, which are a bit smaller.

THINGS TO REMEMBER

Another valuable tool in your chest is the stanine—like a percentile, only a band of percentiles under the distribution of scores. They are a fast and efficient way to report a test score.

When raw scores are converted to stanines (and the conversion itself is beyond the scope of this book, but you can see Appendix A to learn more), the nine stanines have a mean of 5 [(1 + 9)/2 = 5] and a standard deviation of 2. Take a look at Table 5.4 and you can see how stanines relate to percentiles, quartiles, and deciles. In this example, Stu (who is in the 82nd percentile) is in the eighth stanine.

TABLE 5.4 Stanines Related to Percentiles, Quartiles, and Deciles

Percentile	Quartile	Decile	Stanines
1st	1st	1st	1st
2nd			
3rd			
4th			↓
5th			2nd
6th			
7th			
8th			
9th		↓	
10th		2nd	↓
11th			3rd
12th			
13th			
14th			
15th			
16th			
17th			
18th			
19th		↓	
20th		3rd	
21st			
22nd			↓
23rd			4th
24th	↓		
25th	2nd		
26th			
27th			
28th			
29th		↓	
30th		4th	
31st			
32nd			
33rd			
34th			
35th			
36th			
37th			
38th			
39th		↓	↓
40th		5th	5th

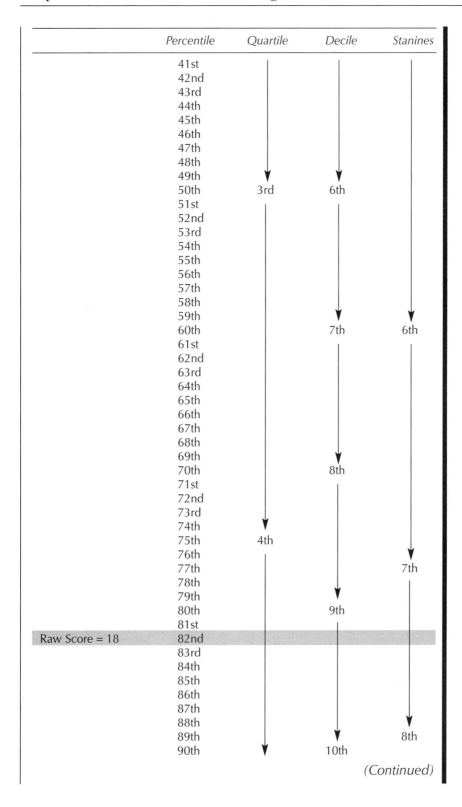

	Percentile	Quartile	Decile	Stanines
	41st			
	42nd			
	43rd			
	44th			
	45th			
	46th			
	47th			
	48th			
	49th			
	50th	3rd	6th	
	51st			
	52nd			
	53rd			
	54th			
	55th			
	56th			
	57th			
	58th			
	59th			
	60th		7th	6th
	61st			
	62nd			
	63rd			
	64th			
	65th			
	66th			
	67th			
	68th			
	69th			
	70th		8th	
	71st			
	72nd			
	73rd			
	74th			
	75th	4th		
	76th			
	77th			7th
	78th			
	79th			
	80th		9th	
	81st			
Raw Score = 18	82nd			
	83rd			
	84th			
	85th			
	86th			
	87th			
	88th			
	89th			8th
	90th		10th	

(Continued)

TABLE 5.4 (Continued)

	Percentile	Quartile	Decile	Stanines
	91st			
	92nd			
	93rd			
	94th			
	95th			↓
	96th			9th
	97th			
	98th			
	99th			
	100th	↓	↓	↓

What's to Love About Stanines

Stanines are useful for the following reasons:

- Stanines are pretty easy to compute.

- Stanines can be represented by a single digit, which communicates lots of information easily and effectively.

- Stanines represent equal units along the continuum being measured. Stanine 3 and Stanine 6 each represent a half standard deviation of scores.

- Unlike percentiles, raw score equivalents for stanines are not disproportionate along the scale being measured. It's the equal-unit thing, unlike percentiles.

What's Not to Love About Stanines

Then, of course (as you expected), there are some not-so-nice things about stanines:

- Stanines tell us little, if anything, about performance differences between people.

- They limit us to nine categories when more would allow greater differentiation.

- They assume that placing people in one of nine categories makes conceptual sense. That is, within the context of the test, getting a "1" or a "5" helps us understand what the score on the test means.

But let's not bicker, because stanines are used and used well.

THE STANDARD (FARE) SCORES

Our next type of normative score involves those that are often referred to as standard scores. A **standard score** is one that (surprise) is standardized based on a certain metric. In both of the following cases, z scores and T scores, the metric is the standard deviation, a measure of the variability within a set of scores (see Appendix A for more information about variability).

Standard scores (which come in different flavors) are cool for one very good reason—they are useful because, like percentiles, they are directly comparable to one another and give us a very clear picture of one's relative position in a distribution. In other words, you can compare scores across different distributions. Better than percentiles? Nope—just different.

Our Favorite Standard Score: The z Score

Although there are several types of standard scores, the one that you will see the most frequently in your tests and measurement work is the **z score**. This is the result of dividing the amount that a raw score differs from the mean of a set of scores by the standard deviation, as shown in the following equation.

THINGS TO REMEMBER

A z score is the most frequently used standard score and, like others, allows the comparison of scores across different distributions.

$$z = \frac{X - \overline{X}}{s}$$

where

z = the z score

X = is the individual score

$\overline{X}$ = is the mean of the set of test scores

s = is the distribution standard deviation

For example, here you can see how the z score is calculated for Stu with a raw score of 18. The standard deviation for the set of test scores you saw in Table 5.4 is 5 and the mean is 13.

$$z = \frac{18 - 13}{5} = 1$$

In Table 5.5, you can see the z scores that are associated with each of the raw scores in the entire set of scores that we have been working with throughout this chapter.

TABLE 5.5   z Scores Associated with Raw Scores

ID	Name	Raw Score	z Score	ID	Name	Raw Score	z Score
1	Bruce	12	−0.20	26	Sabey	17	0.80
2	Chandler	20	1.40	27	David	11	−0.40
3	Susan	17	0.80	28	Maria	14	0.20
4	Zachary	8	−1.00	29	Maureen	19	1.20
5	Danae	15	0.40	30	Keith	13	0.00
6	Talya	6	−1.40	31	Mark	6	−1.40
7	Michael	15	0.40	32	Pam	9	−0.80
8	Noah	5	−1.60	33	Kim	16	0.60
9	Jerry	15	0.40	34	Burce	12	−0.20
10	Faith	8	−1.00	35	Adam	19	1.20
11	David	19	1.20	36	Stu	18	1.00
12	Leni	15	0.40	37	Nancy	17	0.80
13	Sara	8	−1.00	38	David	8	−1.00
14	Micah	11	−0.40	39	Suzie	16	0.60
15	Pepper	14	0.20	40	Jan	12	−0.20
16	Lew	16	0.60	41	Kent	5	−1.60
17	Linda	7	−1.20	42	Annette	5	−1.60
18	Rachael	20	1.40	43	Lisa	9	−0.80
19	Gregory	17	0.80	44	Jim	6	−1.40
20	Russ	11	−0.40	45	Deborah	5	−1.60
21	Sue	19	1.20	46	Sam	16	0.60
22	Max	16	0.60	47	Seth	19	1.20
23	Sophie	14	0.20	48	George	9	−0.80
24	Dave	19	1.20	49	Ann Marie	9	−0.80
25	Lori	7	−1.20	50	John	5	−1.60

I'm sure you're not surprised to learn that any raw score above the mean will have a corresponding z score that is positive, and any raw score below the mean will have a corresponding z score that is negative. For example, a raw score of 15 has a corresponding z score of +.40, and a raw score of 7 has a corresponding z score of −1.20. And of course, a raw score of 13 (or the mean) has a z score of 0 (which it must be because it is no distance from the mean).

Below are just a few observations about these z scores, as a little review:

1. Those scores below the mean (such as 8 and 10) have negative z scores, and those scores above the mean (such as 14 and 16) have positive z scores.

2. Positive z scores always fall to the right of the mean and are in the upper half of the distribution of all the scores. Negative z scores always fall to the left of the mean and are in the lower half of the distribution.

3. When we talk about a score being located one standard deviation above the mean, it's the same as saying that the z score is 1. For our purposes, when comparing test scores across distributions, z scores and standard deviations are equivalent. In other words, a z score is simply the number of standard deviations the raw score is from the mean.

4. Finally (and this is very important), z scores across different distributions are comparable. A z score of 1 will always represent the same relative position in a set of scores regardless of mean and standard deviation and raw score used to compute the z score value. This quality is exactly what makes z scores so useful—they are so easily compared across different settings and different testing situations and tests. z scores are directly comparable across any test situation, making them very handy.

THINGS TO REMEMBER

I love z scores! Why? Because they are so incredibly handy. Best of all, they allow us to compare raw scores from different distributions.

What's to Love About z Scores

You already know the answer to this one—z scores are easily compared across different sets of scores. Want more? OK . . .

- z scores are easily computed.

- z scores are easy to understand as the distance from the mean of a set of scores.

- No more following around with raw scores—z scores tell you exactly where a test score lies and what its relative relationship is to the entire set of scores.

What's Not to Love About z Scores

There is always that nagging flip side:

- z scores may not be easy for naïve parties to understand, such as parents, students, and nontesting professionals.

- Raw scores of any kind, and z scores are a perfect example, always carry the connotation of poor performance.

- It's difficult to interpret any score on a test that has a decimal component such as 1.0 or 1.5. Try explaining, "You did very well on your exam, with a final test score of 1.87."

TECH TALK

z scores and percentile ranks are often used to express a test score position relative to the other test scores in a group. But how do z scores and percentile ranks relate to one another? In an interesting and straightforward way.

You may remember in your basic stat class that the area encompassed below one z score under the normal curve is about 84% of all scores (for a review, see Appendix A). Bingo. A z score of 1.0 corresponds to the 84th percentile or a percentile rank of 84. And, a z score of 0, which would correspond to a raw score equivalent to the mean of the set of scores, corresponds to a percentile of 50%, also known as the median.

Normalized Standard Scores

Finally, the last type of norm-based scale is called a **normalized standard score**. A normalized standard score is one where the z scores, like those we created above, are forced into a distribution that has all the characteristics of a normal curve. For our purposes here, the most important of these characteristics is how scores are distributed, with certain fixed percentages of scores occurring under certain areas beneath the curve.

It's beyond the scope of *Tests & Measurement for People Who (Think They) Hate Tests & Measurement* to go into great depth about this type of score, but you should know that a normalized standard score is approximately the same as a standard z score. However, whereas the distribution of the normalized scores looks like a pretty bell-shaped curve, the distribution of a set of z scores can, and usually does, look much different.

T Scores to the Rescue

Now here's a good idea.

One of the outstanding disadvantages of z scores is the less-than-outstanding value placed on any negative score. So, to get around that concern, why not use a type of standard score that almost never can be negative? That's how T scores, a variant of z scores, were born.

A **T score** is a standard score as well, only one that uses z scores as shown in the following:

$$T = 50 + 10z$$

where

T = the T score

z = the z score

For example, Stu's raw score of 18, which is equal to a z score of 1, is equal to a T score of 60, or $50 + 10(1)$.

You may realize immediately that what this alternative standard score does is eliminate any negative numbers, as well as any fractional scores. For example, take a look at the top and bottom 10 scores from our original set of scores shown in Table 5.1.

ID	Name	Score	z Score	T Score
2	Chandler	20	1.40	65
18	Rachael	20	1.40	65
11	David	19	1.20	62
21	Sue	19	1.20	62
24	Dave	19	1.20	62
29	Maureen	19	1.20	62
35	Adam	19	1.20	62
47	Seth	19	1.20	62
36	Stu	18	1.00	60
3	Susan	17	0.80	58
17	Linda	7	−1.20	38
25	Lori	7	−1.20	38
6	Talya	6	−1.40	36
31	Mark	6	−1.40	36
44	Jim	6	−1.40	36
8	Noah	5	−1.60	34
41	Kent	5	−1.60	34
42	Annette	5	−1.60	34
45	Deborah	5	−1.60	34
50	John	5	−1.60	34

Here, you can see that the best score (20) has a corresponding z score of 1.40 and a T score of 65. And even for the lowest raw score of 5 with a corresponding z score of −1.60, the corresponding T score is 34—a nice, positive number.

TECH TALK

z scores and T scores are similar in that they are both transformed scores, and both are comparable across different distributions. z scores are comparable because they use the same metric—the standard deviation. T scores are comparable because they use the same metric—the z score. Finally, a set of scores generated from a distribution of raw scores has a mean of 0 and a standard deviation of 1, whereas a set of T scores generated from the same distribution has a mean of 50 and a standard deviation of 10.

STANDING ON YOUR OWN: CRITERION-REFERENCED TESTS

Here's the alternative to normative, norm-based, normalized, and so on based tests—criterion-based tests. A **criterion-based** or **criterion-referenced test** is one where there is a predefined level of performance used to evaluate outcomes, and it has nothing to do with relative ranking among a larger set of scores.

For example, if a score of 75 correct is defined as the level at which one may advance to the next lesson, that's the criterion in this criterion-referenced system. You may indeed get just 60 correct, and (relative—here we are back to norms again—to your peers) you're a star because the average score for the entire group was 37 correct. But the importance here is on performance rather than relative position.

Any kind of score that takes into account *absolute performance* within a particular and well-specified topic area (such as physics) or domain (such as mechanical aptitude or culinary skills) is a good candidate for evaluation using an external criterion. The key here is the absolute nature of what is being evaluated—those outcomes that do not make any sense when compared to the same outcome from other members of the group.

The importance of a criterion-based test model should be obvious. We expect people to be able to do thousands of things, and they must be based on an absolute scale of success. We expect police officers to know the rules of law enforcement—not just 50% of the rules. We expect a new nurse to be able to start an intravenous line with a 100% level of success—not just better than his or her classmates, but perfect every time. And, we expect school bus drivers to drive with few miscalculations—not just to be better than the other drivers.

THE STANDARD ERROR OF MEASUREMENT

The last idea that we'll cover in this chapter may be one of the most important when it comes to understanding what a test score means.

No one ever gets the exact same score on a test if that test is taken more than once. You remember our discussion in Chapter 3 on reliability and how there are all kinds of influences that can affect a score on repeated testing.

The **standard error of measurement** (or SEM) is a simple measure of how much a test score varies for an individual from time to time. It's how different one person's test score would be if he or she were repeatedly tested. Using this value can give us an estimate of the accuracy of any one test score.

Let's say that we could have a student take the same test 10 times. In theory, the standard error of measurement is the standard deviation or the amount of spread that each observed score differs from each true score (and remember that true score can never be measured directly). In other words, let's say that Stu really did take a test three times and got three different scores—18, 17, and 19. Because we know his true score to be 19 (that's the true measure of what he really knows), the standard error of measurement would be calculated based on the differences between the true score (19) and the raw scores of 18, 17, and 19.

THINGS TO REMEMBER

Another way to think of the standard error of measurement is that it is the standard deviation of repeated test scores.

But of course, we cannot ask a student to take a test three times of 10, or any more than once, so we use a handy formula that helps us to estimate the standard error of measurement using the standard deviation of the original set of scores and the reliability coefficient, which has already been computed when the test was developed. Here's the formula:

$$SEM = s \sqrt{1 - r}$$

where

SEM = the standard error of measurement

s = the standard deviation for the set of test scores

r = the reliability coefficient of the test

For the example that we have used throughout this chapter, s = 5 and r = .87 (we got the 5 from computing the standard deviation for the set of 50 raw scores and the test-retest coefficient of .87 from two administrations of the test). And the value of the standard error of measurement is 1.80, computed as follows:

$$SEM = 5 \sqrt{1 - .87} = 1.80$$

And because we will use this number later as well, the mean of all these scores is 13.

What the SEM Means

The standard error of measurement is a measure of how much variability we can expect around any one individual's score on repeated testing. For example, what we know about normal curves and the distribution of scores (see Appendix A), we also can apply to the SEM.

For example, Stu got a score of 18 and the SEM is 1.80. This can be interpreted to mean that the chances of Stu's *true score* (remember? his real, real, real score) falling within 18 +/−1.80 (a range from 16.2 to 19.8), is about 68%. We know this because we know from our knowledge of the normal curve that 68% of all scores are contained within plus or minus one standard unit from the mean. Only this time, the standard unit is one standard error of measurement.

OK—so let's put together some of what we learned earlier in the book with what we are learning here.

1. First, if there is no standard error of measurement, then raw scores are equal to true scores and the test is a pretty darn good one.

2. Next, the smaller the SEM, the more reliable the test, because the observed score is more like the true score. Similarly, a larger SEM reflects a less reliable test.

3. Finally, our goal is to minimize the SEM—and in doing so, we make the test a more accurate measure of what we want to assess.

SUMMARY

So what did *you* get? As you can see, there are lots of ways to define and interpret performance on a test, starting with a raw score and ending up by using the reliability of a test to gain some judgment as to what a "good" test score may indeed tell us about an individual's performance. This second part of *Tests & Measurement for People Who (Think They) Hate Tests & Measurement* covered lots of material about the psychometrics, or measurement qualities, of testing. Now it's time to move on in Part III to specific types of test items and how they are used.

TIME TO PRACTICE

1. What are the advantages and disadvantages of using raw scores to report test results?

2. Using the following set of test scores, compute the percentile rank for Test Taker #12, who had a raw score of 64. Remember that you have to rank all the scores before you can use the formula shown on page 85.

ID	Score	ID	Score
1	78	11	67
2	67	12	64
3	66	13	58
4	56	14	87
5	78	15	88
6	89	16	89
7	92	17	90
8	96	18	98
9	86	19	85
10	46	20	68

3. Using the same set of data as shown above, what are the corresponding quartile and decile for a raw score of 89?

4. Emily and Grace are in different groups, and the following shows their test scores on two different tests. If we assume that a higher score is better, which one scored better overall? Here's more information that you need.

   • The mean and standard deviation for Emily's group on Test 1 were 90 and 3.
   • The mean and standard deviation for Emily's group on Test 2 were 92 and 5.
   • The mean and standard deviation for Grace's group on Test 1 were 87 and 3.
   • The mean and standard deviation for Grace's group on Test 2 were 93 and 5.

	Score on Test 1	Score on Test 2
Emily	88	91
Grace	92	94

5. Provide an example of when it is appropriate to use a criterion-referenced test rather than a norm-referenced test. Provide a rationale for your decision.

ANSWERS TO PRACTICE QUESTIONS

1. There's actually no advantage to reporting only raw scores other than that they are easy to understand and give the test taker some idea as to the number (easily converted to a percent) that he or she got correct. As for disadvantages, there are many, but perhaps the most important is that a raw score by itself tells little about performance, either in absolute terms (because you don't know what constitutes a good or excellent raw score) or relative to other test takers.

2. The formula is

$$P_r = \frac{3}{20} \times 100 = 15$$

   A raw score of 65 corresponds to a percentile rank of 15.

3. A raw score of 89 is in the second quartile and the third decile.

4. The first step is to compute the z scores for each of the four raw scores, as you can see we have done here.

	Test 1 Score	Test 2 Score	Average z Score
Emily	0.67	0.20	0.43
Grace	1.00	−0.80	0.10

The next step is to average the z scores. We can do this because these z scores are standard scores, and we can average them because we are averaging scores based on some metric (the standard deviation). As you can see, relative to one another, Emily's average z score of .43 is higher than Grace's score of .10.

5. The owner of a radio manufacturing company needs to be sure that each person on the assembly line can perform his or her assigned tasks with a level of 98% accuracy. The rationale for using a criterion-referenced test is that the owner does not care whether one assembler is better than another, only that each perform at this defined level, which is the criterion.

WANT TO KNOW MORE?

Further Readings

- Mangan, K. S. (2004). Raising the bar. *Chronicle of Higher Education, 51*(3), A35–A36.

Think that test scores don't have wide-ranging implications? This article discussed the imposition of tougher law-exam standards in an effort to get better lawyers. However, there's no proof that requiring higher scores on a standardized test would weed out incompetent lawyers, and it could exclude the minority students whom law schools are eager to attract. Quite a lot to think about.

- Leonard, D., & Frederick, K. (2004). Should we worry about boys? *Times Educational Supplement, 4597*, 13.

Why be concerned about gaps in achievement between the genders? This professor claims that poor test scores will not help male students' lack of self-esteem, but others argue that these differences are meaningless when it comes to future employment and earning potential.

And on the Internet

- Both teachers and parents can benefit from reading through Parenting Perspectives at http://www.teachersandfamilies.com/open/parent/scores1.cfm and learning more on how to understand what test scores mean.

- The National Education Association also provides assistance to parents, teachers, and others in understanding test scores, available at http://www.nea.org/parents/testingguide.html.

PART III

The Tao and How of Testing

Snapshots

"No, seriously. I'm in medicine. Cutting edge stuff.
I work in a measurement lab downtown."

Now that you have the introductory material under your belt and are familiar with such important concepts as reliability and validity, it's time to explore the various types of test items that are used in the creation and administration of all different types of tests.

In working through the chapters contained in this part of *Tests & Measurement* . . . , you should remember that your goal is to learn how to distinguish the different types of test items from one another (such as true-false and matching) and to understand how they are created and when they are best used. For example, assessing achievement might be better done using multiple-choice items (see Chapter 8) rather than a portfolio (see Chapter 11), which in turn would be best for assessing progress in a beginning fine arts class.

The most important thing to remember about the chapters in Part III is that part of your tour consists of many different ways to create, and use, test items. Learn about them, and even practice creating them, and you'll be ready to better understand their value when the time comes, be you a test developer, test giver, or test taker.

6 Short Answer and Completion Items

Baskin Robbins® Has __ Flavors

Difficulty Index ☺☺☺☺ (really pretty easy)

G uess what? The title of this chapter says it all. **Short answer and completion items** are short (and simple). They are generally short in structure and require a short answer as well. Because both of these types of items tend to be used in a very similar fashion and resemble one another in format, we're combining our discussion of both into this one chapter. And as if you didn't know, Baskin Robbins has 31 different flavors.

WHEN WE USE 'EM AND WHAT THEY LOOK LIKE

Short answer and completion items are used almost exclusively to assess lower-level thinking skills such as memorization and basic knowledge. If you want a test taker to know the chemical symbol for hydrogen, a completion item like

---

1. The chemical symbol for hydrogen is ____.

---

is the perfect item (with H being the correct answer).

THINGS TO REMEMBER

Short (and sweet) answer questions work well because they focus on a particular level of understanding of material and should not be used for anything more ambitious than that.

If you want the test taker to know how hydrogen is manufactured—turn to the next chapter on essay questions—that type of test item would better fit your needs.

A similar short answer item more in the form of a question might be

---

1. What is the chemical symbol for hydrogen?

These kinds of items are sometimes called **supply items**, because the test taker is required to supply a response (such as words, numbers, or symbols) rather than selecting one from a list, such as in matching (see Chapter 9) or multiple-choice items (see Chapter 8).

HOW TO WRITE 'EM: THE GUIDELINES

Here are some guidelines for how to write short answer and completion items.

1. *If you have a choice, create a short answer question rather than a completion question.* Instead of asking,

---

1. The precursors of T cells leave the bone marrow and mature in the _____.

---

ask this item as a question, as follows:

---

1. In what gland do T cells mature?

Why ask it as a question? Questions are clearer and more straight-forward, and they leave less room for ambiguity. For example, the answer to the completion or "fill-in-the-blank" item above could be "human body" and would be correct. But the more specific and absolutely correct answer is the thymus gland—and the short answer question much more clearly requires that type of response.

2. *Avoid grammatical clues to the correct answer.* Be sure that the structure and construction of the question makes sense and does not inadvertently provide help. For example, take a look at the following item, which really cues the test taker into understanding what may or may not be the correct answer.

> 1. Hippocrates, the author of the Hippocratic oath, was trained as a _____.

Better would be

> 1. Hippocrates, the author of the Hippocratic oath, was trained as a(n) _____.

The correct answer is mathematician. The first item cues the test taker that the answer has to begin with a consonant (such as "m" for mathematician or "p" for philosopher). The second item allows for an answer that begins with either a consonant or a vowel, decreasing the value of a grammatical cue and the likelihood of guessing.

3. *Do not copy short answer or completion items straight from the study material that test takers are using to prepare.* This strongly encourages memorization beyond what is necessary (entire sentences and phrases rather than just facts). Although most short answer and completion items focus on memorization, you want just the important information to be memorized, not everything verbatim.

THINGS TO REMEMBER

Most people who take tests prepare for them (when they can) and think about what kinds of questions will be asked. So, to level the playing field for all test takers, be careful not to create short answer questions by copying them directly from the teaching or preparation material.

4. *Place the blank for a completion item at the end of the item.* For example, here's a good one:

> 1. The speed of light in meters per second is ____.

Here's a not-so-good one:

> 1. ____ is the speed of light.

The problem here is that when the blank appears at the beginning of an item, a test taker can easily get stuck and not be able to get past it, and the test taker often has to read and reread the item to get the information he or she needs to complete the answer. When the blank comes at the end of the question, the test taker has been prepared by the preceding information (The speed of light is . . .) rather than focusing on what goes in the blank space that precedes any of the information that is needed to answer the question. (And by the way, the speed of light is 299,792,458 meters per second.)

5. *When requiring a numerical answer, be sure to specify the precision of the answer you want and the units in which you want the answer expressed.* In #4 above, you can see how the first example asked for the answer in meters per second, but the second example did not. If you want there to be only one correct answer to a question, you have to ask for it, and you have to ask for it to be expressed as you want it (meters per second, miles per hour, etc.).

6. *Make sure your blank spaces are equal in size across items and kept to a minimum.* Misuse of blank spaces is a punishable offense and often confuses the test taker with insufficient information to answer the question. For example, the following completion item

> 1. "To" is a preposition, whereas ____ and ____ are other parts of speech.

would leave any test taker dazed and confused.
    Much better would be

> 1. "To" is a preposition, whereas other parts of speech that sound the same are ____ and two.

In the second example, some comparisons provide the information the test taker needs to complete the question.

7. *Short answer and completion items should be written so there is only a single and brief answer that is correct.* For example, for the soon-to-be horticulturist, a question like

> 1. What is the scientific name for a popular daisy?

just leaves open too many answers because the test taker could enter the scientific name of any daisy—this question just does not get at the focus of knowledge about scientific names. But the following question does a much better job:

> 1. The scientific name for the Palm Spring Daisy is ____.

(The answer? Cladanthus arabicus.)

THE GOOD AND THE BAD

As with any other item, completion and short answer items have their advantages and disadvantages in everyday use. We'll start with what's good about them. You can see a summary of these points in Table 6.1.

TABLE 6.1 The Good and Bad About Short Answer and Completion Items

Advantages of Short Answer and Completion Items	Disadvantages of Short Answer and Completion Items
• They are very flexible.	• Machine scoring is hard, if not impossible.
• They minimize guessing.	• Scoring can be subjective.
• They lend themselves to computational items.	• Limited scope of cognitive skills can be assessed.
• They are easy to write.	• One-answer questions are tough to create.
• They allow for lots of items to be used.	

Why Completion and Short Answer Items Are Good

1. *Completion or short answer items are very flexible.* They can be used to assess any content area, even if they are somewhat limited by the level of information that can be tested.

2. *Guessing is minimized.* With other types of items, such as true-false or multiple-choice, it's much easier to guess. The likelihood of being right on a true-false item, by chance alone, is 50%. The probability of being correct on a completion item, by chance alone, is a big zero. With completion items, there are no predefined options to select from as a chance effort at getting the item right. This means that the test taker really has to at least have some idea about the content of the material.

3. *Short answer and completion are both very attractive item formats for computational items.* Asking 5 + 5 = ___? is an efficient and straightforward way to find out if the test taker knows the sum of 5 and 5.

4. *Completion and short answer items are relatively easy to write.* When you want to assess how well 100 different facts can be recalled and want to write 50 questions about those facts, completion or short answer items are quick and easy to write.

5. *Completion items allow for increased item sampling.* Remember back in Chapter 3 we pointed out how test reliability increases as the number of items increase? Well, because completion items are easy to construct and test time is usually limited, more of these kinds of items can fit into a standard testing session and provide a broader sample of items that more accurately reflects the overall content being assessed.

Why Completion and Short Answer Items Are Not So Good

OK, then there are the reasons why we would not want to use completion or short answer items even though the above five points are pretty convincing.

1. *There's no machine scoring here.* You have to grade these kinds of items by hand, and it can be a tedious and time-consuming task.

2. *Scoring can be subjective.* Although you may try and create a completion item that has only one correct answer, this is hard, and other answers *might* (and I stress might) have some correct content. It's your call as the test scorer, and, sometimes, if the item is not well written, it can be a tough one. And, you also have to consider that spelling and grammatical errors in an answer influence the scoring, as does illegible handwriting. And (again) to complicate matters even more, you may consider giving partial credit for partially correct answers!

3. *Advanced types of thinking skills cannot be assessed using short answer items.* As we have mentioned several times, short answer and completion items work best when the learning objectives you are assessing are basic and focus on memorization and understanding of simple ideas.

THINGS TO REMEMBER

Don't get too ambitious with short answer questions. They are used mostly for tapping information that is more basic than not. Save the higher-order questions for other types of items such as multiple choice and essay.

4. *One answer being correct may be the requirement for the best of completion items, but it's tough to write those kind of completion items.* Items such as

> 1. The United States Secret Service was created in 1862 to ____.
>
> (counteract counterfeiting)

could also have answers such as "guard the integrity of the currency" or "make sure that only genuine currency is used for commerce," and so on. One answer being correct, when you have a blank space to complete, is a tough order to fill.

SUMMARY

Short answer and completion items are very useful in that they can be easily written, get at the most fundamental of learning outcomes, and minimize guessing. On the other hand, they are hard to score and are limited to the lower level of thinking skills they can assess. But they are still a handy tool in your assessment arsenal, and, for achievement-oriented material, they can be a very effective assessment format.

TIME TO PRACTICE

1. What areas of behavior would you measure using short answer and completion questions, and why?

2. What's wrong with these five completion or short answer items?
   a. ____ is the president on the $50 bill.
   b. Pythagoras' work in mathematics resulted in an ____.
   c. A nanometer is how wide? ____
   d. ____ is made up of the elements ____ and ____.
   e. What is the function of time?

3. In an area of your interest, be it a hobby or your profession, write five completion items. Then share them with a class colleague and use the criteria we defined earlier to evaluate them.

4. Name three of the advantages of using completion and short answer questions in an assessment, and explain why these benefits make this type of item useful.

5. OK, how about the same question as #4 immediately above, only this time discuss a disadvantage.

ANSWERS TO PRACTICE ITEMS

1. Achievement or content areas are probably the best to assess because these general areas (such as physics, history, geometry, and horticulture) lend themselves to short answer and completion-type questions for the evaluation of how much understanding or knowledge the test taker has.

2. a. In a completion or short answer question, the blank should come at the end of the items.
   b. Oops . . . "an" theorem? Nope—a theorem. Watch for grammatical clues.

c. A nanometer is 1/100,000,000th of a meter, but an answer such as the width of a human hair would not be wrong either. Precision and definition are the keys here.

d. Well, H_2O may very well be made up of two molecules of hydrogen and one of oxygen, but you sure won't get a correct answer with so many blanks in an item.

e. No doubt an interesting question, but not one with only one answer.

3. Do this on your own.

4. For example, one advantage is that they are easy to write and the rules for writing them are very clear. For the busy test creator (such as a teacher) who is assessing a clearly defined area (such as general biology), there's a significant advantage to being able to put together 25, 50, or even 100 of these in a relatively short amount of time.

5. One that surely comes to mind, and this is a practical concern, is scoring. These are tough tests to grade, and, if you have 50 items where all of the responses are handwritten, you may be able to distinguish between a right and wrong answer, but once you get to Item 45 of the 76th student, then you're sure to find fatigue interrupting your accuracy and threatening the usefulness of the item.

WANT TO KNOW MORE?

Further Readings

• Kim, H.-S. (2003). Adaptive computer software that supports reading comprehension: An exploratory analysis of instructional and design implications. *Dissertation Abstracts International Section A: Humanities and Social Sciences, 64*(3–A): 868.

Yes, the type of question that is used to collect information can make a difference in the value and usefulness of the response. In this study, the relationship among prior knowledge, learner variables, and interactive reading instruction on multimedia reading outcomes was explored. The lead researcher found that students reading with interactive agent support scored significantly higher on the short answer questions.

• Sadler Smith, E., & Riding, R. (1999). Cognitive style and instructional preferences. *Instructional Science, 27*(5), 355–371.

Why bother about different types of questions such as short answer or completion? Because differences in cognitive styles and instructional preferences may result in different outcomes depending upon the types of questions used, which is what this study is about. The results are discussed in relation to the cognitive style and the practical implications for individual differences and assessment.

And on the Internet

- Find out how to ace any test, including those with short answers, at The Learning Center at http://webster.commnet.edu/pfaculty/~simonds/tests.htm.

7 Essay Items

Hope You Can Write

Difficulty Index ☺☺☺☺ (really pretty easy)

One of the things that we will stress throughout this part of *Tests & Measurement for People Who (Think They) Hate Tests & Measurement* is that the type of item you use as an assessment tool is closely tied to the level of information (or level of thinking skills) you want your test taker to show that he or she does (or does not) have. In Chapter 6, we emphasized how short answer items are best used when trying to assess memorization of factual information. In this chapter on essay items, you'll find other tools that you can use to assess other types of outcomes.

Here, we'll focus on **essay items**—those items where the test taker is expected to write a coherent and informative response to a question. Forget about that Friday spelling test or even the SAT—essay tests are the real thing when it comes to seeing how well test takers integrate ideas and how well they can express them in written form.

WHEN WE USE 'EM AND WHAT THEY LOOK LIKE

Essay questions allow for perhaps the most unrestricted type of written assessment item that we will cover in *Tests & Measurement for People Who (Think They) Hate Tests & Measurement*. What you want to know is how well the test taker can organize information and express his or her ideas in writing. That's why the really, really big exams in one's academic career are usually of the essay type—these types of items just tap more higher-level and complex skills.

THINGS TO REMEMBER

Essay items are the item of choice if you want an unrestricted response and want to access higher-order thinking, such as the relationship between ideas and the pros and cons of a particular argument.

Essay questions come in two basic flavors: open-ended (also called unrestricted or extended) questions and closed-ended (also called restricted) questions.

An **open-ended** (or **unrestricted response**) **essay question** is one where there are no restrictions on the response, including the amount of time allowed to finish, the number of pages written, or material included. Now, it is a bit impractical to allow test takers to have 25 hours to answer one essay question or to write hundreds of pages about anything they like. So, of course there are *practical* limits. It's just that the limits do not define the scope of the response. For example, here's an open-ended essay question.

> 1. Discuss the various theories of human development that have been talked about this semester. Among other things, be sure to compare and contrast the basic assumptions of the theories, the method used to study development, and the criticisms of each. You are free to take as much time as you need. Write as many pages as you like, and organize your answer as you see fit.

That is a nice, open-ended question where the response is unrestricted.

Now, take a look at this closed-ended question where the response is restricted.

> 1. Compare and contrast two of the basic theories of human development that have been discussed this semester. Include a brief summary of each theory, the method used to study development, and the criticisms of each perspective. Limit your response to five written pages, and do not write for longer than 2 hours.

These two types of questions reflect different types of experiences. The first question, which is much less restrictive, gives the test taker a lot more flexibility (among other things) and allows for a more creative approach. The more restricted closed-ended question places definite limits on the content as well as the format.

You might think that almost everyone would like to have as much flexibility as possible, but that's just not the case—many people like a very well-structured and clearly defined task assigned to them.

HOW TO WRITE ESSAY ITEMS: THE GUIDELINES

Here are just a few guidelines that will be helpful when it comes time to write an essay question.

1. *Allow adequate time to answer the question.* By their very design, essay questions can take a considerable amount of time to answer. Earlier in this chapter, we contrasted closed- and open-ended questions, where the nature of the response is restricted or not. Regardless of whether an essay question is closed or open ended (remember, we have to be practical), you need to tell the test taker how much time he or she has to complete the question. And how much time should that be? Keep in mind that essay questions require test takers to *think about*, and then *write*, the response. One strategy is to encourage test takers when they are practicing to plan their response by spending 30%–40% of their time outlining or "sketching" their response, 40%–50% of their time writing the response, and then the last 10%–30% rereading what they have written and making any necessary changes.

Using Outlining Tools

These days, it is not unusual for a test taker to complete an essay using a word processor and not even manually write anything. Test takers in such a situation may also be able to use the outlining feature that many word processors provide. The 30% or 40% of time spent thinking about the response can be used to outline the important major and minor points. Then, the outlining features— such as expanding and contracting headings, moving headings up or back in the outline, and collapsing and expanding sections—can be used to fine tune the response before the actual writing begins. Some essay writers write out their thoughts as an outline and, when finished, create the necessary transitions between thoughts and are done! Figure 7.1 shows you what such an outline might look like.

As you can see, there are different levels of headings. By clicking various buttons on the toolbar right above the outline, the material can be rearranged, expanded, or collapsed, and many other operations can be performed. Are outlines for you? Your word processor has the option—try it and see.

+ Psychoanalytic Theory
    − Historical Period
    − Assumptions
    + Critical Elements
        − Stages
        − Dynamic Nature
        − Structural Elements
    − Evaluation

Figure 7.1   Outline

2. *Be sure the question is complete and clear.* This one sounds simple and it may indeed be, but sometimes essay questions are not very clear in their presentation. Want to know why? Because it's not clear what the person writing the question wants to know. For example, here's an unclear essay question

> 1. Discuss the impact of the Civil War on the economy of the postwar South.

It's not like this question is that poorly designed, but it sure does not reflect a clear notion of what was learned or what is being assessed. This is the kind of a topic that some historian could write seven volumes about! Look how much more clear the following question is.

> 1. Discuss the impact of the Civil War on the economy of the postwar South, taking into account the following factors: reduction in the work force, international considerations, and the changing role of agriculture.

This second example just provides additional direction, which may be exactly what the test taker needs to answer the question more completely.

3. *Essay questions should be used only to evaluate higher-order outcomes, such as when comparisons, evaluations, analyses, and interpretations are required.* Want to know what 64^3 is? (262,144)—The infant mortality rate of the United States in 2001? (6.9 per 1,000 live births)—What the French called tomatoes? (pomme d'amour for apple of love). If so, an essay question is not what you are looking for—you want the kind of item that tackles lower-level thinking skills such as knowledge or memorization. For the higher-order outcomes, such as evaluation and synthesis, you want the essay format and questions such as the following:

> 1. Identify the principle factors that contribute to infant mortality in the United States and discuss and evaluate the success of efforts that have been taken to close the gap between white and nonwhite populations.

Such a question requires a knowledge of rates of infant mortality but goes far beyond the statement of just facts. In fact, here's this chapter's cheat sheet about what kinds of words signal higher-order skills (and these words usually show up in essay items).

Analyze	Generalize
Apply	Infer
Arrange	Integrate
Classify	Justify
Contrast	Organize
Compare	Persuade
Create	Predict
Evaluate	Summarize
Explain	Synthesize

4. *Have all test takers answer the same questions.* This just reduces the burden placed on the developer of the test and, more important, makes the test easier to score—it's just more practical. Why?

Because essay questions should have one correct answer, and (as you will learn shortly) there should be a model answer against which test takers' responses should be compared. Allowing for multiple questions requires the test scores to have multiple standards against which to compare them—too much work! Instead, rotate questions from year to year or test to test so there is a nice collection of questions and model answers.

THE GOOD AND THE BAD

Essay items have their advantages and disadvantages—let's review them. And, you can find a summary of these in Table 7.1.

TABLE 7.1 The Advantages and Disadvantages of Essay Questions	
Advantages of Essay Items	*Disadvantages of Essay Items*
• They help find out how ideas are related to one another.	• They emphasize writing.
• They increase security.	• They are difficult to write.
• They provide increased flexibility in item design.	• They provide an inadequate sampling of subject matter.
• They are relatively easy to construct.	• They are hard to score.
	• They emphasize writing skills over content.

Why Essay Items Are Good

1. *It's doubtful that you can come up with a better way of finding out not only what test takers know, but also how they relate ideas to one another.* You've defined your learning goals, and the essay question is your choice of assessment tool because you are interested in finding out how well a test taker understands ideas and can relate ideas to one another. Essay questions most definitely tap into how well test takers can organize and integrate information. And essay questions also provide opportunities to demonstrate creativity.

THINGS TO REMEMBER

Among the many reasons why essays are particularly useful is that they are very flexible in both form (the size and complexity) and purpose (relate simple ideas or elaborate a complex argument).

2. *The use of essay questions increases security because it is very difficult to plagiarize during an essay item examination.* And, along the same lines, it is almost impossible for test takers to effectively guess the correct answer—so guessing is removed as a legitimate concern.

3. *The essay item format has unparalleled flexibility.* Take the time necessary to create a really good question—one that is exciting to consider and one that gives the test taker a fair chance at success.

4. *Essay questions can be relatively easy to construct.* If you know your material well (and we would sure assume such), you can put together four essay questions in less than an hour that can effectively tap higher-order learning. Sure beats creating 100 multiple-choice items at 10 minutes each (yep, about 15 hours).

Why Essay Items Are Not So Good

1. *They emphasize writing.* Well, no kidding—that's what they are supposed to do. But what they don't do well at all is tapping the test taker who is knowledgeable about ideas and their relationship to one another, but just cannot express it in words. For these kind of test takers, evaluating them fairly and accurately is always a challenge.

2. *They can be tough to write.* But didn't we just say above that they were easy to write? Well, we said they *can* be. They can be a bear as well! The test designer has to invest a great deal of time in creating each essay question and making sure that it taps the objectives that are to be tested, but does so in a way to encourage the expression of ideas that you can't find in a true-false or matching test.

3. *Precision in sampling counts.* Because essay questions take a good deal of time to create and even more time to complete as part of a test, it's tough for the test to adequately sample the entire universe of what the test taker might have learned. This should always be a consideration in the overall evaluation of knowledge and understanding of any topic.

4. *Essay questions are not easy to score.* Think about it—in a class of 25 students, each of whom completes five essay questions—that's more than 120 questions that have to be graded. No teacher will begrudge grading them (well, maybe a few), but all will have some serious problems remaining neutral, staying on task, and being consistent.

5. *Writing can become more important than content (see #1 above).* Because essays are written, some students can bluff their way through the answer by virtue of their excellent writing ability. Just about the only way to counter this is through the use of model answers, as discussed in the next section.

HOW TO SCORE ESSAY ITEMS

Essay items are absolutely terrific and almost indispensable for sampling higher-order thinking. I've mentioned that several times throughout this chapter. But they are a bear to score—time consuming and very demanding of all the scorer's attention.

With that in mind, here are a few tips that might make the scoring process more efficient and result in a fairer assessment.

1. *Scorers should provide plenty of time to score an essay item.* Each of the items has to be read and then scored, and often the scorer will read the items more than once—the first time for a general overview of the content, and the second time for a more detailed analysis, including an assessment of content (again) and writing skills (such as grammar, transitions, and sentence usage).

THINGS TO REMEMBER

 There's one thing about scoring essay items that you have to be especially careful of, and that's allowing yourself to be swayed by the very first question you evaluate. If the handwriting is difficult to read, if you inadvertently know the test taker (which may be very easy given the handwriting), and so on—you may be biased one way or the other. Biased about what? All the grading that follows. A very good, or a very poor, response can create expectations (which may or may not be appropriate), and it's not easy to shed those as you grade. Unless you are able to approach some (acceptable) level of objectivity, then you should seriously consider creating a model you can follow point by point, argument by argument.

2. *Take your time.* This is related to #1 above, but it is critical to pace yourself when scoring essay items. If you have 50 students, each writing four essay responses, it would be impossible to grade these 200 (yes, 200) responses in one sitting. Fatigue is a huge threat to the integrity of the assessment process, so grade essay exams in batches. Perhaps one question at a time, with 30 minutes or something else in between (like a walk around the block, or a stretch, or get yourself a cookie as a reward for your good work!).

3. *Use a model correct answer to have a basis for comparison.* Having a model greatly increases the likelihood that you will evaluate each answer fairly and have as objective a standard as is possible because you can compare what is there (the test taker's response) to what should be there (your model response). Answering your own questions is not fun, especially when you know you have to do a terrific job, but this is about the only method you can use to avoid a totally subjective approach to scoring these kinds of questions. When's the best time to create these model answers? When you're initially writing the question, of course!

You can also develop your own system of scoring. Susan M. Brookhart, a grading expert from Duquesne University, suggests that essay questions should be evaluated on three criteria:

- Thesis and organization

- Content knowledge

- Writing style and mechanics

Each of these elements, for example, could be scored separately. A model too difficult for you to do? Then at least have the important points listed on a separate sheet of paper against which you can compare test takers' responses.

4. *Score each question across all test takers.* Given that you have a model answer, go through each test focusing the same question each time. For example, score the answer to Question 1 across all test takers, and then go back and score Question 2 across all test takers. This allows you to make absolute judgments in comparison to your model answer, but also to make relative judgments (if necessary) within any one item.

Essay Items and Unreliability

You remember from Chapter 2 that our discussion about reliability focused in part on the reduction of error variance. The more error variance that is removed from the entire testing situation, the higher the reliability.

OK—given that thought, there are a lot of sources of error variance when it comes to essay items, and perhaps the largest source is differences in grading. By its very nature, an essay item has so many indefinite things associated with it (objectivity of the grader, student's writing skills, etc.) that it is even more important to control what you can. So, do try and ensure anonymity, use a model for scoring, and standardize conditions whenever possible. You'll have a more reliable test, and the test takers will be treated more fairly.

5. If possible, *grade the responses without knowing the test taker's identity.* Because a subjective element can enter into the grading of essay questions, not knowing who the test taker is (and avoiding that possible bias) can be a great help. There are a bunch of ways to do this—using code numbers keyed to names rather than just names is one example—but another way is to have the test taker put his or her name on the back (and blank) side of the first page of the responses. The grader won't see it and any conflict can be avoided.

SUMMARY

Essay questions are terrific to get at those more sophisticated thinking skills that we have to assess to find out if an individual understands more complex ideas and how these ideas relate to one another. But although they might be relatively easy to create (they are short, after all, and only a few are needed), they can underrepresent content, they are tough to score, and there are lots of reasons why they could be considered unreliable. So, use 'em only when they need to be used!

TIME TO PRACTICE

1. In your area of interest, write one stunningly terrific essay question. Then, exchange it with a classmate and evaluate it according to the guidelines that were presented in this chapter.

2. Explain why essay questions are more useful for tapping higher-order thinking skills than just straight memorization.

3. Name two advantages of essay items and provide an explanation as to why they are advantages.

4. Write three essay items that violate at least one of the guidelines we identified in this chapter, and indicate what's wrong.

5. Name two disadvantages of essay items and discuss how you might compensate for them.

ANSWERS TO PRACTICE QUESTIONS

1. Here's my question:

    Discuss the origins of the testing movement in the United States, and be sure to identify how the social and political events of the times helped encourage the growth of the testing industry (45 minutes).

2. Unlike test items such as short answer or completion (or many other types you have yet to learn about), essay questions provide the flexibility to explore ideas and not just require memorization or the repetition of facts.

3. First, good performance on an essay question demands an understanding of ideas and how they relate to one another. That's very important in topics where there is a premium on relationships between ideas and concepts rather than rote memorization of those concepts. Second, they are very flexible in that they can be adjusted to meet the needs of the assessment setting. One set of essays might be used to look at a description of a particular historical event, whereas a more

ambitious one (for the test taker, that is) might be used to look at how certain unhistorical events had an impact on others and what the consequences of each event was for future policy decisions.

4. Here are mine:
   a. What are some of the important things that happened in American history? (unclear and incomplete)
   b. Name the planets in order of their distance from the sun, with the closest first. (not an essay question)
   c. When she didn't establish a foundation for the foundation, she made a terrible mistake that angered her mother. Relate that to how she furthered her career. (Uh—very unclear and include).

5. My two are as follows:
   a. There's no getting around the fact that the writing component to essay questions can be very important. But one way to compensate for that is to make sure the test takers are capable of expressing themselves in writing before administering such an exam. Or, provide adequate outlining assistance and extensive practice organizing and writing such a response. These are tough to get by, but perhaps worth it.
   b. Essay questions are no fun, tedious, and very draining to score—especially if you have a lot of them to do. One way to help with this task is to use a model answer (as we discussed earlier in this chapter) and to work in small chunks of time so that you remain refreshed.

WANT TO KNOW MORE?

Further Readings

• Hamberg, K., Risberg, G., Johansson, E. E., & Westman, G. (2002). Gender bias in physicians' management of neck pain: A study of the answers in a Swedish national examination. *Journal of Women's Health and Gender-Based Medicine, 11*(7), 653–665.

Essay questions can be used in many different settings as exemplified here, where these researchers examined gender differences in the diagnosis and management of neck pain. Modified essay questions were used to record suggestions about management of neck pain.

• Bridgeman, B., & Morgan, R. (1996). Success in college for students with discrepancies between performance on multiple-choice and essay tests. *Journal of Educational Psychology, 88*(2), 333–340.

The title says it all. Students in the top third on the essay portion of a test and the bottom third on the multiple-choice portion of the examination were compared with students with the opposite pattern (top third on the multiple-choice questions and bottom third on the essay questions). Part of the findings? Students who were strong in the essay format and weak in the multiple-choice format were as successful in their college courses as students with the opposite pattern. Guess if you know it, you know it.

And on the Internet

- The Advanced Placement people at the University of Georgia can show you some real live essay questions from previous years dating back to the early 1960s at http://apbio.biosci.uga.edu/exam/Essays/. This is a perfect place to see what essay questions look like in the area of biology at some of the most advanced levels.

- Computers grade the prose of an essay question? Maybe. Read all about it at Salon.com's technology section, located at http://www.salon.com/tech/feature/1999/05/25/computer_grading/.

8 Multiple-Choice Items

Always Pick Answer C and You'll Be Right About 25% of the Time

Difficulty Index ☺☺☺☺ (a bit difficult because of the math—but don't worry too much)

WHEN WE USE 'EM AND WHAT THEY LOOK LIKE

Multiple-choice items are the ones that you see all the time—most often as items on achievement tests used to assess some area of knowledge such as introductory chemistry, advanced biology, the written part of the Red Cross CPR test, the national boards in internal medicine, and so on. They are so easy to score, easy to analyze, and so easily tied to learning outcomes that multiple-choice items are, by far, the preferred way of testing achievement-oriented outcomes.

But beyond all the other great things about multiple-choice items, they are hugely flexible. And by that we mean that it is very easy to create an item that exactly matches a learning outcome.

In Chapter 13, we will emphasize the importance of taxonomies (such as Benjamin Bloom's taxonomy, which we will cover there) and how these hierarchical systems can be used to help you define the level at which a question should be written. Well, what multiple-choice items allow you to do is to write an item at any one of these levels. You can do this, for example, with short answer and completion items as well, but it is much more difficult. Why? Because multiple-choice items provide you with much more flexibility.

THINGS TO REMEMBER

Multiple-choice items are most often used to assess knowledge of a particular topic, and they typically appear on achievement tests.

For example, such items can target simple memorization, like the following multiple-choice item from an undergraduate research methods course:

---

1. Another name for research that occurs "post hoc" is

    a. experimental.
    b. correlational.
    c. quasi-experimental.
    d. historical.

Choice C is the correct answer.

There's nothing more required here than memorizing that another name for post hoc research is quasi-experimental. On the other hand, the following item taken from the tests for the same course taps a bit of higher-level thinking.

---

1. A nondirectional research hypothesis is similar to a directional hypothesis in that both

    a. specify the direction of the difference between groups.
    b. reflect differences between groups.
    c. are nonspecific regarding the direction of group differences.
    d. make no allusion to group differences.

Choice B is the right one here.

In this example, the test taker has to understand the similarities and dissimilarities of directional and nondirectional research hypotheses and select the ones that both types of hypotheses have in common—much more thinking is involved.

You can see in both of the above examples how a multiple-choice item can easily handle simple or complex ideas.

Multiple-Choice Anatomy 101

Multiple-choice items consist of three distinct parts: a stem and a set of responses, which in turn consists of the correct answer and alternatives. Let's look at the following items from a high school geology class and identify these parts.

---

1. If the hanging wall has moved down, the fault is

   a. reversed.
   b. normal.
   c. strike-slip.
   d. indeterminate.

Choice B is it.

The **stem** sets the premise for the question and comes before any of the alternatives appear (in this example, the stem is "If the hanging wall has moved down, the fault is").

An **alternative** is a sentence or a part of a sentence that is used to complete the stem or answer the question being asked. For example, answers A through D above are all alternatives. And, there is only one **correct alternative**, which in this example is B. Sometimes, the correct alternative is called the **key** or the **key alternative**.

Distracters are a special type of alternative. These are the incorrect alternatives whose job it is to distract the test taker into thinking that the incorrect alternative is correct, but not to be so distracting that if the test taker knows the correct answer, he or she cannot identify it.

This is a pretty cool idea. Come up with a set of alternative answers to a question, one of which is correct and some of which are not. But, make the ones that are not correct sound pretty good so that if someone knows only a bit about the topic, then the incorrect ones may seem attractive enough to select. However, for the test taker who is knowledgeable and understands the material, even though the distracters may appear to have some merit, they have less merit than the one correct answer. That's what you get for being smart.

THINGS TO REMEMBER

The key to a great multiple-choice question is a set of terrific distracters—those alternatives that could be, but are not, correct.

Why such a cool idea? Because the primary job of achievement tests that use multiple-choice items is to discriminate between those who know the material and those who do not. A really easy test and everyone gets 100%? (Oops—test didn't do a very good job of discriminating.) A really hard test and no one gets any right? (Oops—same problem.) Much more about this later under item analysis, because it is a really important aspect of how multiple-choice items work.

Your job is to

- write terrific multiple-choice items that have clear, well-written stems that reflect the learning objective you want tested
- create adequate alternatives that are all appealing
- make sure that within those alternatives, there are distracters that are almost as appealing as the correct answer

Let's find out how to do this.

HOW TO WRITE MULTIPLE-CHOICE ITEMS: THE GUIDELINES

As the Great Oz said, the best place to start is at the beginning.

1. *List alternatives on separate lines and one right after the other.* It makes the items easier to read and is much less confusing, especially if the alternatives are of any length.
    Here's the way it should not be done:

> 1. The first president of the United States was
>   a. Washington b. Jefferson c. Lincoln d. Kennedy

And the way it should be is as follows:

---

1. The first president of the United States was

   a. Washington

   b. Jefferson

   c. Lincoln

   d. Kennedy

---

2. *Be sure that each item reflects a clearly defined learning outcome.* This is a biggie for sure. The key here is to be sure that your defined learning objective (and, for example, its level of complexity) is reflected in the items you write.

3. *Be sure that the position of the correct alternative varies such that each position is represented an equal number of times.* Let's say you have created a 100-question multiple-choice test, and you inadvertently keyed the correct answer to be in position D for each item. If the test taker selects D for each item, by chance alone he or she will get a score of 25% correct. And indeed, when those bubble scoring sheets are used, some test taker who did not prepare just goes right down the sheet, marking off whatever column he or she wants. If you denote a correct response for each item (A, B, C, or D) such that there is an equal chance of any one of them being correct by chance alone, you reduce the impact that guessing can have.

4. *Use correct grammar and be consistent.* This may sound like a no-brainer, but many multiple-choice items are constructed in such a way that the test taker can easily figure out what the correct answer is or at least can eliminate some of the distracters. For example (and for those of you who are aspiring cooks),

---

1. Mirepoix is a

   a. Mixture of onions, carrots, and celery

   b. Ingredients for fondant icing

   c. Entrée served in France

   d. Alternative to flour used in baking

The only reasonable answer based on grammar alone is A. All the other alternatives are grammatically incorrect where a vowel "a" is followed by another vowel (such as "i," "e," or "a"). See, you don't even have to know a whisk from crème anglaise to answer the above question correctly.

TECH TALK

Other Species of Multiple-Choice Items

In this chapter, we are concentrating on only one type of multiple-choice item—the one that has only one correct answer—but there are several other types of more complex multiple-choice items that you may want to consider. Some multiple-choice items are *context dependent,* where the questions can be answered only within the context in which they are asked, such as when the test taker is asked to read a passage and then answer a multiple-choice item about that passage. Then, there's the *best answer* type of multiple-choice item, where there may be more than one correct answer, but only one that is best. *Danger, Will Robinson!*—both of these may work quite well, but they should be used only with additional training and experience. If you're just starting, stick to the basic type of multiple-choice items where there is only one correct answer.

---

5. *The stem of the item should be self-contained and written in clear and precise language.* Everything the test taker needs to know about the question's topic should be contained in the stem so that he or she does not have to read redundant information in each of the alternatives. Remember, you want to know if someone has the knowledge that the question is tapping, not if they can read the same material over again quickly. For example, here's an item that contains not enough in the stem and too much in each alternative.

---

1. New York City is the site of the next Olympics and

   a. has a new stadium for track and field.
   b. is building a new stadium for track and field.
   c. will be using only the Jets stadium in New Jersey.
   d. hasn't yet completed plans for where stadium events will take place.

The following question sets a better set of conditions for anyone who knows the correct response:

> 1. The current population of New York City is
>
>   a. More than 15,000,000
>   b. Less than 15,000,000
>   c. More than 25,000,000
>   d. Indeterminate

6. *Negatives, absolutes, and qualifiers in question stems are no-nos.* Not only are negatives confusing, but there is rarely an absolute case of anything, so test takers can easily get confused. And qualifiers (such as *only, although, perhaps,* etc.) drive test takers nuts. In addition, almost any good test taker who might miss a question where an absolute is involved could probably argue for his or her answer. For example, here's a confusing multiple-choice item that contains negatives. This is so confusing that all or none of these answers could be correct.

> 1. Not only do cicadas come every 17 years, but they never arrive
>
>   a. during the rainy season.
>   b. only if the temperature is sufficiently warm.
>   c. whenever the ground is just about soft enough for them to merge.
>   d. after June 1.

7. *Be sure that all distracters are plausible.* If a distracter does not even seem possibly correct, it is eliminated, and the value of the item decreases substantially because the likelihood of guessing correctly increases substantially. For example, in the following items, two of the four alternatives (A and C) are implausible, leaving B and D as possibilities. So, rather than a 25% chance of getting the item correct by guessing, the odds are now 50–50.

> 1. The square root of 64 is
>
>   a. 64
>   b. 8
>   c. 642
>   d. Infinity

8. *Items need to be independent of one another.* Multiple-choice items need to stand alone, and the answer on one item should not inform

the test taker as to what the correct answer might be on another item. For example, an item early in a test may provide a clue or even an answer to an item that comes later.

THE GOOD AND THE BAD

Multiple-choice items have their advantages and disadvantages—let's review them, and they are summarized in Table 8.1.

TABLE 8.1 The Advantages and Disadvantages of Multiple-Choice Questions	
Advantages of Multiple-Choice Items	*Disadvantages of Multiple-Choice Items*
• They can be used to measure learning outcomes at almost any level.	• They take a long time to write.
• They are easy to understand (if well written, that is).	• Good ones are difficult to write.
• They deemphasize writing skills.	• They limit creativity.
• They minimize guessing.	• They may have more than one correct answer.
• They are easy to score.	
• They can be easily analyzed for their effectiveness.	

Why Multiple-Choice Items Are Good

1. *Multiple-choice items can be used to measure learning outcomes at almost any level.* This is the big one, and we have mentioned it before. This allows multiple-choice items to be very flexible and to be useful anytime you are sure that test takers can adequately read, and understand, the content of the question.

2. *They are clear and straightforward.* Well-written multiple-choice items are very clear, and what is expected of the test taker is clear as well. There's usually no ambiguity (how

many pages should I write, can I use personal experiences, etc.) about answering the test questions.

3. *No writing needed.* Well, not very much anyway, and that has two distinct advantages. First, it eliminates any differences between test takers based on their writing skills. And, second, it allows for responses to be completed fairly quickly, leaving more time for more questions. You should allot about 60 seconds per multiple-choice question when designing your test.

4. *The effects of guessing are minimized, especially when compared to true-false items.* With four or five options, the likelihood of getting a well-written item correct by chance alone (and that's exactly what guessing is) is anywhere between 20% and 25%.

5. *Multiple-choice items are easy to score, and the scoring is reliable as well.* If this is the case, and you have a choice of what kind of items to use, why not use these? Some of the techniques used to score tests are discussed in Appendix A, but being able to bring 200 bubble scoring sheets to your office's scoring machine and having the results back in 5 minutes sure makes life a lot easier. And, when the scoring system is more reliable and more accurate, the reliability of the entire test increases.

6. *Multiple-choice items lend themselves to item analysis.* We'll talk shortly about item analysis, including how to do it and what it does. For now, it's enough to understand that this technique allows you to further refine multiple-choice items so that they perform better and give you a clearer picture of how this or that item performed and if it did what it was supposed to do. For this reason, multiple-choice items can be diagnostic tools to tell you what test takers understand and what they do not.

Why Multiple-Choice Items Are Not So Good

Those just-mentioned advantages sound pretty rosy, but there's a down side as well.

Guess What? No, Don't Guess . . .

You already know from the reading in this chapter that guessing may have a significant impact on a test taker's score, which is why we need to consider some kind of correction for guessing. Remember that the standard four-alternative multiple-choice item already has a probability of being correct one out of four times by chance alone, or 25%, or 0.25. So, we'd like to even the playing field and get a more accurate picture as to what's going on.

The correction for guessing looks like this:

$$CS = R - \frac{W}{n-1}$$

where

CS = corrected score

R = number of correct responses

W = number of wrong responses

n = the number of choices for each item

For example, on a 60-item multiple-choice test with four alternatives, you can expect a score of 15 by chance alone, right? (0.25 × 60 = 15). Russ gets 15 correct on this 60-item test, and Sheldon gets 40 correct. How can we adjust these scores such that Sheldon's performance is encouraged (because it is way above chance) and Russ is gently punished for lots of guessing? When we are correcting scores (using the above formula), it turns out that Russ's new score is 15–(45/3), or 0!, and Shel's is 40–(20/3), or about 33. Russ is clearly "punished" for guessing.

1. *Multiple-choice items take a long time to write.* You can figure on anywhere between 10 and 20 minutes to write a decent first draft of a multiple-choice item. Now, you will be able to use this same item in many different settings, and perhaps for many different years, but nonetheless it's a lot of work.

2. *Good multiple-choice items are not easy to write.* Not only do they take a long time, but unless you have very good distracters (written well, focused, etc.), and you include one correct answer, then you will get test takers who can argue for any of the alternatives as being correct (even though you think they are not), and they can sometimes do this pretty persuasively.

3. *Multiple-choice items do not allow for creative or unique responses.* Test takers have no choice as to how to respond (A or B or C or D). So, if there is anything more they would like to add or show what they know beyond what is present in the individual item, they are out of luck!

4. *The best test takers may know more than you!* Multiple-choice items operate on the assumption that there is only one correct alternative. Although the person who designs the test might believe this is true, the brightest test taker may indeed find something about every alternative, including the correct one, that is flawed.

Multiple-Choice Items: More Than Just "Which One Is Correct"

Throughout this chapter, we are emphasizing the importance of the type of multiple-choice item that has only one correct alternative. But, there are others with which you should be familiar.

- *Best-answer multiple-choice items.* These are multiple-choice items where there may be more than one correct answer, but only one of them is the best of all the correct ones.

- *Rearrangement multiple-choice items.* Here's where the test taker arranges a set of items in sequential order, be it steps in a process or the temporal sequence in which something might have occurred or should occur.

- *Interpretive multiple-choice items.* Here, the test taker reads through a passage and then selects a response where the alternatives (and the correct answer) all are based on the same passage. Keep in mind that although this appears to be an attractive format, it does place a premium on reading and comprehension skills.

- *Substitution multiple-choice items.* This is something like a short answer or completion item (see Chapter 6), but there are alternatives from which to select. The test taker selects those responses from a set of responses that he or she thinks answers the question correctly.

ANALYZING MULTIPLE-CHOICE ITEMS

OK—you've got your multiple-choice items created, you understand very well the advantages and disadvantages and feel pretty comfortable that the test you just gave did what it should have—separate those who know the material from those who do not. Now's the time to find out if you are right.

Multiple-choice items (as do other types) allow for an in-depth analysis of whether the item did what it was supposed to—discriminate between those who know the material and those who do not. This can be done through the completion of an **item analysis**, which consists of generating two different indexes for each item: a difficulty index and a discrimination index.

By looking at how well the distracters work, the multiple-choice question format can be diagnostic in nature. For example, if all the people who did very well on the test selected the incorrect distracter, there's got to be a good reason and one well worth exploring.

Let's explore both of these using the following item (for all you baseball lovers) as an example. Let's say this is Item 14 on a test that contains 25 multiple-choice items, and 50 people took the test.

---

1. Who was the first president to dedicate a new baseball stadium?

    a. John F. Kennedy
    b. Lyndon B. Johnson
    c. Calvin Coolidge
    d. Chester Arthur

It was Lyndon Johnson.

First, we are going to show you the final scores for all 50 people as shown here.

Individual	Score	Individual	Score	Individual	Score	Individual	Score	Individual	Score
#1	21	#11	25	#21	23	#31	24	#41	25
#2	24	#12	21	#22	24	#32	21	#42	20
#3	23	#13	21	#23	13	#33	21	#43	12
#4	18	#14	12	#24	16	#34	11	#44	14
#5	15	#15	9	#25	14	#35	9	#45	14
#6	21	#16	23	#26	13	#36	19	#46	9
#7	24	#17	7	#27	4	#37	18	#47	23
#8	15	#18	21	#28	13	#38	3	#48	21
#9	18	#19	22	#29	21	#39	18	#49	24
#10	19	#20	3	#30	24	#40	5	#50	8

So, Individual 12 got 21 correct out of 25, and Individual 40 got 5 correct out of 25.

Now, here are the results for Item 14 that we are using as an example. You can't see these individual results in the above listing—you can only see what's there, which is the score for each individual test taker.

Alternative	Total Times Selected
A	4
B	26
C	8
D	12
Total Responses	50

So, of all 50 people who took the test, 26 selected the correct response B, and 24 (4 + 8 + 12) selected one of the alternatives.

As you learned earlier, the rationale behind doing an item analysis is to find out how well an item discriminates between those who know the material and those who do not. In order to do this, we will create two groups of test takers—yes—those who know the material and those who don't.

How do we do this? Simple. We order all the test scores from highest to lowest and take a percentage of the top performers and call that our high group and take a percentage of low performers and call that our low group. What percentage of the group do we take? 27%. Why 27? Because various studies have shown that this percentage maximizes the difference between those who know the material and those who do not—just what we want to find out.

TECH TALK

50% Will Do Just Fine

OK—you've seen the recommendation—take the top and bottom 27% from the groups that are used in an item analysis. But, for all practical purposes, and especially for the classroom teacher, splitting the entire group in half (so you have the high group and the low group, each consisting of 50% of the entire group) is just fine, especially because classrooms often have relatively small numbers of students, and 27% would result in just too small a number to be useful in the analysis.

Here's how we create these two groups.

1. Place all of the scores for all test takers in descending order (from highest to lowest).

2. Select the top 27% of scores and identify that as the high group. In this case, 27% of 50 is 14, so the highest 14 test takers constitute the high group.

3. Select the bottom 27% of scores and identify that as the low group. In this case, 27% of 50 is 14, so the lowest 14 test takers constitute the low group.

4. Here are the final scores of the high and low group.

#11	25	High Group
#41	25	High Group
#2	24	High Group
#7	24	High Group
#22	24	High Group
#30	24	High Group
#31	24	High Group
#49	24	High Group
#3	23	High Group
#16	23	High Group
#21	23	High Group
#47	23	High Group
#19	22	High Group
#1	21	High Group
#26	13	Low Group
#28	13	Low Group
#14	12	Low Group
#43	12	Low Group
#34	11	Low Group
#15	9	Low Group
#35	9	Low Group
#46	9	Low Group

#50	8	Low Group
#17	7	Low Group
#40	5	Low Group
#27	4	Low Group
#20	3	Low Group
#38	3	Low Group

5. Finally, for these 28 different test takers (and remember, we are doing an item analysis, so we are looking at just one item, which is #14 in our example), we get the following results, again for that one item only.

Item 14					
			Alternative		
	a	*b**	*c*	*d*	*Total*
High Group	2	21	2	4	29
Low Group	2	5	6	8	21
Total	4	26	8	12	50

So, on Item 14 (and only Item 14), a total of 26 test takers selected Alternative B (which is correct); 21 of those were in the high group, and 5 of them were in the low group. Similarly, a total of 12 test takers selected Alternative D (which is an incorrect alternative); 4 of those were in the high group, and 8 of them were in the low group. For our upcoming item analysis, all we care about are the responses to Alternative B.

Ok, let's get to the analysis.

THINGS TO REMEMBER

One of the most common mistakes made by new users of item analysis is that they believe the analysis is of the *entire test* and not individual items. Indeed, the analysis is for each item, one at a time. So, if you have a 50-item test, then a difficulty index and a discrimination index can be computed for *each* item on that test. One might average these two indexes across all items to get an overall set of numbers, but the purpose of this item analysis is to get feedback on how good an individual item is, then to revise that item so that it will be even better next time you use it.

Computing the Difficulty Index

The **difficulty index** tells us how difficult the item is or how many people got that the item correct. It is a percentage reflecting the number of responses in the both the high and low group that got the item correct. Here's the formula

$$D = \frac{N_h + N_l}{T}$$

where

D = difficulty level

N_h = the number of correct responses in the high group

N_l = the number of correct responses in the low group

T = the total number of responses to the item

If we plug in the number to the above formula, we find that the difficulty level for Item 14 is 52%.

$$D = \frac{21 + 5}{50} = 52\%$$

Fifty-two percent (52%) of the responses to Item 14 were correct. If the difficulty level were equal to 100%, it would mean that everyone got the item correct (far too easy), and if the difficulty level were equal to 0%, it would mean that everyone got the item incorrect (far too hard).

And, that's the story of the difficulty index—but only half the entire story of item discrimination. Let's move on to the discrimination index.

Computing the Discrimination Index

Where the difficulty index is a measure of the percentage of responses in the high and low groups that are correct, the **discrimination index** is a measure of how effectively an item discriminates between the high and low groups.

Here's the formula

$$d = \frac{N_h - N_l}{(.5)T}$$

where

d = discrimination level

N_h = the number of correct responses in the high group

N_l = the number of correct responses in the low group

T = the total number of responses to the item

If we plug in the number to the above formula, we find that the difficulty level for Item 14 is 0.64.

$$D = \frac{21 - 5}{25} = 0.64$$

As you can see, the discrimination index is expressed as a decimal.

Right off the bat, you should recognize that when *d* is positive, more people in the high group than in the low group got the item correct (the item is doing what it should). And, if *d* is negative, it means that more people in the low group than in the high group got the item correct (the item is not doing what it should).

TECH TALK

Another Way to Compute the Discrimination Index

The method we show you in this chapter to compute *d* (the discrimination index) for any one item is straightforward and pretty easy to calculate. There's another way you may see mentioned and one that is especially good for longer tests. It's called the point biserial method, which is the correlation between a dichotomous variable (right or wrong for the item under analysis) and a continuous variable (the test score). Here's the formula:

$$d = \left[\frac{\overline{X}_1 - \overline{X}}{S_y} \right] \sqrt{\frac{P_x}{1 - P_x}}$$

where

d = discrimination index

$\overline{X}_1$ = the mean score on the test for all those test takers who got the item correct

$\overline{X}$ = the mean score for the test

S_y = the standard deviation for the test

P_x = the proportion of people who got the item correct

So, for example, suppose that 67% of test takers got Item 17 correct, and the mean score on the test was 83 and the standard deviation 7.5. For those who got Item 17 correct, also suppose that the mean score for their tests was 79. The formula for *d* would then look like this:

$$d = \left[\frac{79 - 83}{7.5} \right] \sqrt{\frac{.67}{.33}} = -.757$$

Not a great item because the negative value indicates that those who knew less overall did better on this item than those who knew more overall.

THINGS TO REMEMBER

Multiple-choice questions are used for many reasons, but among the most important is that they lend themselves to a thorough quantitative analysis using the item analysis we talk about in this chapter.

How the Difficulty and Discrimination Index Get Along: Quite Well, Thank You

As we move to understanding the relationship between the difficulty and discrimination indexes and what that means for any one item, remember that the perfect item has a discrimination index of 1.00, which means that 100% of the test takers in the high group got it correct and 100% of the test takers in the low group got it incorrect. And in order for this to occur, guess what? Read on . . .

The perfect item has two characteristics. First, the item is sufficiently difficult such that 50% of all the test takers get it correct and 50% of all the test takers get it incorrect. Guess which 50% get it correct?

That's right. The second condition is that all the test takers in the high scoring group (the "smarter" folks) get the item correct and all the test takers in the low scoring group get the item incorrect.

Now for the prize question. If the two conditions are met, then what is the value of D and d? That's right . . . $D = 50\%$ (half got it right and half got it wrong), and $d = 1.00$ (the half that got it right scored best on the test). And that's how they get along.

But there's more—in fact, the *only* possible way for an item to have perfect outcomes for the item analysis is if these two conditions are met, because *discrimination level is constrained by the value of the difficulty level.* That's right, the only way you can have perfect discrimination is if the difficulty level is equal to 50%. The more the difficulty level varies from 50%, the less well the item discriminates.

For example, the only way that the highest half of the total number of test takers can get the item right is if 50% of all the test takers get it right and the other 50% get it wrong. Similarly, if the item doesn't perfectly discriminate between the two groups, it means that some test takers in the high group got the item incorrect and some of the test takers in the low group got the item correct—not what we want.

Now, we all know that nothing's perfect, so let's look at five different items (1, 2, 3, and 4) with different difficulty and discrimination indexes and try and understand what they are like.

You can see each of them in Figure 8.1 represented by a star (★) and an item number (★1 through ★4). And, to make everyone's day just perfect, there's the happy face ☺, indicating the absolute perfect item with a difficulty level of 50% and a discriminating level of +1.00. Isn't that cute?

Item ★1 has a difficulty level of about 25% and a discrimination level of about 50%. Not bad—about 25% of the test takers got it correct and it positively discriminates, meaning that more in the group that got better scores got it correct than those in the lower group. This item is doing a pretty good job.

Item ★2 has a difficulty level of about 75% and a discrimination level of about 50%. Like Item ★1, this item positively

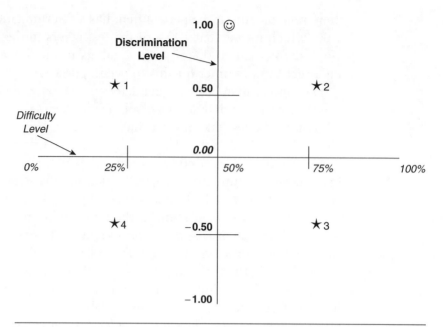

Figure 8.1 Difficulty and Discrimination Indexes

discriminates, but, with a difficulty level of 75%, it's getting a bit too easy.

Item ★3 isn't one that we particularly want to take home and show our friends and relatives—nor, of course, use again on a test. With a negative discrimination level around –.50, which means that more test takers in the low group got it correct than those test takers in the high group, and a pretty high difficulty index of 75%, indicating that it may be a bit too easy—it's time to go back to the drawing board.

THINGS TO REMEMBER

Remember that the only way to maximize an item's discrimination is to have 50% of the test takers get it correct, and those 50% be the ones who have the highest performance.

Finally, Item ★4 does not discriminate very well either (it's also negative), and it's too hard—only 25% of the entire group got it correct. Yuk.

For a perfect item, then, we shoot for $D = 50\%$ and $d = 1.00$. Do we reach those levels of perfection? Not usually, but we surely can come close. But how do we come closer? Read on.

The reason why an item fails to discriminate and has an unacceptable level of difficulty is because one or more of the rules for writing items (discussed earlier in this chapter) has been violated. For example, if you do not have one clearly correct answer, it's unlikely that there will be uniform agreement about the test takers in the high group as to which is correct. Similarly, if you have distracters that are not effective and are all implausible, the item becomes too easy, and if it is too easy (or too hard, for that matter), then discrimination is restricted (look at Figure 8.1 and you can see that if difficulty level is around 0% or 100%, then there can be little discrimination).

But most of all, if you want great items, create clearly correct answers and have terrific distracters. That ensures that the folks who know the material show such on a test and the folks who don't know it show their skills (or lack thereof) as well!

Each time you create a new multiple-choice item, place the stem and alternatives on the front of an index card. Each time you use the item in a test, enter the difficult and discrimination indexes on the back of the card along with the date the item was used and any other special circumstances (pop quiz, final exam, pretest, etc.). Then, the next time you want to use that item again, you know what it is that needs to be changed. If the difficulty and discrimination indexes are not what you want them to be, you can fine-tune the item more and more. With multiple uses of the same item that is constantly modified, you can eventually come up with very well-written and effective multiple-choice items.

SUMMARY

There's nothing like a dip in the lake on a hot and humid summer day or that favorite dessert of yours on Thanksgiving. And, there's nothing like a multiple-choice item (or a set of them, actually) to give you a fairly accurate and unbiased assessment of someone's level of knowledge about a particular area. Multiple-choice items have been used for decades with great success, and the simple and straightforward tools of item analysis have led to refinements that make these types of items simply the best for finding out what others know.

TIME TO PRACTICE

1. What are the three parts of a multiple-choice question, and what purpose does each serve?

2. In your area of expertise (your area of professional training, a hobby, or just personal interest), write five multiple-choice questions. Then, share these five with a class colleague, and go through the criteria presented in this chapter to evaluate how well each question meets the set of criteria on our cheat sheet for writing multiple-choice items.

	Alternative			
	A	B	C*	D
High Group	12	6	25	7
Low Group	18	15	5	12

3. Evaluate the following item based on the difficulty and discrimination indexes.

4. Jim is pretty smart, but he didn't prepare very well for his multiple-choice test and guessed his way to 23 out of 50 items correct with five alternates to each item. Chris is also pretty smart as well, and she studied and got 43 correct. What are their corrected scores for guessing?

5. In order for an item to be perfect (discriminate efficiently and have the appropriate level of difficulty), two conditions have to be met. What are those conditions?

ANSWERS TO PRACTICE QUESTIONS

1. The stem, a set of alternatives, and distracters. The stem sets the premise for the question. The alternatives consist of alternative answers that make up distracters and include the correct alternative or answer.

2. This is done on your own.

3. $D = .3$ and $d = .6$ (30% of all test takers got the item correct, and it does discriminate positively, approaching the ideal item characteristics of $D = 50\%$ and $d = 1.00$).

4. The formula used to compute the corrected score for guessing is

$$CS = R - \frac{W}{n - 1}$$

Jim's corrected score is $CS = 23 - \dfrac{27}{5 - 1}$ or 16.25.

Chris's corrected score is $CS = 43 - \dfrac{7}{5 - 1}$ or 41.25.

5. One half of all test takers have to get the item correct, and that one half is all the people in the high group—that way, the difficulty level is 50% and the discrimination index is 1.00 or perfecto!

WANT TO KNOW MORE?

Further Readings

• Elstein, A. S. (1993). Beyond multiple-choice questions and essays: The need for a new way to assess clinical competence. *Academic Medicine, 68,* 244–249.

You may think that multiple-choice questions are great, but not everyone shares that perspective. This article talks about alternatives and why other techniques might be a better choice for assessing knowledge than multiple-choice questions.

• McG, H. R., Brown, R. A., Biran, L. A., Ross, W. P., & Wakeford, R. E. (1976). Multiple choice questions: To guess or not to guess. *Medical Education, 10*(1), 27–32.

This is a pretty old study, but one that raises a question that every multiple-choice test giver and test taker should ask (and answer). These researchers found that the "don't know" option in multiple-choice question papers favors the bold and test-wise student.

And on the Internet

- From the University of Illinois at http://www.las.uiuc.edu/students/advising/practical_study/mult_choice.html, 22 ways to help increase your score on a multiple-choice exam—strategies for taking them and doing well.
- And more of the same from George Washington University at http://gwired.gwu.edu/counsel/asc/index.gw/Site_ID/46/Page_ID/14561/.

9 Matchmaker, Matchmaker, Make Me a Match

Matching Items

Difficulty Index ☺☺☺☺☺ (easy)

The multiple-choice type of item is absolutely perfect for finding out how much test takers know about a particular topic. As you learned in Chapter 8, they are easy to administer, easy to score, and well regarded by others as an acceptable tool for assessment.

So are matching items—except they are somewhat easier to construct and can be used for very special applications. But in many other ways, they are just like multiple-choice items. And in fact, some test experts treat them as one and the same because, basically, matching items are multiple-choice questions that share the same alternatives (as you will shortly see).

WHEN WE USE 'EM AND WHAT THEY LOOK LIKE

Matching items are used to assess a content area—be it of history, biology, statistics, or the regulations governing NASCAR races. Like multiple-choice tests, they are basically assessment tools that assess an individual's knowledge of a particular subject and the associations between ideas. And like multiple-choice items and true-false items (see Chapter 10), they involve *selection,* where the test taker needs to select one answer from a set of at least two alternatives. However, in matching items, the number of alternatives is usually more than five (the case for multiple-choice items) or more than two (the case for true-false items).

THINGS TO REMEMBER

Multiple-choice items are wonderful, but matching items can be just as good, especially when you have lots of possible answers and you do not want to be constantly repeating them.

Here's a typical matching item from a test on basic statistics.

Directions: Column A contains a list of statements that describe different measures of central tendency or variability. On the line to the left of each of the items in Column A, write the letter of the item in Column B that best matches the statement.

Column A	*Column B*
___ 1. The sum of a set of scores divided by the number of observations.	a. The mean
	b. The median
___ 2. The most frequently occurring score in a set of scores.	c. The standard deviation
	d. The range
___ 3. The difference between the highest and lowest scores in a set of scores.	e. The average score
	f. The mode
___ 4. The point in a set of scores where 50% fall below that point and 50% are above.	g. The deviation score
	h. The variance
___ 5. The point about which the sum of the deviations equals zero.	
___ 6. The average amount that any one score falls from the middle-most score in a set of scores.	

The statements in Column A are called **premises**, and the statements in Column B are called **options** or **responses**. So, there is a premise to the question that the test taker considers, and there are various options or responses from which the test taker can select what he or she thinks is the correct answer.

Traditionally, the premises in a matching item are designated using numbers, and the options or responses are designated using letters (either capital or lower case). So, the same information is presented in a more compact format without any of the repetition that may threaten the type of multiple-choice item you learned about in Chapter 8.

Matching items are also often used instead of multiple-choice questions when you want to use the same response in more than one question and such a practice would threaten the independence of each question and the integrity of the test.

For example, take the following two questions written first as multiple-choice questions:

---

1. The Declaration of Independence was signed in

   a. 1774
   b. 1775
   c. 1776
   d. 1777

---

2. The important historical document that was a response to the repression felt by the founders of the United States was called

   a. The Magna Carta
   b. The Declaration of Independence
   c. The Constitution
   d. The Framer's Document

In these examples, the correct answer (C for Question 1 and B for Question 2) biases the test taker toward that one response—the Declaration of Independence.

If we were to create the questions as matching items, the same information could be tested as follows. Notice how four options in Column B are all you need to answer the two questions in Column A.

Column A	Column B
___ 1. This historical document was signed in 1776.	a. The Magna Carta
	b. The Constitution
___ 2. This historical document was a response to the repression felt by the founders of the United States.	c. The Declaration of Independence
	d. The Framer's Document

HOW TO WRITE 'EM: THE GUIDELINES

Let's get to the construction of matching items. Keep in mind that the first rule of constructing matching items (or any item for that matter) is that the item type (matching) best fits the objectives you have. Here, we're after a measure of achievement or knowledge of a particular subject, be it the discovery of circulation in the human body (history of medicine), cloning (biotechnology), or who hit more home runs than Willie Mays (baseball).

And the winning guidelines (drum roll, please) for writing matching items are as follows:

1. *There are two columns, one containing premises and the second containing options or responses.* The number of options or responses does not matter as long as this number is more than the number of premises, which helps reduce the effects of guessing. For example, two premises and four possible responses works quite well, as you saw above.

2. *As with any test, provide complete directions.* This is important because, in some cases, the test taker may be able to use a response more than once, and in others, he or she may not. Let the test taker know exactly what is allowed and supposed to be done. For example, here are well-written directions:

> **Directions:** In Column A, there are five statements about 20th-century American writers. In Column B are the names of eight 20th-century American writers. Match the name of the writer in Column B with the statement in Column A that best describes the writer by placing the letter in Column B on the line next to the number in Column A.

3. *All premises and all responses should be reasonable.* The lightbulb box that follows on page 162 talks about this a bit, but you should not have premises that are too simple, such as

Column A	Column B
____ 1. Ducks like to swim in this.	a. water
____ 2. Yummy in the winter.	b. soup
	c. motor oil

4. *Responses should not be listed in the same order as the corresponding premise.* This might sound obvious, but it could be an easy mistake to make. This would allow a test taker to just go right down the premise list and enter a, b, c, d, etc., and be correct. Also, be sure that the responses do not have a pattern to them, such as a, b, c, a, b, c in a six-item matching test. For example, here's a pattern you want to avoid where the correct response is adjacent to the premise.

Column A	Column B
___ 1. The only president to be unanimously elected.	a. George Washington
___ 2. John Adams's friend who died on the same day.	b. Thomas Jefferson
___ 3. First president to have a photograph taken.	c. John Quincy Adams
___ 4. First president to receive a patent.	d. Abraham Lincoln

And the answers, of course (and you knew this all along, right?), are 1a, 2b, 3c, and 4d.

5. *A premise should contain more words than an option.* The premise is the part of the question that contains the idea, concept, term, or fact that the item is evaluating. It's where the meat of the question lies. You don't want test takers spending their time reading possible answers when it is the premise to which they should be paying attention and thinking about. For example, here's a violation of this how-to:

Column A	Column B
___ 1. Analysis of variance	a. The inferential technique that is used when you want to test the difference between the strength of two correlation coefficients and the assumptions of normality are not violated.
___ 2. t test	b. The inferential technique that allows you to determine whether there is a difference between the means of two or more samples.

> When creating and organizing matching items, try to make sure that they appear in homogeneous groups—that is, groups that are similar in content and level of difficulty. For example, if the test contains matching items on physics and meteorology (a subset of physics), don't mix questions from the two topics in the same set of possible answers.

6. *To help all test takers respond efficiently, place the premises in some logical order, such as alphabetical or chronological.* For example,

Date	Event
____ 1. July 21, 1861	a. Battle of Wilderness
____ 2. September 17, 1862	b. Battle of Shiloh
____ 3. May 6, 1864	c. Battle of Antietam
	d. Battle of Gettysburg
	e. Battle of 1st Bull Run

So, how well do you remember your American history dates? Correct answers are 1e, 2c, and 3a.

7. *Make sure that all premises and responses appear on the same page.* How crazy would it make you to have to keep flipping pages back and forth to read and reread premises and possible responses?

8. *Make sure that each premise has only one correct response.* This increases both the reliability and the validity of the test (and cuts way down on argument with test takers!).

9. *Columns should be labeled to orient and assist test takers.* In the example you see above about Civil War dates, the two columns are labeled Date and Event. Note that if the premises aren't homogeneous in content, you can't label the columns because the content covered bridges different areas.

THE GOOD AND THE BAD

Now that we know how to write matching items, it's time to look at their advantages ☺ and disadvantages ☹. Like any other type of item, they have their share of both, and here are the ones that I think are the most important.

Table 9.1	Advantages and Disadvantages of Matching Questions
Advantages of Matching Items	*Disadvantages of Matching Items*
• They are straightforward and clear in their presentation. • They are easy to administer. • They allow for comparison of ideas and facts. • Responses are short and easy to read. • The value of guessing is decreased.	• The level of knowledge tested is limited. • The test can be difficult to machine score. • The test emphasizes memory.

Why Matching Items Are Good

1. *Matching items are easy to score because the format of the premises and responses is straightforward and very clear.* The response on a matching item is absolutely unambiguous. Most of the time, test takers enter the letter of a response that matches a premise, but you can also have them draw a line connecting the two items that match. And, because these items are so straightforward in their presentation, the test format tends to be reliable.

THINGS TO REMEMBER

Matching items are terrific because they are easily administered and are easy to format securely.

2. *Matching items are easily administered to a large number of test takers.* The directions can be very straightforward, and, if the items are written following the guidelines we identified above, the testing sessions should go smoothly.

3. *Matching items allow for the comparison of ideas or facts.* The responses can consist of several different ideas, facts, or observations—all of which need to be compared to one another.

4. As we mentioned earlier, *when multiple-choice items need to have the same response, matching items are perfect.*

5. *Responses are short and easy to read* (or at least they should be!).

6. *Matching items deemphasize writing ability.* This is true, of course, with all objective (multiple-choice, true-false, etc.) types of items. You just don't have to write well to be able to demonstrate a knowledge of the material. And, if you are interested in whether a medical student knows the name of the cervical nerves in the spinal column, whether he or she can write poetry becomes irrelevant.

7. *Finally, the matching item format actually decreases the value of guessing.* With most multiple-choice items, there's a 25% (1 in 4) or a 20% (1 in 5) chance of getting it right by guessing. When you are matching, there are probably 6–10 options for each premise—the odds are then reduced to about 17% (1 in 6) or even 10% (1 in 10).

Why Matching Items Are Not So Good

Then, there's the dark side . . .

1. *When matching items are used, the level of knowledge tested is limited.* We're dealing mostly with factual information here, so it's pretty easy to test the year in which *Gone With the Wind* was published (1936), who invented the lightbulb (Thomas Edison), or how much $10^{4.5}$ equals (31622.78). But, if you want a comparison between different theories of development or a discussion of the advantages and disadvantages of socialism, go elsewhere, such as short answer or essay items.

2. *Matching items are useful only when you can generate a sufficient number of options.* You may be testing a topic that is so finite and narrow there are not very many attractive options that are incorrect, and it would be difficult to write a good item that fairly assesses the test taker's knowledge of the topic at hand. In other words, you end up short on options.

3. *Scoring can be a problem.* Although matching terms are presented in an objective framework, it is more difficult to

machine score them because the test taker usually writes directly on the test itself and not on some scoring sheet, such as those used with multiple-choice or true-false tests.

4. *If your memory is good, then matching items are for you.* One of the criticisms of matching items is that they emphasize memorization of facts rather than higher-order thinking skills. OK, that's a legitimate concern, but that's also usually why people create such items—to test basic knowledge.

SUMMARY

So, with the end of this chapter, we've finished with two of the three selection item formats (multiple-choice and matching), and it's time to move on to the last type of selection format we'll discuss, which is true-false. Remember that once you know the substantive objectives you want to assess on your test, then the type of format you want to use should become evident.

TIME TO PRACTICE

1. What are the advantages of matching items over multiple-choice items?

2. Why should matching items be homogeneous?

3. In your area of interest (be it a hobby, profession, or just an interest), write five matching items. Once you have finished, use the following chart to evaluate each one. Place a plus where the item meets the criterion and a minus where it does not. Then, go back and revise the items where necessary so you have a nice collection of all pluses.

Criterion	+ or −
1. There are two columns, one containing premises and the second containing options or responses.	_____
2. Complete directions are provided.	_____
3. All premises and all responses are reasonable.	_____
4. Responses are not listed in the same order as the corresponding premise.	_____
5. Premises contain more words than do the options.	_____
6. Premises are not in some logical order, such as alphabetical or chronological.	_____
7. Premises and responses appear on the same page.	_____
8. Premise has only one correct response.	_____

4. In your area of interest, write five more matching items and then give them to a classmate or a colleague and have that person evaluate them based on the criteria that are listed in the above chart.

5. Use the criteria listed in #3 above and indicate what's wrong with the following set of matching items on the planets and stars:

Column A	Column B
___ 1. Mizar	a. Jupiter
___ 2. The planet that rotates around its axis once about every nine hours.	b. Also known as the "red planet"
	c. Venus
___ 3. The hottest planet in the solar system.	d. Krypton
___ 4. The only planet other than Earth that may have been subject to massive flooding.	e. The star in the Big Dipper that has another star revolving around it.
	f. Pluto
___ 5. Mars	

ANSWERS TO PRACTICE QUESTIONS

1. Here are at least three:
   a. Matching items lower the odds of guessing correctly.
   b. Responses can be short and easy to read.
   c. Repetition is minimized.

2. One of the uses of matching items is to allow for the same answer to be used for multiple questions. If the items are not homogeneous, in that they cover the same content area, this use would be impossible.

3. Complete this form and be sure you go back and correct the items that do not meet all the criteria.

4. You're on your own on this one.

5. The following criteria aren't met:
   a. No instructions have been given.
   b. Columns are not labeled.
   c. Not all premises contain more words than options.
   d. Some of the options are implausible (Krypton?).

WANT TO KNOW MORE?

Further Readings

• Fenderson, B. A., Damjanov, I., Robeson, M. R., Veloski, J. J., & Rubin, E. (1997). The virtues of extended matching and uncued tests as alternatives to multiple choice questions. *Human Pathology, 28*(5), 526–532.

So what works best? These researchers compared the reliability and validity of multiple-choice, uncued, extended matching, and true-false tests and evaluated the effects of uncued examinations on long-term retention of medical knowledge. The results? Matching and uncued tests have considerable advantages over multiple-choice and true-false examinations in that they are more reliable and better discriminate the well-prepared from the marginal student.

• Bastick, T. (2002, April). *Gender differences for 6–12th grade students over Bloom's cognitive domain.* Paper presented at the annual meeting of the Western Psychological Association, Irvine, CA.

Item format may very well matter. The possibility that different types of test questions (multiple-choice, true-false, and matching) favor males or females was investigated. There was only one statistically significant advantage—for females using matching questions—because of females' advantages at the Analysis and Synthesis levels (i.e., they're smarter).

And on the Internet

• At http://www.usd.edu/esci/exams/matching.html (matching questions on minerals and rocks), you can see how easily adaptable matching questions are to an interactive electronic format.

10 True-False Tests

T or F? I Passed
My First Measurement Test

Difficulty Index ☺☺☺☺☺ (easy breezy)

Of all the types of items that we cover in this part of *Tests & Measurement for People Who (Think They) Hate Tests & Measurement*, true-false items might seem like they are the easiest to write (because they are the shortest) . . . but beware.

Short does not mean easy. Short can mean difficult to write because you have little space to be very precise and say exactly what you mean. In other words, as your mother told you, "Say what you mean and mean what you say," and it is perhaps more the case with true-false items than with any other type of item.

WHAT WE USE 'EM FOR

True-false items are most often used for achievement-type tests when there is a clear distinction between the two alternatives, true and false. For example, the item

A minute is 60 seconds.

can be either true or false, but it cannot be both.

One of the best criteria for judging the value of a true-false item is whether the correct answer (be it true or false) is, unequivocally, the right one, the only one, and the correct one (get the picture?). If you're studying time warps or the speed of nanomunchies, then perhaps "your" minute does not have 60 seconds. But for all practical purposes, there can't be both a "true" and "false" answer to a good true-false question such as the one we showed you above.

HOW TO WRITE 'EM: THE GUIDELINES

As with the other chapters in this part of *Tests & Measurement . . .* , we're going to give you the basics of how to write these types of items.

1. *True-false items are always stated as declarative sentences.* Here's an example of what you don't want to do.

> 1. True? or False? Is it true or false that a leap year occurs every 4 years?

Here's a true-false item stated as a good, declarative sentence:

> 1. True? or False? (circle one) A leap year occurs every 4 years on the lunar calendar.

2. *The alternative answers can be true-false, right-wrong, yes-no, like-dislike, or whatever—as long as they are very clear choices.* Just remember that there are only two choices and one of them is correct, and the other—you guessed it—is incorrect. Why use the yes-no format rather than the true-false format? It might better fit the nature of your item and may even present a less dramatic set of alternatives (true is always a tough concept to grasp).

Here's what you don't want to do:

> 1. Maybe? or Not? B. F. Skinner's studies focused on short-term memory.

And here is the same question as a simple yes-no item.

> 1. Yes? or No? B. F. Skinner's studies focused on short-term memory.

3. *A good true-false item focuses on one and only one idea, concept, or specific topic.* Too many ideas and the test taker can get confused.

If the focus is too general, the test taker will start overanalyzing the possible answers and how that declarative sentence may very well be both true and false (and then he or she is in trouble, along with you for the crime of lousy item writing).

Now, here's a crummy item:

> 1. True? or False? A roux is prepared using fat and flour, and is always used as the first step in the preparation of a sauce.

Not only might a roux be prepared using other ingredients (such as an alternative to flour), but it may be the first step in another preparation, other than a sauce. Here's a much better version of the same item.

> 1. True? or False? A roux can be prepared using fat and flour.

THINGS TO REMEMBER

Perhaps the most important rule to remember about constructing true-false items is that the statement is clearly true or false. When items are not created with this quality, they not only drive the test taker nuts but also don't give a very fair appraisal of the test taker's knowledge.

4. *Be careful about using statements of opinion.* You can use opinions in true-false items, but they become like-dislike. But be careful, because it is easy for items to become far too full of the item writer's perspective, such as in the following:

> 1. Like? Dislike? In the video, I liked the way the teacher masterfully handled the interaction between the child and his overbearing father.

Next, we have a *relatively* unopinionated alternative true-false item:

> 1. Like? Dislike? In the video, I liked the way the teacher handled the interaction between the child and his father.

There's no room for opinion in true-false items because such statements as the one shown first above violate the rule that there is one answer and that answer is right or wrong. Such items are best left for the realm of short answer or essay.

> Lee Cronbach, one of the most famous measurement specialists in the history of the discipline, did a study in 1950 where he found that when students do not have any clues to what the right choice is on a true-false item, they will, more often than not, select "true." That, coupled with the fact that he also found that most items on a true-false test are true (because these items are easier to write), leads one to believe that unless you intentionally create an equal number of true and false items for any test, you will not get a true or fair picture of performance using true-false items. Pretty cool observation, no?

5. *Double negatives might be fun, but not as part of a true-false question*—they only confuse the test taker. For example, here's a true-false item that is so confusing, it is almost easy to see how a true or false response could be argued to be correct! This is truly a terrible item.

> 1. Yes? or No? Neither Technique #1 or Technique #2 should be used with caution.

Here's a similar one in much better form.

> 1. Yes? or No? Technique #1 should be used with caution.

6. *Be careful of qualifiers such as "always," "never," "sometimes," "unquestionably," "none," "best," and so on.* They not only limit your ability to write precisely (because they are absolute statements), but also are not necessary—if the statement is true, then it's true, always, forever, and longer.

> 1. True? or False? The earth absolutely, without a doubt, and most assuredly revolves around the sun.

Here it is again, in much better form.

> 1. True? or False? The earth revolves around the sun.

7. *Do not include clues to the answer in your item.* Those qualifiers can also serve as inadvertent clues for the test taker to get a slight advantage over other test takers. Any test-wise student knows that the statements that contain words such as "always," "never," "sometimes," and others are usually false—based, of course, on the assumption that the item is poorly written and there is little that is never true or never false or sometimes true or sometimes false. Another clue is if true items are of a different word length than are false items. Keep them the same.

8. *Leave the more complex material to different types of items other than true-false that can more easily tap higher-order thinking.* Why? Because the very nature of complex material does not lend itself to such unambiguous answers as "correct" or "incorrect." For example, here's a topic that would have been better asked couched within a short answer or essay question rather than the true-false one you see here.

> 1. Correct? or Incorrect? Given that the internal combustion engine is a significant source of carbon monoxide emissions, and that there are more than 200,000,000 cars in the United States used on a daily basis, the only answer to reducing these gases is through alternative energy sources and hydrogen-powered cars.

9. Our last guideline? *Have an equal number of true and false items on the test*—this minimizes the role that chance will play.

THINGS TO REMEMBER

 True-false items also fall under the general category of dichotomous format—items that have two, and only two, responses.

THE GOOD AND THE BAD

As always, there are reasons to use true-false items and reasons not to use them. Here's my take on why they are good and why they are not so good. And, you'll find a summary of such in Table 10.1.

TABLE 10.1 Advantages and Disadvantages of True-False Questions

Advantages of True-False Items	Disadvantages of True-False Items
• They are convenient to write.	• The "truth" is never quite what it seems to be.
• They are easy to score.	• The items emphasizes memorization.
	• The items are easy to guess right.

Why True-False Items Are Good

There are lots of reasons why true-false items fit the bill and are very useful for a variety of applications. Here are the two main ones.

1. *They're convenient.* A bunch can be administered in a short amount of time because they are relatively short.

2. *They are very easy to score.* If well written, the answers are either correct or incorrect. In the physical construction of such an exam, there are a few different alternatives, such as a word True? or False? Like this:

> 1. True? or False? The sun revolves around the earth.

Or a blank space to the left of the item like this, where the test taker indicates "T" or "F."

> 1. ___ The sun revolves around the earth.

And then there's the always popular "circle the alternative," such as

> 1. Ⓣ F The sun revolves around the earth.

What's nice about this aspect of true-false items is that they are easy for the test taker to respond to and easy for the test scorer to score.

Why True-False Items Are Not So Good

OK, that's the good news. Here's the not-so-good news about using true-false items.

1. *How "true" is true?* You read above how one of the things that a good true-false item should do is present one idea clearly and unequivocally—yep, that's the case. But, it is a double-edged sword. How "true" is true? Take a look at the following item:

> 1. Water is a liquid.

Well, it is, and it could be argued fairly effectively that this is true. But it is not always a liquid—it can also be a gas (a vapor) or a solid (ice). So, although the statement is true under one condition (liquid), others might argue otherwise. It's tough to write in absolutes unless the most basic of facts are being considered, and, often, finding out what the test taker knows as the most basic of facts (also called memorization—see #3 below) is not the objective of the test.

2. *True-false items place a premium on memorization.* It's tough to get beyond the most basic levels of knowledge with true-false items without violating some of the write 'em rules we mentioned earlier. Now, in some ways, that's OK, if your goal is to sample from a universe of items that is knowledge based, but you should recognize this limitation and not think that you can easily tap into the higher levels of knowledge about neuro-anatomy or higher mathematics using true-false items.

TECH TALK

It's pretty obvious that true-false tests are scored based on the number correct and that's the end of that, right? Not so fast.

There is a way that true-false test scores can be corrected for guessing (and that's the chance outcome of getting 50% correct by guessing alone). This is a useful adjustment to make so that scores reflect more truly those who really do know more versus those who just guess.

Let's propose a scoring system where students get 1 point for being correct, 1 point for being incorrect, and nothing for leaving the item blank. So, the formula for correction (or CS for corrected score) becomes

$$CS = R - W$$

where

CS = corrected score

R = number correct

W = number incorrect

For example, let's take a 50-item test where you would expect a score of 25 by chance alone, right? (0.5 × 50 = 25). Bruce gets 35 correct on a 50-item test, and Bill gets 25 correct. How can we adjust these scores such that Bruce's performance (which is way above chance) is recognized?

Correcting the scores, it turns out that Bruce's new one is 35 – 15 = 20, and Bill's is 25 – 25 = 0. Hmm—Bill is clearly "punished" for guessing.

Take a look at this chart. It shows the number right on a 50-item test, the number wrong, and the corrected score.

# Right	# Wrong	Corrected Score
50	0	50
45	5	40
40	10	30
35	15	20
30	20	10
25 (chance)	*25 (chance)*	*0*
20	30	–10
15	35	–20
10	40	–30
5	45	–40
0	50	–50

So, when you do correct for guessing, you really place a premium on being correct. As chance becomes less of a factor (and the test taker gets more correct), there is a smaller discrepancy between the regular scoring procedure and the corrected score. The lesson? Don't guess, but, if you have to guess, guess correctly ☺.

3. *It's pretty easy to guess right.* Now this may seem a bit silly, because it's pretty easy to guess wrong on a true-false item as well, right? The probability of being right (or wrong) is 50%, and, by chance alone, if the test taker selects T or F on a somewhat random basis, the final score will be about 50%. But the odds of guessing right are much higher than for any other type of item we have or will cover. As long as you realize this limitation, true-false items can still do a good job. So, it would be wise that you have a standard for passing way, way above 50%.

SUMMARY

True or false? You now know everything you need to about the true-false item format. True, but you still need lots and lots of experience writing true-false items and thinking through the type of content best suited to scoring and correction. This is a cool format, but in a relatively limited setting—mostly knowledge based. Given that you can evaluate a test taker's basic knowledge, let's move on to a more expressive way of assessing outcomes—the portfolio.

TIME TO PRACTICE

1. Identify one thing wrong with each of these true-false items.
   a. Do you think that the Yankees will win this year's World Series?
   b. Cold fusion always works.
   c. Health care and child care are major concerns for our society.
   d. Students would not be better off if they couldn't take advantage of school tutoring.
   e. It's always best to make sure you are early to an appointment.
   f. Music rocks.

2. Write out five poor true-false items that violate some of the basic principles we noted in this chapter and then identify what's wrong with them.

3. Write out five excellent true-false items that demonstrate the nine item-writing principles we discussed above. Then, show them to a colleague in class and have that person evaluate them. Then, you do the same for your colleague (be kind).

4. Here are the results of a 100-item true-false test. Compute the corrected score and tell us why the corrected score is a more accurate indicator of someone's performance.

Name	Raw Score	Corrected Score
Bruce	76	
Vicki	55	
Trish	82	
A. J.	79	

5. OK, your job is to assess junior high students' knowledge of basic biology, and one of your colleagues is arguing that true-false items are too easy and that they can't fairly assess knowledge-level information. Because you're smarter than he, what's your correct response?

ANSWERS TO PRACTICE QUESTIONS

1. One can always argue that a question that has a flaw might be pretty good—I think the flaws carry more weight.
   a. No questions please—only declarative statements.
   b. Cold fusion may indeed work—whatever work means, and that's the problem. It may work under different and selected conditions, and the question might have a different answer depending upon those conditions.
   c. One or the other, but not both.
   d. No double negative please—this is really a lousy item.
   e. Rarely is anything always the case—and this is not an item of a factual nature.
   f. Music might rock, but the short nature of the item might act as a clue.

2. Do this on your own.

3. Do this on your own.

4. For a 100-item true-false test, you can expect a score by chance alone of 50 correct, right? The formula for correct that we discussed is the number right minus the number wrong, and the closer you get to chance (50 correct), the smaller your score gets because that factor is taken into account. Here they are:

Name	Raw Score	Corrected Score
Bruce	76	52
Vicki	55	10
Trish	82	64
A. J.	79	58

5. If written and administered well, true-false questions can be as effective as any other form of question for assessing basic knowledge. So there.

WANT TO KNOW MORE?

Further Readings

- Loftus, E. (1975). Leading questions and the eyewitness report. *Cognitive Psychology, 7,* 550–572.

This is a pretty old study but one that is very interesting and points out the importance of considering many factors when designing and using true-false questions. This research examined how the working of questions asked immediately after an event influenced answers to other questions asked much earlier. The format? Modified true-false questions. The findings? The response (it happened or didn't) depends upon whether the earlier question was a true statement. Fascinating.

• Gaskell, G., Wright, D., & O'Muircheartaigh, C. (1993). Measuring scientific interest: The effect of knowledge questions on interest ratings. *Public Understanding of Science, 2*(1), 39–57.

How interested the public is in science, and what the public knows about science is always of interest to policymakers. These researchers looked at context effects in testing which occur when a question influences responses to later questions. They found that context effects raised some concerns about interpreting findings from surveys of the public understanding of science.

And on the Internet

• More about true-false items at http://captain.park.edu/faculty development/true-false.htm and a nice checklist to make sure you're creating them correctly.

11 Portfolios

Seeing the Big Picture

Difficulty Index ☺☺☺☺☺ (easy)

"T ests" (you know—you come into a room and take one) are not necessarily always the best way to evaluate an individual's performance. Later on (in the next chapter) in *Tests & Measurement for People Who (Think They) Hate Tests & Measurement,* we'll deal with case studies, a particularly historic way of understanding and assessing behavior.

But for now, let's turn our attention to portfolios, a relatively new way to assess outcomes, especially outcomes that do not necessarily lend themselves to the more traditional ways we have been describing in the previous chapters and in this entire part of *Tests & Measurement. . . .* Interestingly, portfolios are also being used to assess others in the educational profession, including teachers and administrators.

This isn't a very long chapter because the practice of using portfolios (especially in the classroom) has not been going on very long, and there is not a great deal written about them (although there is sure to be in years to come). Where they have been used (in the fine arts, for example), there's not much interest in the psychometric characteristics of portfolios, so they haven't received much attention there either. This chapter, however, will give you a very good introduction to what portfolios are, how they are used, and how they can benefit all parties (student and teacher, boss and employee, trainer and trainee, etc.).

WHAT PORTFOLIOS ARE AND HOW THEY WORK

A **portfolio** is a collection of work that shows efforts, progress, and accomplishment in one or more areas. For example, a student's lab manual, plans for experiments, results of experiments, data, ideas about future research, and lab reports might be the contents of a portfolio in a chemistry class. Or, a student's poetry, journal, essays, and impressions of other students' work might be the contents of the portfolio for a student in a creative writing class.

THINGS TO REMEMBER

Portfolios are performance-based assessments. So, for those of you who are considering this tool for assessment, remember that the outcomes you see are meant to be a true reflection of the individual's performance on the relevant tasks.

Actually, portfolios were born into the music, art, dance, and other creative activity settings, where traditional means of assessment just didn't work. From there, portfolios (because they seemed like a good idea) made their way to the more traditional classroom and are used now across every academic subject and in business settings as well, both formal and informal. For example, want to evaluate how well a student in social work interviews a client? Why not have him or her tape the interview and then discuss it? The student learns what he or she did right and wrong, others watching (perhaps classmates or colleagues) learn about the same elements of a good interviewing technique, and the teacher learns what to expect and how goals and objectives may have to be refined to work better.

THINGS TO REMEMBER

Portfolios are an alternative to more traditional ways of evaluating performance and had their birth in the music and art disciplines.

As a means for assessment, postfolios are clearly different from a traditional achievement test, which examines one's knowledge of an area. Where a traditional achievement test is more or less time and content bound (such as introductory earth science), a portfolio allows the student and the teacher to expand the format of the material being evaluated. But, of course, along with that comes a price—the effort needed to create a portfolio and the effort needed to evaluate it. Portfolios take a great deal of time and energy to design and then create, and the evaluation takes an equally long amount of time to judge fairly each element in the portfolio.

And, as you might expect, this evaluation can be very subjective— a major criticism of portfolios. But for topics where subjectivity seems to be less important (as in evaluating poetry vs. math performance), then portfolios may very well allow for more artistic expression and be much more user friendly. In this sense, portfolios might be the perfect antidote to the test(osterone) craziness that pervades almost any educational endeavor these days.

What's a Good Portfolio?

A good portfolio has certain characteristics regardless of the area of focus. But, do beware, using portfolios—because they are less objective—doesn't let the teacher and others off the hook as far as defining clear objectives. *Au contraire* (that's French), because the evaluations of portfolio products can be subjective in nature, then every effort has to be made to have ever more objectives to at least level the playing field so that every student knows what is expected.

Table 11.1 contains a summary of advantages and disadvantages of using portfolios.

TABLE 11.1 Advantages and Disadvantages of Using Portfolios

Advantages of Using Portfolios	Disadvantages of Using Portfolios
• They are flexible.	• They are time consuming to evaluate.
• They are highly personalized for both the student and the teacher.	• They do not cover all subjects well, nor can they be used with all curriculum types.
• They are an alternative to traditional methods of assessment.	• They can be relatively subjective.
• They are possibly a creative method of assessment when other tools are either too limiting or inappropriate.	

THINGS TO REMEMBER

 You can read here what a good portfolio is. But it is very important to remember that a good portfolio is not just a collection of an individual's work. It's a systematically organized and documented group of elements and goals that meets predefined objectives. And, it includes a final phase where students and their teachers reflect upon what has been accomplished.

1. *A good portfolio is both formative and summative in nature.* What this means is that the evaluation is continuous; the efforts and accomplishments are evaluated as the portfolio is being created (say, every 3 weeks or every four elements of the portfolio) and summative in that there is a final evaluation.

2. *A portfolio is a product that reflects the multidimensional nature of both the task and the area.* For example, the art student who is applying to a college-level art school has to assemble a portfolio that reflects his or her interests and abilities. The task at hand is to exhibit one's ideas, so the student should think broadly in creating that portfolio and include lots of different media (works of drawing, clay, painting) and not limit the content to functional pottery (how about some sculpture?) or abstract drawings. The portfolio invites the student to be expressive and think big—that's the beauty of this as an evaluation tool.

3. *Portfolios allow students to participate directly in their own growth and learning.* While being closely monitored (by teacher or supervisor), the student can participate (with feedback) in the process of creating each element and get to think and consider the direction in which his or her work is going and make adjustments as needed (given teacher feedback as well as changing ideas on the student's part). This is a pretty cool characteristic, because with most items we evaluate outcomes in a rather abrupt fashion, where the student gets a grade and that's it. The student does not participate in the actual evaluation. Using a portfolio, the student gets a chance to participate directly in the evaluation process, and through this dialectic (or give-and-take), he or she becomes an indispensable part of the process of determining what direction future work will take. Very cool indeed.

4. Finally, *portfolios allow teachers to become increasingly involved in the process of designing and implementing curriculum.* In many educational settings, teachers are told what they need to teach and even how. By using portfolios, the "what" becomes much more a part of the teacher's everyday activities, and the "how" results in a close integration of classroom activities and materials.

How Portfolios Work

At its most basic, a portfolio is an opportunity to collect work, organize it, and show it off. And those three steps can surely take many different forms as a result of the student's desires and the teacher's expectations and needs.

But there are two fundamental dimensions that must be considered in the use of portfolios: first, the content, and second, the age or developmental level of the student.

A Very Summary Judgment

Most students are pack rats—they save everything. Why not take this "everything" and turn it into a well-organized representation of a student's ongoing (formative) and final (summative) set of work? It means that there's a method to the madness of all those papers and projects—instead of a disorganized collection, it becomes evidence of accomplishment and, best of all, insight on the part of both the teacher and student as to the process involved in learning.

The *content* of a portfolio usually reflects class assignments that are keyed to the particular curriculum that is being studied. If the lesson is on the reliability of achievement tests, then perhaps one entry into the student's portfolio would be a journal article and a summary of how the authors deal with establishing the reliability of the tests being used. Or, for the student studying creative writing, perhaps a portfolio entry might be a biography of a writer whom that student feels has influenced his or her work. And, such content need not be in any one particular area, but many. What if the skill being developed is reading? Why not have the student accumulate materials that show evidence of reading skills in history, science, and current affairs, showing the skill across many different curricula?

The age, grade, or developmental level speaks to the way in which the portfolio is created and used by the teacher. For example, for the first grader who is just beginning the reading process, perhaps oral reports on which simple books have been read over a 2-week period are sufficient (and the reports can be taped and included in the portfolio). But for the junior high student, perhaps a 2- to 3-page book report on each book read, plus a peer evaluation of an oral report, might reflect well on that student's ability to comprehend and then synthesize the ideas put forth in the readings.

And finally, there is the purpose to which the portfolio will be used. Teachers (and administrators), for example, can use portfolios in a variety of ways. We already know that portfolios can serve students very well in that they allow for the student to track his or her own work, get feedback, and then incorporate that feedback into the body of work represented in the portfolio.

For the teacher, portfolios can do any one or more of the following:

- Allow for comparison across students, classrooms, and even schools

- Allow for specific feedback and possibly improve student learning

- Involve parents (they love to see their children's work) in the process of learning, knowledge of expectations, and progress (or lack thereof)

SUMMARY

There's nothing like a portfolio to point up the difference between the more traditional (relatively, at least) way of assessing outcomes and a newer way that focuses more on student or learner involvement. Are portfolios meant for every teacher and student in every setting? Absolutely not. But do they provide an alternative for the assessment of certain topics where traditional methods of objective measurement might fall short? Absolutely.

TIME TO PRACTICE

1. What disciplines and subjects do you think lend themselves to assessment through a portfolio, and why?

2. What are some of the advantages and disadvantages of portfolios?

3. Go to the library or online and find at least one journal article that used portfolios, and then write a brief paragraph as to the portfolio's effectiveness or ineffectiveness. If it was ineffective, what else might have been done?

4. Pick a subject topic and list 10 elements you find in that portfolio.

5. Why do you think portfolios can be an effective means of assessment?

ANSWERS TO PRACTICE QUESTIONS

1. The arts, music, and other creative endeavors. The reason is that these subject areas often have to be judged using subjective criteria, and, if the portfolio is well designed, its objectives can be evaluated fairly.

2. a. Some of the advantages are as follows:
   i. They are flexible.
   ii. They are highly personalized for both the student and the teacher.
   iii. They are an alternative to traditional methods of assessment.
   iv. They are possibly a creative method of assessment when other tools are either too limiting or inappropriate.

   b. Some of the disadvantages are as follows:
   i. They are time consuming.
   ii. They do not fill all subjects well, nor can they be used with all curriculum types.
   iii. They can be relatively subjective.

3. Do this one on your own!

4. Consider the high school senior who wants to major in art in college and has to prepare a (guess what?) portfolio to send in along with his application. Here's what he included (and he did get into the college of his choice):
   a. A brief rationale for why he assembled this collection of elements the way he did
   b. The objectives of the portfolio and how he believes these objectives were met
   c. A brief letter from his primary high school art teacher discussing his performance in the various art classes he took, and his character as well
   d. Photographs of 10 works he completed in an introductory jewelry class
   e. Photographs of 10 works he completed in an intermediate jewelry class

f. Photographs of his abstract paintings, two from each year of high school
g. A critique of his artwork by fellow students and faculty completed during his junior year of high school
h. A paper on the influence of politics on the art of the Impressionist painters
i. A biography of Alexander Calder, including a critique of his work
j. A 2- to 3-page statement of his plans to be an artist and why he believes he can make a contribution to the world of art

5. There are many different answers to this question, but perhaps one good one is that the more that students are involved in the learning and evaluation process, the more meaningful the entire experience is for them.

WANT TO KNOW MORE?

Further Readings

• McGrath, D. (2003). Rubrics, portfolios, and tests, oh my! Assessing understanding in project-based learning. *Learning & Leading With Technology, 30*(8), 42–45.

This author presents an overview of those features that are central to project-based learning, a close cousin to portfolios. All kinds of assessment strategies are discussed, and some of the high-tech tools that can help are discussed as well.

• Nickerson, J. F. (2003). Deaf college students' perspectives on literacy portfolios. *American Annals of the Deaf, 148*(1), 31–37.

Nickerson's article demonstrates how useful portfolios are for teaching people with special needs; namely, deaf college students. Here, reading comprehension, writing processes, and products were evaluated using a portfolio model, and the results support the use of literacy portfolios.

And on the Internet

• Electronic portfolios at http://webcenter1.aahe.org/electronic portfolios/index.html is brought to you by the American Association for Higher Education. It features a host of chapters on portfolios and how their online or electronic version can be used.

12 So, Tell Me About Your Childhood

Interesting Interviews

Difficulty Index ☺☺☺☺ (really pretty easy)

W e have talked about supply-type items (see Chapter 6 on short answer and completion items) and selection-type items (see Chapter 8 on multiple-choice items), but we now have a type of assessment item that has been used for thousands of years (and perhaps longer than any other type) and may provide us with the richest source of information available about human behavior.

It's called the interview, and whether it is a star soccer player or a Nobel laureate in chemistry being interviewed, there are guidelines we need to follow and the associated advantages and disadvantages of the technique. Let's explore all of these.

TABLE 12.1 Advantages and Disadvantages of Using Interviews

Advantages of Using Interviews	Disadvantages of Using Interviews
• They provide rich and detailed results.	• They are highly individual and do not allow for generalization.
	• They are very involved and time consuming (and expensive).

WHEN WE USE 'EM AND WHAT THEY LOOK LIKE

An **interview** is a set of questions that elicits answers about material that is not accessible through more traditional assessment techniques (such as multiple-choice items, essay questions, or portfolios). We use interviews when we want to get to know the story behind the story.

THINGS TO REMEMBER

Want to get way into motives, aspirations, ideas, feelings, perceptions, and perspectives (among others)? That's what an interview does—it allows you to assess on the broadest and richest of scales.

For example, it may be a simple task to find out how police officers deal with a violent arrest (we can just check their report), but how do they prepare for one in their training, and what kind of psychological and emotional toll might such an event take on the officer? More importantly, in his or her own words, the police officer can express ideas about, the impact on, and possibly lasting effects about the incident. A simple set of short-answer questions would never provide us with the information needed to make changes in training or help after the fact—such questions would totally miss the mark and leave little opportunity for follow-up.

Interviews: A Flavor for Everyone

There are several different types of interviews, all fitting a particular need.

A **highly structured interview** is sort of like an oral questionnaire, where the questions (and the direction) are predefined and all the interviewer need do is just ask away and record the responses. Here are some examples of questions that you might find in a highly structured interview. These are also called a **closed interview** or a **fixed response interview**.

1. Where were you born?

2. Who was your favorite teacher? Why?

3. When did you find yourself interested in science, and what led you to study it in college?

4. Why did you select chemistry as a major rather than some other physical science?

5. How did you think of the idea that eventually led to the Nobel Prize-winning research that you did?

In a **guided interview**, the interviewer guides the interviewee in a particular direction (and there is a beginning set of questions that is used along the way, but not necessarily in a prescribed order). The interviewer is not necessarily restricted to a *particular* set of questions, but the questions are restricted to specific subject areas. These kinds of interviews are also called **general interviews**.

For example, one might begin with a question such as,

1. Who was the most significant influence on your decision to study chemistry?

Perhaps this question is followed up by another question that is based on the response to the first. Let's take a look at the transcript from this brief sample interview where we illustrate this type of interview.

Q. Who was the most significant influence on your decision to study chemistry?

A. It was probably my first geometry teacher.

Q. Why was that? Geometry and chemistry seem pretty far apart.

A. Well, we were solving a simple problem using a variety of methods one day and someone asked, "Why can't we just use the one method and leave it at that?" The teacher's response was that as good mathematicians, we have to understand that there is always more than one way to "skin a cat." It's an old expression, but it made sense to me. The more I learned, the more perspectives I could bring to a problem, and perhaps a new perspective is fresh enough that it might make all the difference. Once I started studying chemistry and physics (and I really liked what the topics of chemistry had to offer), I was hooked on the subject and the idea of solving problems in that field.

Then we have the last kind of interview we will discuss here, the **nondirective** or **unguided interview**. Here, there may be nothing other than a starting set of questions that the interviewer begins with and then lets the individual being interviewed take it from there. And by "take it from there," I mean that the person being interviewed is given free rein to say and include whatever he or she thinks is necessary and pertinent. There is very little guidance from the interviewer. These interviews are also called **unstructured** or **conversational interviews**.

For example, the first question might be (and by definition, this first question is a very open-ended invitation to have the interviewee just think out loud):

> Q. Tell us about your early experiences with science and how those experiences shaped your interest in chemistry later on. And, please also let us know what factors were important in your decision to study this particular field of chemistry and who acted as your primary source of encouragement.

Interviews should be used when the testing person, like yourself, wants to know the behind-the-scenes answers to questions that have yet to be asked. Sound a bit of a conundrum? **Hang on— we'll explain this paradox as we proceed through this chapter.**

TECH TALK

The Validity and Reliability of Interviews

Here's a good lesson. There's no way to collect interview-type data other than through an interview—the richness and depth are just not obtainable any other way. And, you probably won't be surprised to learn that both the validity (or the trustworthiness of the data) and the reliability of interview results are greater when the questions are structured or closed rather than when they are open or nondirective. Why? Well, the more controlled the interviewing process is, the less likely it is that error variance can sneak into the situation and muck things up. On one extreme, a question such as "How old are you?" is very structured and highly reliable. On the other hand, a very open "question" such as "Tell me a bit more about your first anxiety attack" is not at all structured and very open to interpretation.

And other problems can sneak into the entire interview process that can easily erode the value of the experience and the information that is collected. Errors such as:

- asking the wrong type of questions

- failing to follow up on a question that obviously leads in a new direction, and

- incomplete recording of responses

are only three of many pitfalls along the way.

The lesson? The results of unstructured or open interviews can be highly variable and may be data that the interviewer can get only through that technique. However, there can be virtually no agreement among judges as to what the question or the response should be, and that the results have limited generalizability to other settings and limited usefulness unless the interviewer is looking specifically for certain responses or types of responses.

HOW TO DO 'EM: THE GUIDELINES

The first thing we need to do when planning an interview is preparation, which includes a good deal of time thinking ahead and becoming familiar with the subject of the interview and/or the topic.

For example, in the case of a multiple-choice test, we need to make sure that the room is well lit, the temperature is not too hot or too cold, there are plenty of sets for test takers, etc. For an interview, however, there's a bit more to do, and how well we plan at this stage often accounts for the success or failure of the interview.

When planning for your interview and actually conducting the interview, keep the following in mind:

1. *Before you begin the interview process, explain the nature of the interview to the individual being interviewed.* How long will it take? What kinds of question will you ask? What is this about? What do I do if I feel uncomfortable about answering some of these questions? Will the results be shared? Who are you? Why are you doing this? When will we be done? Do I have to answer truthfully?—and about 100 more—all questions that one or more interviewees will have and ones for which you have answers.

2. *Practice, practice, practice.* You won't be an expert when you first start, so take your time; practice on people other than the real interviewee (friends, family, and colleagues); and get a general

sense of what types of questions might best lead to responses that are useful. Write down the best set of questions you can from a discussion with a practice friend, and then refine those as you practice with others. It doesn't matter what type of interview you want to conduct, be it open ended or very structured—there's no substitute for being well prepared, and there's no saving grace when you're not.

3. *Ensure confidentiality.* Make sure—absolutely, uncategorically, forever and ever—that the anonymity of the person being interviewed and his or her statements will be absolutely, without a doubt, and for sure maintained. This is a very sensitive topic and one that you have to be very aware of. Whatever the nature of the topic or the content, nothing goes beyond you and the immediate need-to-know folks. Who are need-to-know folks? Professional audiences and professional colleagues and no one else. The foundation and success for any interview are based on the interviewer's assurance that anything said remains in confidence. In fact, for some professionals, interviews are a mainstay method of assessment (such as psychiatry and counseling), and there is a legal provision (and this information cannot even be accessed by law enforcement people) that anything shared is strictly between the therapist and the patient. Think of Las Vegas—what happens here stays here.

What a Slob! Oops—The Validity of the Interview

It's always a challenge—separating your personal judgment from your objective judgment about the people you are interviewing. And, it's a validity issue as well. How well can you interview an individual when you keep noticing his dandruff or unwashed hair, or the clashing clothes, or the nose that needs to be wiped with a tissue or the food in his beard? Hmm . . .

Well, these inadvertent biases have been recognized and named. One famous researcher, X. Hollingsworth, way back in 1922, called it "standoutishness" to indicate how people tend to judge others based on one outstanding characteristic. Not good for an interviewer.

What to do? Note it, be professional, and go beyond the physical appearance and any other possibly unrelated characteristics that would get in the way of your producing an interview that focuses on the topic at hand rather than appearance or some other physical characteristic.

And while you're at it, be very sensitive to cultural differences. Don't ask people who cover their heads for religious reasons if they would like to take their hat or scarf off to be more comfortable, and avoid putting people in uncomfortable situations. In some cultures, unmarried women are not allowed to be alone with unmarried men. Know the group from which your interviewees come, and know a bit about their culture *before* you begin. How? Visit the neighborhood; read the local paper; talk with people at the coffee shop; and ask, ask, ask when you are first planning your activities.

4. *Choose your setting wisely.* You want the interview to take place in a setting where the interviewer is comfortable (and where you are as well, of course); where there is little distraction; and where it is quiet and pleasant if at all possible (no broom closets turned into research offices).

5. *Allow more time than you think you will need.* Depending upon how structured your interview is, you may need exactly 15 minutes or anywhere from 15 minutes to 90 minutes. In any case, allow sufficient time for the interviewee to get to the place you've identified, but also for all those open-ended questions to be asked and answered. There is nothing more frustrating than being on the verge of an inspired question and a terrific answer and having to say, "Well, we're out of time. See ya!"

6. *Take notes, take notes, take notes.* Even if you have a memory like the Amazing Kreskin, you are much better off taking (a copious amount of) notes and even using a recording device of some kind (with the interviewee's permission, of course). You can use a simple tape recorder or one of those very cool digital recorders. With a digital recorder, you can dump the entire interview onto your computer as a sound file and even use software that can transcribe it (fitfully, but it does work somewhat). And, of course, ask permission before you start recording.

7. *Stay in touch.* Let the interviewee know that he or she can ask you questions after the interview about any aspect of the interview, or he or she can ask such questions at a later time (and you give him or her contact information).

8. *Get them and keep them talking!* This means that you talk less and listen more, but it also means that you continue to encourage

interviewees to talk more about the important topics. If people tell you about their first day in the classroom as a teacher, encourage them by nodding your head, asking them to continue if they stop as if they are finished, following up on questions, and pursuing leads. One way to kill an interview is to respond to their responses in a negative fashion by showing disgust, disagreement, or emotions that don't have any place. Be positive at best and neutral at worst.

9. *Put on a happy face.* Well, it does not have to be happy, but remember this. Interviews are like no other type of assessment for many different reasons, but the most important one is that there is a very human element involved—the interviewer. And that interviewer sets the tone and the direction of the interview. Imagine a brusque and impolite interviewer asking you personal questions about your love life. Not a very good start. As the interviewer, you need to be civil, polite, interested (or at least act as such), on task, prepared, ready to answer questions, tolerant, and totally focused on what you are doing. Do not chew gum, make sure you dress the part, and be there on time.

10. *Use transitions to keep things going.* OK, you have your interviewee talking about her experiences with the glass ceiling in a primarily male employment situation, and she has said some very interesting things but has now stopped. Get her talking again, but refer back to her last response or even an earlier one. For example, how about, "Thanks for telling me about that one experience you had when you got your own office and were made partner. But, can you tell me a bit more about the other partners' reactions to your promotion?"

11. *All done? Say thank you, wrap up the interview, and pay attention to details.* Once the interview has ended, write down any important observations you might have or even areas in which you may want to follow up in a subsequent interview with this individual or others. Ask permission to follow up via phone or e-mail once you get back to your office, home, or lab, and ask those questions that were raised by statements during the interview, but you might have missed the opportunity. You want to do your homework and try to have all these questions consolidated so that you do not have to keep going back to the person who was interviewed. Remember, the best place to find new interview questions (which can be used if you are interviewing another person about the same general area) is the responses you have gotten to earlier questions.

Electronic Interviews

There's nothing like the real thing, and that's the case with interviews as well. Meeting with an individual, observing the nuances in his or her responses and facial expressions, being able to ask an additional question on the spot, judging whether he or she is comfortable and whether you should pursue a certain direction—all are advantages of interviewing in person.

But, that's not always possible because of geographic or time constraints. These days, both e-mail and instant messages can be used for interviews, with a few modifications.

1. Lay out the set and sequence of questions well before the interview.

2. Specify the ground rules, such as, "I would like to interview you for 30 minutes and then take another 15 minutes 1 week later to follow up."

3. Set up a specific time for the interview, and call ahead to confirm it. Remember that time zones can kill you. What you think is a great time of day to get started (8 a.m. on the East Coast) may not be for your interviewee (it's 1 a.m. in New Zealand). See http://www.timeanddate.com to find out what time it is right now, anywhere on the planet.

4. If you want to conduct the interview using instant messages (be it through MSN, Yahoo, or iChat), be sure they have access to the same tool and, most important, be sure the interviewee is comfortable using the tool. There's nothing like having that famous person on the other end of the line and not being able to get an answer to your brilliantly framed question.

5. Yes-no questions are a cinch for anyone to answer in an e-mail, so try to get those out of the way during an earlier session. For the interview itself, try to ask more open-ended questions—and instant messaging lends itself especially well to that purpose. You get an immediate response, and it's somewhat like the person being in the same room as you.

THE GOOD AND THE BAD

There's not a big list here, but these reasons are certainly worth some comments.

Why Interview Items Are Good

1. *They can be rich, detailed, and full of worthwhile information.* The primary advantage of the interview is that it provides rich detail that is often impossible to obtain using any other assessment technique—where else can you find out what and who were the inspiration for a great novel or a great experiment?

2. *Interviews are personal.* Assessment procedures in general are pretty objective and far removed from personal interaction. Interviews provide the opportunity to "get the inside story" and to get to know the people being interviewed as well— both rewarding takes.

Why Interview Items Are Not So Good

On the other hand . . .

1. *Interviews are subjective.* Well, sure they are, and that's the nature of the process. In all fairness, to call them subjective is to misunderstand the utility of the technique. They are not so much subjective as they are highly individualized and should be used as such.

2. *Interviews are time consuming.* No doubt about that, and probably no way to get around the expense.

3. *Interviews allow little generalizability.* This may very well be true, but if one does enough interviews about a very circumscribed topic (such as why one enters the social work field) and is careful when assembling and analyzing the data, some generalizability will be present.

SUMMARY

"So, what do you think about school vouchers and their effectiveness?" is just one of many types of interview questions that one might ask to get the whole story about how one person (at a time) thinks about this topic. Interviews, like no other technique, let us get really deep into a person's thoughts, ideas, and feelings about a host of topics that could not be assessed fairly using any other technique. Do interviews have their problems? Sure, but what technique doesn't? With this technique, though, we end this part of *Tests & Measurement* . . . and move away from different items toward different tests.

TIME TO PRACTICE

1. When would you use an interview as opposed to some other technique for collecting information or assessing some outcome?

2. What's the advantage of open-ended versus closed-ended interview questions?

3. Name one crucial step that one should take in preparation for an interview.

4. Using an interview format, assess a classmate's beliefs about his or her political affiliation. Be sure not to leave the information you collect just at the "yes" or "no" level, but press your interviewee beyond the first response to provide more information.

5. Visit http://thinktwice.com/famous.htm on the Internet and read the interview with Thomas Jefferson (he's dead, I know). What do you think the interviewer did well? What could the interviewer have done better?

ANSWERS TO PRACTICE QUESTIONS

1. Interviews should be used when the question that you are asking requires an assessment that, first, cannot be completed using more traditional methods such as essay or multiple-choice questions and, second, requires an interaction between the interviewer and the interviewee such that a complete and thorough revealing of as much information as possible is accomplished.

2. Open-ended questions can require a more complex and detailed response revealing information that the interviewer may not have anticipated, thereby suggesting other and new directions in which to proceed.

3. There are certainly many, but among the first could be
   a. Having a well-thought-out and clear question that you want answered. This is not necessarily one that has a "correct" or specific answer but provides information that bears on the question you are asking and relates to the concept, idea, knowledge, etc., you are assessing.
   b. Preparating by knowing the topic well enough to ask the right questions.
   c. Preparing a setting that is conducive to an effective interview, including a quiet place without distractions.

4. This one is on your own, and be sure to take notes and compare the responses to others in the group.

5. One thing the interviewer did well was using President Jefferson's responses to lead to additional questions. This is a very effective technique. However, she let him set the stage for the content of the questions by allowing him to set the tone and content. That would be fine if it fits the interviewer's needs—otherwise, he told the interviewer what he thought she wanted to hear and not what she needed to know.

WANT TO KNOW MORE?

Further Readings

- Halasz, G. (2004). In conversation with Dr. Albert Ellis. *Australasian Psychiatry, 12,* 325–333.

This is the perfect example of how an interview can reveal ideas and commentary that go far beyond a more restrictive item. Here, the author interviews Albert Ellis, founder of rational emotive behavior therapy, and explores the impact of many different factors, including childhood illness, sibling relationships, and parental divorce, on his pacifist philosophy and the creation of rational emotive behavior therapy.

- Ohtani, T., Iwanami, A., Kasai, K., Yamasue, H., Kato, T., Sasaki, T., & Kato, N. (2004). Post-traumatic stress disorder symptoms in victims of Tokyo subway attack: A 5-year follow-up study. *Psychiatry and Clinical Neurosciences, 58,* 624–629.

Some things you just can't get through any means other than interview. These authors used structured interviews to obtain the mental and physical symptoms of the 34 victims of a sarin gas attack 5 years later.

And on the Internet

- An increasingly large part of doing research and other intensive, more qualitative projects involves specially designed software. At http://www.scolari.com/ you can find a listing of several different types and explore which might be right for you if you intend to pursue this method (interviewing) and this methodology (qualitative).

PART IV

What to Test and How to Test It

Snapshots

You just finished learning all about different types of test items, how they are constructed, and how they might be used. So, now you know more than a bit about important test and measurement concepts such as reliability and validity (from Part II) and a great deal about different types of test items.

But the rubber really meets the road when we start talking about what areas of behavior, growth, learning, human performance, and change (you get the picture) we want to test. Perhaps we want to find out how aggressive someone is (personality), how "smart" he or she is (ability), or for what career his or her skills and interests would be best suited (career development).

Now, it's time to turn our attention to different types of tests and what they do. The best way to do this is to tell you a bit about what kinds of tests there are (such as achievement and personality tests), what they measure, and how they are constructed.

This information won't make you the newest girl or guy psycho-metric tsar on your block or in your dorm, but what it will do is give you a very basic but pretty broad overview of just what kinds of tests are out there, what they look like, and how they work.

Here's the simple skinny on what each type of test does.

- Achievement tests (which we cover in Chapter 13) test knowledge and previous learning.

- Personality tests (which we cover in Chapter 14) assess a person's enduring characteristics and disposition.

- Aptitude tests (which we cover in Chapter 15) test the potential to learn or acquire a skill.

- Ability tests (which we cover in Chapter 16) test intellectual potential, and we know them best as intelligence tests (which come in all shapes and forms).

- Career choice tests (which we cover in Chapter 17) cover the types of tests that are taken to determine level of interest in various occupations and the skills associated with those occupations.

Finally, in the last chapter in this part of the book, Chapter 18, we provide some of the general tips and tricks for taking tests that might be useful for you to come closest to that true score we talked about earlier in Chapter 3.

This is solid stuff, and knowing what's in these next seven chapters will increase your skill and understanding for designing, and using, tests effectively.

13 Achievement Tests

Who Really Discovered America?

Difficulty Index ☺☺☺ (moderately easy)

Columbus, of course, in 1492. Or, maybe it was the Chinese in 1421, as some recent archaeological digs suggest. Or, maybe it was Asiatic people, who then became Native Americans, or even Norse explorers around 986.

The subject here is history, with a little anthropology thrown in perhaps for good measure. And the kind of test that you would write to measure whether or not someone knows who discovered America could be an achievement test.

Achievement tests measure how much someone knows or has learned—how much knowledge he or she has in a particular subject area, be it mathematics, reading, history, auto mechanics, biology, or culinary science. Achievement tests are the most common tests given—more of these are administered each year than any other type of test—by far.

More Than One Test at a Time

Many achievement tests are called **multilevel survey batteries** because they test material at more than one level (multilevel) and in several different topic areas at once. But just as many tests, and perhaps more, are teacher-made tests that focus on only one level or topic area.

WHAT ACHIEVEMENT TESTS DO

By the time you get to high school, and even more so college, you have probably taken thousands of achievement tests. That every-Friday spelling test was an achievement test, as was the SAT test you took in your junior or senior year of high school. They all test how much you know. And for the most part, achievement tests are administered in educational (school) or training institutions.

Achievement tests have some very well-defined purposes. You already know that the first purpose is to measure or assess how much someone knows about a certain topic. But other purposes are equally important, and, as you will see, these do overlap with one another.

1. *Achievement tests help define the particular areas that teachers believe are important to assess.* They help pinpoint those topics that are important and those that are not. This can be done through what is called a table of specifications, which we will talk about later in this chapter.

2. Achievement tests tell teachers and testers whether an individual has accomplished or achieved the necessary knowledge to move to the next step in study. Passing such a test might be a prerequisite to move on to a more advanced course. Perhaps at your school you can "test out" of Calculus 1 or Biology 101 by taking a test designed just for that purpose—to see if you have the prerequuisite knowledge to move on.

3. *Achievement tests can allow for the grouping of individuals into certain skill areas.* If the teacher has an accurate assessment of a student's skill, instruction can be targeted more precisely at current levels of achievement, and further achievement can be facilitated.

4. *Achievement tests may be used diagnostically in that they help identify weaknesses and strengths.* Once a student's deficiencies or weaknesses are identified, it's so much easier to help that individual by targeting those specific areas for remediation.

5. *Achievement tests can be used to assess the success of a program or a political initiative on a school- or district-wide basis.* Such an assessment or evaluation hopefully can help teachers, administrators, and trainers adhere more successfully to legislated policies (such as No Child Left Behind—see Chapter 19 for more on this).

6. Finally, *achievement tests inform.* This helps everyone who is trying to help the child (or a student of any age) address levels of progress (or lack thereof) and what weaknesses need to be addressed. If the test is sufficiently diagnostic, even better because it becomes even more clear how these weaknesses should be addressed.

HOW ACHIEVEMENT TESTS DIFFER FROM ONE ANOTHER

Achievement tests are pretty similar in what they do—they assess knowledge. But they differ in some important ways as well. Here's how.

Teacher (or Researcher) Made Versus Standardized Achievement Tests

Teacher-made tests are constructed by a teacher, and the effort placed in establishing validity or reliability, norming, or the development of scoring systems varies from nonexistent to thorough. The midterm you took in your introductory psychology class was probably a teacher-made, multiple-choice test. There's nothing at all wrong with teacher-made tests—they are just very situation specific and defined to suit a particular need. These are very specific assessment instruments.

> **Textbook Tests?**
>
> There's nothing wrong with teacher-made tests. Most books come with an instructor's or teacher's manual, so if the teacher follows the book material closely enough, then the items should track to the curriculum. And, what teacher couldn't use more time to teach rather than create tests? But there may be some question as to whether the book publisher provides questions that are very good (these question banks are usually done at the last minute in the publication process as an afterthought, and there are few guidelines for administration and scoring). And, because the test question writer does not know what goes on in the classroom, it may be difficult to map the questions to classroom objectives. So, these tests may be a bit more convenient but also a bit more problematic to use.

A **standardized test** is one that has undergone extensive test development—meaning the writing and rewriting of items; hundreds of administrations; development of reliability and validity data; norming with what is sometimes very large groups of test takers (for example, upwards of 100,000 for the California Achievement Tests); the development of consistent directions; and administration procedures and very clear scoring instructions.

Most achievement tests that are administered in school for the purposes we listed earlier are standardized. Standardization is a very long, expensive, and detailed procedure, but it is the gold standard for creating achievement tests that are reliable, valid, and appropriate for the population of test takers being assessed. Standardized tests such as the Iowa Test of Basic Skills are also usually published by some commercial establishment (in this case, Riverside Publishing).

Group Versus Individual Achievement Tests

This distinction has to do with the way in which the tests are administered. The majority of achievement tests are administered in a group setting (such as in a classroom), although some achievement tests are given individually (especially those that are used for diagnostic purposes or those that are used to evaluate the status or progress of individuals who have special needs).

Criterion- Versus Norm-Referenced

Achievement tests can be norm-referenced or criterion-referenced. **Norm-referenced tests** allow you to compare one individual's test performance to the test performance of other individuals. For example, if an 8-year-old student receives a score of 56 on a mathematics test, you can use the norms that are supplied with the test to determine that child's placement relative to other 8-year-olds. Standardized tests are usually accompanied by norms, but this is usually not the case for teacher- or researcher-made tests.

Criterion-referenced tests (a term coined by psychologist Robert Glaser in 1963) defines a specific criterion or level of performance, and the only thing of importance is the individual's performance, regardless of where that performance might stand in comparison with others. In this case, performance is defined as a function of mastery of some content domain. For example, if you were to specify a set of objectives for 12th-grade history and specify that students must show command of 90% of those objectives to pass, then you would be implying that the criterion is 90% mastery. Because this type of test actually focuses on the mastery of content at a specific level, it is also referred to as a **content-referenced test**.

TECH TALK

Choose Your Criterion Carefully

Criterion-referenced tests use that one measure of "success," but what that criterion is can be very different for different tests. For example, on an achievement test, it might be a certain percentage of correct answers. But the criterion can also be how fast a certain number of items can be completed, how accurate the individual's performance is, or the quality of the responses. The specific criterion used, of course, depends on the goal of the test and the assessment objectives.

HOW TO DO IT: THE ABCs OF CREATING A STANDARDIZED TEST

Robertson (1990) wrote a terrific piece on the practical aspects of developing a standardized test.

Warning—this is a brief overview of a very time-intensive, expensive, and demanding experience. Understanding these steps will surely help you appreciate how refined and well planned these tests are, and, to a large extent, why you can have a high degree of confidence in them when you participate in their administration.

So, although you may not go into the business of creating achievement tests, you should have some idea of how it's done so you can appreciate the amount of work and the intensity of the experience. A more informed consumer makes a better practitioner. What follows is a summary of some of the most important points that Robertson made.

First, there is the development of *preliminary ideas*. This is the stage where the test developer (perhaps a professor like the one teaching this class) considers the possible topics that might be covered, the level of coverage, scope, and every other factor that relates to what may be on the finished test. For example, perhaps high school-level biology, or elementary school-level reading.

Second, *test specifications* should be developed. This is a complex process that allows the test developer to understand the relationship between the level of items (along one of many dimensions) and the content of the items. We'll show you more about developing specifications in the next section of this chapter. These tables are usually created based on curriculum guides and other information that informs the test developers as to what content is covered in what grades.

Third, the *items are written*. In most cases, a large pool of item writers (who are experts in the content area) are hired and asked to write many, many items. At the end of this stage, these items are reviewed, and the most inappropriate ones are discarded. These items are then reviewed for bias and cultural insensitivity.

Next, Step 4 finds the *items being used in a trial setting*. Instructions are drafted, participants are located, actual preliminary tests are constructed, items are tried, and items are analyzed. This is a l-o-o-o-ng process and very expensive.

Step 5 finds the test developers *rewriting items* that did not perform very well (poor discriminators, for example) but still hold some promise for being included. A new item may be written to take this item's place, or those not-yet-acceptable items may be revised. This step in the development of a standardized test is over when the test developers feel that they have a set of items that meets all important criteria to move forward.

Sixth, the *final tests are assembled*, but it's not soup yet.

Seventh, an *extensive national standardization effort* takes place that includes selection of more participants, preparation of the materials, administration of the tests, analysis of the data, and development of norm tables.

Finally, the last step involves the *preparation of all the necessary materials*, including a test manual, the preparation of the actual test forms, and printing.

Phew—these eight steps not only take a lot of time (years and years) and cost a lot of money, but, because the nature of knowledge changes so often (what's expected of sixth graders in math, for example, or the newest mechanical specs for low-pollution engines), these tests often have to be rewritten and renormed, etc.—lots and lots of work. This results in lots and lots of potential profit for the test industry, which recognizes the value of revisions.

There are a few more steps that we could throw in, including what occurs if the test developers want to publish the test. Because creating the test is such an expensive undertaking, publishing it usually involves including a commercial or university publisher in the process. And more often than not, these publishers are involved very early in the game and provide funding for the test developers to take time off from their other teaching and research responsibilities. For this funding, of course, the publisher gets to sell the test and keep the majority of the profits.

TECH TALK

IRT or Bust

Scoring is scoring is scoring, right? Well, sort of. If a student gets a score of 89 out of 100, then he or she got 89% correct—and that is "sort of" the standard way in which achievement tests have been scored (and then this raw score can be transformed into a standard score, adjusted for norms, and so on). But there's another way of looking at scores on achievement tests. **Item response theory** (or IRT) derives scores based on patterns of responses. Most simply, this means that two students might get the same score on a test, but, because their pattern of responding may be different (one student answered more difficult questions correctly more often than another student), then that student would receive a higher score. Want to know more about IRT? Take a few more measurement classes. It's complex but fascinating stuff.

THE AMAZING TABLE OF SPECIFICATIONS

By any measure, the table of specifications is a fascinating idea and a terrific guideline when it comes to the creation of any kind of achievement test—be it teacher-made or standardized.

In the most simple terms, a **table of specifications** is a grid (with either one or two dimensions, and we'll get to that soon) that serves as a guide to the construction of an achievement test. As you can see below, one of the axes can represent various learning outcomes that are expected or the areas of content that are to be covered. The other axis can represent some dimension that reflects the different levels of questions, and this can be anything from the amount of time spent in the classroom on the topic to a very cool taxonomy of educational objectives such as the one proposed by Benjamin Bloom.

Here's a very simple table of specifications for a tests and measurement midterm (like the one you might get!).

Topic	Amount of Time Spent in Class	Questions
Measurement Scales	35%	1, 2, 3, 4, 5, 6, 7, 8, 10, 11, 13, 14, 15, 16, 17, 18, 20
Reliability	15%	9, 12, 19, 21, 22, 23, 24, 28
Validity	20%	25, 26, 27, 29, 30, 31, 32, 33, 34, 35
Writing Short Answer Items	15%	36, 37, 38, 39, 41, 42, 44
Creating True-False Tests	15%	40, 43, 45, 46, 47, 48, 49, 50
Total	100%	

Once this grid is created, the instructor then knows that 15% of all 50 test questions (and exactly what questions) should deal with reliability, and 20% should deal with validity, which also would reflect the amount of time that the instructor spent on these topics in class. Then, the questions that are in the particular area of interest are listed as well so that the instructor knows which questions relate to which topic area and can be sure that the percentages are correct.

OK. That's the simple table of specifications. A more sophisticated one would look at topic areas and learning outcomes. In 1956, Benjamin Bloom created his taxonomy of learning outcomes or objectives that can be categorized into six different categories of abstraction, from the most basic factual level to the most abstract and cognitively sophisticated level.

The six levels from least sophisticated to most sophisticated are

- Knowledge
- Comprehension
- Application
- Analysis
- Synthesis
- Evaluation

Here's a brief summary of each level and some of the key words you might expect to see in achievement-test questions at each of these levels. In Table 13.1, you can also see the levels and key words summarized.

TABLE 13.1 The Six Levels of Bloom's Taxonomy and Key Words to Look for in Achievement Test Items at Those Levels

Level of Bloom's Taxonomy	Key Words to Look for
Knowledge	list, define, tell, describe, identify, show, label, collect, examine, tabulate, quote, name, who, when, where
Comprehension	summarize, describe, interpret, contrast, predict
Application	apply, demonstrate, calculate, complete, illustrate, show
Analysis	analyze, separate, order, explain, connect
Synthesis	combine, integrate, modify, rearrange, substitute
Evaluation	assess, decide, rank, recommend, convince

TECH TALK

Who's Literate?

This surely is the age of information. No longer do students (like you) go to the library to check out a book on the topic of that term paper. These days, it's the Internet all the way.

Now, to assess how "literate" students are in their use of electronic resources, comes the Information and Communications Technology literacy assessment from our friends at the Educational Testing Service (who also bring us the SAT and GRE tests). This test measures students' ability to manage exercises like sorting e-mail messages or manipulating tables and charts, and also assesses how well they organize and interpret information. It's only one of many sins that we are leaving the industrial age for the information age.

---

1. *Knowledge-level questions* focus on, for example, the recall of information; a knowledge of dates, events, and places; and a knowledge of certain major ideas. All of these reflect a broad base of facts. Knowledge-based questions might contain words such as *list, define, tell, describe, identify, show, label, collect, examine, tabulate, quote, name, who, when,* and *where*; all, of course, in question format.

2. *Comprehension-level questions* focus on the understanding (not just the knowledge) of information and require the test taker to interpret facts, compare and contrast different facts, infer cause and effect, and predict the consequences of a certain event. Comprehension-based questions might contain words such as *summarize, describe, interpret, contrast,* and *predict*.

3. *Application-level questions* require the use of information, methods, and concepts, as well as problem solving. Application-based questions might contain words such as *apply, demonstrate, calculate, complete, illustrate,* and *show.*

4. *Analysis-level questions* require the test taker to look for and (if successful) see patterns among parts, recognize hidden meanings, and identify the parts of a problem. Analysis-based questions might contain words such as *analyze* (surprised?), *separate, order, explain,* and *connect* (as in connect the dots).

5. *Synthesis-level questions* require the test taker to use old ideas to create new ones and to generalize from given facts. Synthesis-based questions might contain words such as *combine, integrate, modify, rearrange,* and *substitute.*

6. *Evaluation-level questions* require that the test taker compare and discriminate between ideas and make choices based on a reasonable and well-thought-out argument. Evaluation-based questions might contain words such as *assess, decide, rank, recommend,* and *convince.* That's what you did on debate team in high school. Evaluation questions do not lend themselves easily to the multiple-choice type format.

As you read through these levels, I am sure you will see how much more sophisticated a question is at the higher levels. For example, knowledge-level questions (Level #1) ask for nothing more than memorization, whereas evaluation-level questions (Level #6) require full knowledge of a topic, an understanding of the relationships between ideas, and the ability to integrate and evaluate them all.

For example, here's a multiple-choice *knowledge*-based question, the least sophisticated of all six levels:

1. The ingredients in a roux are

   a. flour, liquid, and salt.
   b. flour, salt, and mushrooms.
   c. flour, liquid, and shortening.
   d. flour, shortening, and ground nuts.

For all you culinary fans, the answer is C, and a roux is used to thicken a sauce, such as a white sauce.

Here's an example (on the other end of the continuum) of an evaluation-based question, the most sophisticated of all six levels:

Create a recipe where a roux is a central part of the finished dish, and explain the role it plays in the finished dish. (Want a terrific macaroni and cheese recipe? Write the author.)

Earlier we showed you a simple table of specifications. What follows is a much more sophisticated one that doesn't focus on the amount of time spent on a particular topic but instead focuses on the *level* of Bloom's taxonomy. The same measurement topics are being taught, but, this time, the items and the various levels of Bloom's taxonomy that they represent are shown as table entries.

As you can see, there are no synthesis or evaluation questions for the topics of writing short answer questions or writing true-false items. In this case, the instructor did not have learning objectives at this level, and the test, as it should, does not reflect such.

THINGS TO REMEMBER

In general, a table of specifications should be designed to account for the amount of time spent on a particular topic within a course. And, the amount of time should reflect the percentage of questions that appear. Also, any other dimension should be treated in the same way. If it is a taxonomy to which you are trying to map, then the various levels should reflect the various levels of the taxonomy as introduced in the course material. You simply multiply the amount of time in one dimension (such as topic) by the other dimension (such as level of question) to determine the number of content/level items you need in the test.

	Level of Taxonomy					
Topic	Knowledge	Comprehension	Application	Analysis	Synthesis	Evaluation
Measurement Scales	1, 2, 3, 4, 5	6, 7, 8, 10, 11	13, 14	15, 16	17, 18	20
Reliability	9, 12	21, 22	23, 24	26		28
Validity	25, 26, 27	29, 30, 31	32		33, 34	35
Writing Short Answer Items	36, 37	38, 39	41, 42, 44			
Creating True-False Tests	40, 43, 45, 46	47, 48	49	50		

WHAT THEY ARE: A SAMPLING OF ACHIEVEMENT TESTS AND WHAT THEY DO

You're taking this class to learn about tests and measurement and not necessarily to become a psychometrician (one who designs and analyzes tests). So, although I give you a good deal of information about testing principles and the development of test items, in this part of *Tests & Measurement for People Who (Think They) Hate Tests & Measurement*, it's good to be familiar with what some of the most popular and successful achievement tests are.

At the end of every chapter from this one through Chapter 17 on career choices, I'll be providing you with an overview of some of the most common tests used in this country over the past 50 years and still very much in use today. You can see the set for this chapter in Table 13.2.

As you continue your education, you are bound to run into these in one setting or another. And now you'll know something about them—isn't school great?

SUMMARY

Achievement tests are the first kind of test you've learned about in *Tests & Measurement for People Who (Think They) Hate Tests & Measurement*, and they're also the type of test that you are most likely to encounter as someone taking the test as well as someone giving the test. Achievement tests focus basically on knowledge; are constructed using a variety of items you learned about earlier; and can be used as diagnostic, remedial, or just assessment-type tools. In almost every way, they can be powerful allies in the learning process.

TIME TO PRACTICE

1. What are the advantages of a teacher-made test as opposed to a standardized test?

2. Why is the development of any standardized test so expensive?

TABLE 13.2 A List of Some Widely Used Achievement Tests

Title/Acronym (or What It's Often Called)	Purpose and What It Tests	Grade Levels/ Ages Tested	Versions	Conceptual Framework	What's Interesting to Note	Publisher (and Where You Can Get More Information If You Want It)
California Achievement Test Fifth Edition (CAT5)	"Designed to measure achievement in the basic skills taught in schools throughout the nation." Reading (Visual Recognition, Word Analysis, Vocabulary, Comprehension); Spelling, Language (Mechanics, Expression); Mathematics (Computation, Concepts and Applications); Study Skills; Science; Social Studies	Kindergarten– 12th grade for the Complete Battery	The CAT5 comes in two versions. One is the Survey, which contains 20 items per subset, and one is the Complete Battery, which contains 24-50 items per subtest.	The test developers organized items to reflect six types of thinking processes: 1. Gathering information 2. Organizing information 3. Analyzing information 4. Generating ideas 5. Synthesizing elements 6. Evaluating outcomes	1. The developers of the test have created a scoring system such that each student can be scored in the six types of thinking processes. So, the teacher assesses not only achievement–but also the process that goes into thinking about the items on the test. Each student has a set of Integrated Outcome Scores that reflects these thinking processes. 2. Practice tests are available so that students, especially those in the lower grades, can have some idea of how these tests work and what is expected of them.	CTB/McGraw-Hill 3260 Peachtree Industrial Blvd Suite 20 Duluth, GA 30096-2547 or http://www.ctb.com/.
Comprehensive Test of Basic Skills (CTBS4)	"Designed to measure achievement in . . . reading, language, spelling, mathematics, study skills,	K–12	There are three test formats: Complete Battery, Survey, and Benchmark. Each is used for a different testing purpose.	The items on the CTBS4 are classified using the familiar six-category cognitive taxonomy based on Bloom's original taxonomy:	1. The use of a "locator test," which is a pretest that is used to determine the appropriate test level for each student. This can be a very useful diagnostic and remedial tool.	CTB/McGraw-Hill 3260 Peachtree Industrial Blvd Suite 20 Duluth, GA 30096-2547 or http://www.ctb.com/.

(Continued)

TABLE 13.2 (Continued)

Title/Acronym (or What It's Often Called)	Purpose and What It Tests	Grade Levels/ Ages Tested	Versions	Conceptual Framework	What's Interesting to Note	Publisher (and Where You Can Get More Information If You Want It)
	science, and social studies." Reading, Mathematics Concepts and Applications, Language, Science, Social Studies, and Study Skills			1. Gather information 2. Organize information 3. Analyze information 4. Generate ideas 5. Synthesize elements 6. Evaluate outcomes	2. "Functional-level testing," which allows for information about a student's strengths and weaknesses. 3. Short practice tests for Grades 4 through 6.	
Graduate Record Exams– General Test (GRE)	"Designed to assess the verbal, quantitative and analytical reasoning abilities of graduate school applicants." Verbal Reasoning, Quantitative Reasoning, Analytical Reasoning	College juniors and seniors making application to graduate school	Seven sections that take 30 minutes each, with two verbal, two quantitative, and two analytical sections, and the final section reserved for pretesting new questions and gathering information used in research.	The verbal sections consist of four different types of items: antonyms, analogies, sentence completions, and reading comprehension. The quantitative sections consist of three types of items: discrete quantitative questions, data interpretation items, and quantitative comparisons. The analytical sections contain two types of items: analytical reasoning items and logical reasoning items	1. Very high-security practices make it impossible to cheat (cool for the exam giver anyway). 2. This is the most popular and best documented test of its kind, and virtually everyone who applies to graduate school takes it.	Educational Testing Service Rosedale Road Princeton, NJ 08541 or http://www.ets.org/.

Title/Acronym (or What It's Often Called)	Purpose and What It Tests	Grade Levels/ Ages Tested	Versions	Conceptual Framework	What's Interesting to Note	Publisher (and Where You Can Get More Information If You Want it)
Iowa Test of Basic Skills (ITBS)	"To provide a comprehensive assessment of student progress in the basic skills." The core battery is composed of sections for listening, word analysis, vocabulary, reading, language, and mathematics. The complete battery adds social studies, science, and sources of information. A writing assessment and a listening assessment are available.	K–8	Forms K, L, and M	The ITBS samples those fundamental skills that are necessary for a student to make satisfactory progress through school. This includes higher-order thinking skills such as interpretation, classification, comparison, analysis, and inference.	1. One of the first in that it was first administered in 1935 as the Iowa Every Pupil Test of Basic Skills. 2. Lots of extra information is available to users, making test administration and interpretation much more meaningful. 3. This is one test where the authors really tried to base the content and presentation on good curricular planning. For example, two examples are that the ITBS helps teachers determine which students have the knowledge and skills needed to deal successfully with the curriculum, and it provides information to parents that will enable home and school to work together to best fit the student's interests.	Riverside Publishing 425 Spring Lake Drive Itasca, IL 60143-2079 or http://www.riverpub .com/.

(Continued)

TABLE 13.2 (Continued)

Title/Acronym (or What It's Often Called)	Purpose and What It Tests	Grade Levels/ Ages Tested	Versions	Conceptual Framework	What's Interesting to Note	Publisher (and Where You Can Get More Information If You Want It)
Tests of General Education Development (GED)	The GED was designed to "assess skills representative of the typical outcomes of a traditional high school education." Areas tested are writing skills, social studies, science, literature and the arts, and mathematics.	No level specified	One	Like many other achievement tests, the GED uses an adaptation of Bloom's Taxonomy of Educational Objectives Levels, with items mainly from the categories of comprehension, application, and analysis.	1. First developed in 1942 to assist veterans who did not have the time to complete high school. 2. In 1988, more than 700,000 (yikes!) tests were administered with more than 70% of takers passing. 3. New additions include a writing sample, an emphasis on critical thinking, items related to computer technology, and the assessment of consumer skills in common adult settings.	General Educational Development Testing Service of the American Council on Education One Dupont Circle NW, Suite 250 Washington, DC 20036 or http://www.acenet .edu/clll/ged/ index.cfm.

3. Go to the library and find a research article that uses a standardized test, and then answer these questions:
   a. What is the name of the test?
   b. To what purpose was the test used in the research you are reading?
   c. How do you know the test is reliable and valid?
   d. If the test is reliable and valid, why is the test the appropriate one for the purpose of the research?

4. Interview one of your current or past teachers and see if you can get him or her to share what his or her test practice development philosophy is like. Ask him or her about how he or she decides which questions to ask. How does he or she ensure fair scoring? What does he or she do if a particular question is not very good (for example, it does not accurately discriminate or it is too easy)? Don't forget to take good notes.

5. Draw up a simple table of specifications for the area in which you are studying using the topic as one dimension and the degree of difficulty (easy, medium, and hard) for the other. What can you learn from creating such a table, and why are tables of specifications important?

ANSWERS TO PRACTICE QUESTIONS

1. They are less costly, easier to create, and more specific to the task, and they can be under the teacher's complete control.

2. Not only are there many different people involved (all of whom presumably get paid), but the item writing, scoring, rewriting, and norming process can take years and cost many, many thousands of dollars.

3. Do this one on your own.

4. Do this one on your own as well.

5. Your table might look something like this:

	Topic				
Difficulty	Fluids	Gases	Solids	Formulas	Total
Easy	7 items	4 items	2 items	1 items	14
Medium	3 items	7 items	5 items	7 items	22
Hard	2 items	9 items	2 items	1 items	14
Total	12	20	9	9	50

WANT TO KNOW MORE?

Further Readings

- Krug, S. (2003). Maybe we learned all we really needed to know in kindergarten: But how could anybody be sure until we took the test? (ERIC Document Reproduction Service No. ED480069)

Krug argues that testing is an integral part of the learning process, and unless testing is done as part of a broad feedback loop, then the instructional process and learning are both shortchanged.

- Bowker, M., & Irish, B. (2003). Using test-taking skills to improve students' standardized test scores. (ERIC Document Reproduction Service No. TM035279)

This is a nice research project where a program was developed to improve test-taking skills to increase standardized test scores. The treatment? Simple—preparation for taking standardized tests. Students showed an improvement on tracking during tests and students' scores increased.

And on the Internet

- FairTest—The National Center for Fair and Open Testing at http://www.fairtest.org/index.htm has as its mission to "end the misuses and flaws of standardized testing and to ensure that evaluation of students, teachers and schools is fair, open, valid and educationally beneficial." A really interesting site to visit.

- Preparing Students to Take Standardized Achievement Tests (at http://pareonline.net/getvn.asp?v=1&n=11) was written by William A. Mehrens (and first appeared in *Practical Assessment, Research & Evaluation*) for school administrators and teachers and discusses what test scores mean and how they can be most useful in understanding children's performance.

Personality Tests

Type A, Type B, or Type C?

Difficulty Index ☺☺☺☺ (moderately easy)

T his is the most interesting thing about personality. Everyone has one, and, by definition, it tends to be pretty stable across the entire life span (and that's a really long time). Some of us are happier than others, some more reflective, some angrier, and some just don't like to be in crowds very often. No wonder it's such a rich area for psychologists, educators, and other social and behavioral scientists to explore.

Some of us are very shy and not interested in meeting others, and some of us like to rock 'n roll at large gatherings, meeting all kinds of new people and being very adventurous. And what's also interesting is that in spite of the fact that personality testing is, in many ways, not as "accurate" as other forms of testing (such as achievement), it is used in hundreds and hundreds of different settings. For example, the top Fortune 100 companies regularly use tests such as the Thematic Apperception Test, trying to find out how well job applicants might be able to work with management, how flexible they are in their thinking, and how well they get along with others.

You can find these tests used in the business world and the military, as criteria for admission into educational and training programs of various sorts, and in other areas where a good "reading" on what someone is like and perhaps even why takes on importance.

WHAT PERSONALITY TESTS ARE AND HOW THEY WORK

Personality tests measure those enduring traits and characteristics of an individual that are nonmental and nonphysical in nature—such things as attitudes, values, interpretations, style, and, of course, individual characteristics. And, with the increasing emphasis on "performance," managers, company presidents, and even dating services are looking for ways to get the edge and assess people's behaviors as accurately as possible. The better the measure, the more accurate the prediction and the more can be understood about these complex systems of enduring traits. The thinking is that if an employer or manager can understand another individual, then the employer or manager can best fit that person into the exact position where he or she might thrive—or, of course, not hire or consider that person in the first place.

> **Traits and Types**
>
> Although everyone has his or her own personality, we can get a bit more specific and talk about personality traits and personality types. A **personality trait** is an enduring quality, like being shy or outgoing. A **personality type** is a constellation of those traits and characteristics.

Objective or Projective: You Tell Me

There are basically two types of personality tests: those that are objective and those that are projective.

Objective personality tests have very clear and unambiguous questions, stimuli, or techniques for measuring personality traits. For example, a structured item might be when a test taker is asked to respond "yes" or "no" to the statement

I get along with others.

These are test items where there is no doubt about how the test taker can respond: yes or no, agree or disagree. The logic behind personality tests that are constructed like this is that the more items that are agreed with, or checked off, or somehow selected, the more of that trait or characteristic the test taker has. For example, here's an item from the 192-item NEO 4, a widely used personality test published by Psychological Assessment Resources (and this item is used with their permission).

I usually prefer to do things alone.

Figure 14.1 Inkblot

The test taker indicates whether he or she strongly agrees, agrees, is neutral, disagrees, or strongly disagrees with the item.

Projective personality tests have ambiguous or unclear stimuli, and the test taker is asked to interpret or impose his or her own meaning onto these events. The most common example of this is the Rorschach inkblot test, where the test taker is shown what appears to be a blot of ink on a card and is asked to tell the test examiner what he or she sees. Here's an example of a Rorschach-like inkblot in Figure 14.1.

The idea behind projective tests is that individuals can impose their *own* sense of structure on an unstructured event—the inkblot—and in doing so, they reveal important information about their view of the world and the characteristics that are associated with that view. Obviously, the inkblot is not a very structured stimulus, and such tests take a great deal of education and practice to interpret adequately.

Another very common projective personality test is the Thematic Apperception Test (or TAT), where the test taker is shown black-and-white pictures of "classical human situations" (there are 31 of them, with one card being blank). The person who is taking the test is asked to describe the events that led up to the scene in the picture, what is going on, and what will happen next. Test takers are also encouraged to talk about the people in the pictures and what they might be experiencing. You can tell from this description how much of a challenge it is to analyze such test taker responses and then interpret what they mean regarding an individual's personality.

Early Personality "How Do You Feel?" Tests

The earliest forms of personality tests were projective in that physicians interviewed patients, asking them questions about their emotions, feelings, and experiences. No particular response could have been expected, and it was the test giver's skills at interpreting the patient's statements that allowed some conclusion to be reached about the test taker's well being.

DEVELOPING PERSONALITY TESTS

There are many different ways in which items for a personality test can be developed. The two most popular are first, base the items on content and theory, and second, use a criterion group. Let's look briefly at both.

Using Content and Theory

Let's say you want to develop a test that measures someone's willingness to take risks as a personality characteristic. You'd probably say that this is a personality trait among people who like to do things such as climb mountains, go caving, drive fast, and participate in activities that many of us think could be dangerous. For us non-risk takers, we're just as happy to be at home with a good book.

In particular, theories (and all the literature on this topic) of risk taking lead us to believe that we can predict what kinds of behaviors risk takers will exhibit. We can then formulate a set of questions that allows us to take an inventory of one's willingness to take risk through simple self-report questions such as

I would rather climb a mountain than play a noncompetitive sport.

or

I like to spend most of my spare time at home relaxing.

If we follow a theory that says people with certain personality traits would rather do one than the other, we have some idea of what type of content can assess what types of traits. We would probably ask people if they agreed or disagreed with each item. The more items pointing in a particular direction that the test taker agreed with, the more evidence we have that that trait or characteristic is present. And, within this same way of constructing personality test items, we could also ask one of our experts on this particular trait we are calling risk taking whether he or she thinks that this item fairly assessed the trait. Sort of like the content validity we talked about in Chapter 4.

THINGS TO REMEMBER

Content or face validity plays just as important a role in the development of a personality test as it does for the development of an achievement test. The question is whether what you are testing for is evident in the items that you are creating.

The strategy that we just described is the way in which the very well-known Woodworth Personal Data Sheet (the earliest formal personality test) was developed. Woodworth went around and talked with psychiatrists about what they say in their practice as he also consulted lots and lots of literature on symptoms of neuroses. He then created items from the long list of comments he got and information he gleaned from what others had written.

Using a Criterion Group

The use of a criterion group is even more interesting. Here, the test developer looks for a group of potential test takers that differs from another group of potential test takers. And on what do they differ? Those personality traits and characteristics that are being studied!

This is a process of discriminating between different sets of people who have already recognized that they belong to a certain group of people who may behave or work in a particular fashion or may even be in a particular occupation.

For example, let's say we are interested in developing a set of personality items that taps into whether people are deeply religious—perhaps a test of degree of religious faith. Well, one way to create and test such items might be as follows:

1. Explore the previous empirical literature on faith and get some idea of what characterizes one group from the other.

2. Generate a bunch of test items from this review of literature. For example, the literature you read may indicate that very religious people tend to be more empathetic and can identify more easily with others in need.

3. Review items and make sure they make sense—do they tap into the trait or characteristic you want to test?

4. Use the good items (those that are clear and really focus on empathy and have good psychometric qualities) in the first draft of the test.

5. Most important, administer the set of items that has been created to two groups—those people whom you think well represent the criterion group (perhaps those people who go to the church, mosque, or synagogue on a regular basis) and those who have no interest in such activities.

6. Now, in theory, you have these two groups, and you should be able to fairly well decide which of the items that you created for the test discriminate best. These become your items of choice. There's a lot more work ahead, but this is a good start.

For example, a terrific historical example of this method is exemplified by the development of the 567-item Minnesota Multiphasic Personality Inventory (MMPI), first published in 1943.

1. The authors started at the beginning, where they generated as well as collected items from a variety of different sources, including their own case studies, books, journals, and anything else they thought might work.

2. All the items were reviewed, and they settled on 1,000 statements, which were then reduced to 504 after all similar types of questions and such were eliminated.

3. Criterion groups were selected: what the authors defined as a normal group (undergraduates at the University of Minnesota

where the test was invented), and a clinical group consisting of patients in the psychiatric clinic at the university's hospital.

4. Each of the 504 items was given to all participants.

5. The items that discriminated best were kept, and the ones that did not were either revised or discarded.

6. These best items were used to create the test.

7. The final scales themselves were created, and one would expect the participants in the clinical sample to score different from the participants in the "normal" group, and they indeed did. In fact, today's MMPI contains 10 different scales that represent the areas in which the groups distinguished themselves from one another. These areas are as follows:
   a. Hypochondriacs (concerns about illness)
   b. Depression (clinical depression)
   c. Hysteria (converting mental conflicts into physical attributes)
   d. Psychopathic deviate (history of antisocial or delinquent behavior)
   e. Masculinity femininity (masculine and feminine characteristics)
   f. Paranoia (concerns about being watched or persecuted)
   g. Psychoasthenia (obsessive behaviors)
   h. Schizophrenia (distortions of reality)
   i. Hypomania (excessive mood swings)
   j. Social introversion (high degree of introversion or extraversion)

And these 10 scales become the factors or dimensions along which each taker of the MMPI is rated. (And why is the last one not #10? One of the great mysteries of test development.)

Understanding the Results of Personality Tests

Administering (and understanding the results of) personality tests is not for mere mortals like you and me. We could give them, sure, but understanding the results is a whole different story. Almost all users of these tests have undergone years of extensive training; they usually have an advanced degree in clinical, counseling, or school psychology; and they are approved by the American Psychological Association. These are definitely not for the arm-chair psychologist. Want more information about becoming one of these talented folks? Visit http://www.apa.org/apags/profdev/careers.html and read about a career as a psychologist.

Using Factor Analysis

Now, factor analysis surely is a mouthful of words.

First, a bit about the technique. Factor analysis is a technique for looking at relationships between variables and helping to identify which of those variables relate to one another. And if they do relate to each other more than to other variables in the set, we might call this group of variables a **factor**.

For example, if you found that Variables 1, 3, and 6 in a set of 10 are related to one another, and then examined them closely for what they measure (let's say that Variable #1 measures reading comprehension, #3 measures reading fluency, and #6 measures reading strategies), we might collectively call this a factor and name it reading ability. When we use factor analysis, we look for patterns of commonality.

The strategy for developing a test based on factor analysis is to administer a whole bunch of tasks—which may be structured or projective—and then correlate scores on one task with all other tasks. Next, you look for similarities about sets of tasks and give them a factor name, such as shyness or confidence.

The Sixteen Personality Factor Questionnaire (also known as the 16PF and now in its fifth edition) is one such test that was developed based on the research of Raymond Catell. After the collection of many items, administration, and factor analysis, the following 16 factors (on all of which people can and do differ) form the structure of the test.

- Warmth
  (Reserved vs. Warm)

- Reasoning
  (Concrete vs. Abstract)

- Emotional Stability
  (Reactive vs.
  Emotionally Stable)

- Dominance
  (Deferential vs. Dominant)

- Liveliness
  (Serious vs. Lively)

- Rule Consciousness
  (Expedient vs. Rule
  Conscious)

- Social Boldness
(Shy vs. Socially Bold)

- Sensitivity
(Utilitarian vs. Sensitive)

- Vigilance
(Trusting vs. Vigilant)

- Abstractedness
(Grounded vs. Abstracted)

- Privateness
(Forthright vs. Private)

- Apprehension (Self-
Assured vs. Apprehensive)

- Openness to Change
(Traditional vs. Open to
Change)

- Self Reliance
(Group-Oriented vs.
Self-Reliant)

- Perfectionism
(Tolerates Disorder vs.
Perfectionistic)

- Tension
(Relaxed vs. Tense)

The Neo 4 (and you saw a sample item earlier) is also a very well-known personality test that was constructed based on a factor analytic framework. It's based on a five-domain model, as follows:

- Neuroticism

- Extraversion

- Openness

- Agreeableness

- Conscientiousness

Some more examples of items that tap into these domains are

> 17. I often crave excitement.
>
> 50. I have an active fantasy life.
>
> 127. Sometimes I trick people into doing what I want.

Using Personality Theory

In the development of personality tests using this approach, the identification and adherence to a particular personality theory is the most important element.

One of these tests is the (Allen) Edwards Personal Preference test based on the personality research by Murray and first presented in 1938. Edwards created an inventory of items based on the characteristics or needs that Murray identified. The current form of the Edwards scale consists of 210 pairs of statements and 15 different scales such that the test taker chooses which of the two statements most characterizes him- or herself. The scales are as follows:

- Achievement
- Deference
- Order
- Exhibition
- Autonomy
- Affiliation
- Interception
- Succorance

- Dominance
- Abasement
- Nurturance
- Change
- Endurance
- Heterosexuality
- Aggression

Interception? Succorance? Abasement? What Am I Missing?

Those Edwards scales have some interesting names, don't they? Most are self-explanatory, but here's some help on those that may not be. *Interception* is the need to analyze other people's behaviors, and *succorance* is the need to receive support and attention from others. And just in case you're really curious, *abasement* is the need to accept blame for problems and confess errors to others.

WHAT THEY ARE: A SAMPLING OF PERSONALITY TESTS AND WHAT THEY DO

Table 14.1 shows you five personality tests and some information about what they do and how they do it. A useful thing would be to look at the diversity, especially in their format—from an inkblot (the Rorschach) to a test where the test taker draws a person. Interesting indeed.

TABLE 14.1 A List of Some Widely Used Personality Tests

Title/Acronym (or What It's Often Called)	Purpose and What It Tests	Grade Levels/ Ages Tested	Conceptual Framework	What's Interesting to Note	Publisher (and Where You Can Get More Information If You Want It)
Minnesota Multiphasic Personality Inventory (MMPI-2)	The assessment of a number of the major patterns of personality and emotional disorders	Ages 18 and over	Based on the distinction between normal and pathological groups	• Rejected by several publishers in the 1940s, but it went on to become one of the most popular tests • Widely used as a research tool • The original Minnesota normal sample consisted of 724 relatives and other visitors at the University of Minnesota Hospitals	University of Minnesota Press PO Box 1416 Minneapolis, MN 55440 or http://www.pearsonassessments.com/
Neo	The measurement of five major dimensions or domains of normal adult personality	Ages 17 and over	Five-factor model of personality: Openness to Experience, Conscientiousness, Extraversion, Agreeableness, and Neuroticism	• Based on original Neo personality test • Normative group consisted of volunteers	Psychological Assessment Resources, Inc. PO Box 998 Odessa, FL 33556 or http://www.parinc.com
Rorschach inkblot	A tool for clinical assessment and diagnosis	Ages 5 and over	Psychoanalytic conceptual basis (based on Freud's theory that human behavior is conflicted)	• Hermann Rorschach experimented with inkblots for 4 years; he died at age 37, within months of his book's publication, and never saw the further development of his test • This test has always been controversial in its use, but also quite popular	Hogrefe and Huber Publishers PO Box 2487 Kirkland, WA 98083 or http://www.hhpub.com/

(Continued)

TABLE 14.1 (Continued)

Title/Acronym (or What It's Often Called)	Purpose and What It Tests	Grade Levels/ Ages Tested	Conceptual Framework	What's Interesting to Note	Publisher (and Where You Can Get More Information If You Want It)
16PF Adolescent Personality Questionnaire (APQ)	The measurement of normal personality of adolescents and identification of personality problems	Ages 11 to 22	Based on the earlier 16PF, which assesses 16 "bipolar" dimensions • Warmth (Reserved vs. Warm) • Reasoning (Concrete vs. Abstract) • Emotional Stability (Reactive vs. Emotionally Stable) • Dominance (Deferential vs. Dominant) • Liveliness (Serious vs. Lively) • Consciousness (Expedient vs. Rule Conscious) • Social Boldness (Shy vs. Socially Bold) • Sensitivity (Utilitarian vs. Sensitive) • Vigilance (Trusting vs. Vigilant) • Abstractedness (Grounded vs. Abstracted) • Privateness (Forthright vs. Private)	• Assesses normal personality • Assesses adolescents' reasoning ability and work activity preferences • Can provide career counseling information	Institute for Personality and Ability Testing, Inc. PO Box 1188 Champaign, IL 61824-1188 or http://www.ipat.com/

Title/Acronym (or What It's Often Called)	Purpose and What It Tests	Grade Levels/ Ages Tested	Conceptual Framework	What's Interesting to Note	Publisher (and Where You Can Get More Information If You Want It)
			• Apprehension (Self-Assured vs. Apprehensive) • Openness to Change (Traditional vs. Open to Change) • Self-Reliance (Group-Oriented vs. Self-Reliant) • Perfectionism (Tolerates Disorder vs. Perfectionistic) • Tension (Relaxed vs. Tense)		
Draw a Person (DAP)	Originally developed to assess the personality-emotional characteristics of sexually abused children	Ages 7-12	Examines four constructs • Preoccupation With Sexually Relevant Concepts • Aggression and Hostility • Withdrawal and Guarded Accessibility • Alertness for Danger/ Suspiciousness and Lack of Trust	• Very difficult to establish the reliability and validity for such tests and quantifiable scoring procedures have recently been developed • Author cautions that allegations about sexual abuse should not be based on only one test • A very unique approach to testing for personality and emotional difficulties that may be related to sexual abuse	Psychological Assessment Resources, Inc. PO Box 998 Odessa, FL 33556 or http://www.parinc.com

SUMMARY

Personality is a fascinating dimension of human development. The assessment tools that test developers have created over the past 100 years reflect the ideas and theories that underlie various explanations of individual differences in personality. And, even though personality testing is not as precise as we might like (interpretation goes a very long way), these kinds of tests are being used more often than ever in our society for everything from placement in a new job situation to finding a lifelong partner.

TIME TO PRACTICE

1. Why do you think that personality is such a fascinating concept to study and assessing it is so very difficult?

2. Name one way to develop a personality test, and provide an example of how you would do it.

3. What is the primary difference between an objective and a projective personality test, and why would you use one over the other?

4. Go to the library and find a journal article that reports an empirical study on some aspect of personality. What test did the authors use? What variables were they interested in studying? Were the reliability and validity data about the personality test they used reported? Do you think that the results reflected an accurate picture of what role personality plays in what was being studied?

5. Have some fun. Write 2–3 sentences for each of five friends describing his or her personality. Try to do them as independently as you can without a description of one friend interfering with a description of another friend. Now, see if you can draw some similarities and contrasts in your descriptions. What do they have in common? How are they different? Good! You've started creating a taxonomy of important variables to consider in describing personality—the first step on the way to creating a test of personality.

ANSWERS TO PRACTICE QUESTIONS

1. There are many different ways to answer this question, but personality is such an interesting topic because everybody has one, and, basically, there's nothing any better or worse (on the whole) of having one type versus another. So, it's like a constant in all of our lives, and, through an understanding of individual differences and such in personality, we can better understand human nature.

2. One way that we discussed in this chapter is through the use of a criterion group. For example, if you were interested in studying shyness, you would locate groups of people who are shy and those who are not and design items that discriminate between the two.

3. An objective personality test uses structured stimuli and often closed-ended questions (I enjoy eating alone). A projective personality test uses very open-ended items where the test taker constructs a response based on the indefinite and ambiguous nature of the item. In both cases, there is no right or wrong—just a different way of accessing information about one's distinct personality traits and characteristics.

4. This one is on your own.

5. Have fun with this one, and be sure to keep your results confidential.

WANT TO KNOW MORE?

Further Readings

• Varela, J. G., Boccaccini, M. T., Scogin, F., Stump, J., & Caputo, A. (2004). Personality testing in law enforcement employment settings: A meta analytic review. *Criminal Justice & Behavior, 31,* 649–675.

How well can personality measures predict the performance of law enforcement officers? That's one purpose of the study, which used meta analysis as an analytic tool, and the researchers found a statistically significant relationship between personality test scores and officer performance.

• Panayiotou, G., Kokkinos, C. M., & Spanoudis, G. (2004). Searching for the "Big Five" in a Greek context: The NEO FFI under the microscope. *Personality and Individual Differences, 36,* 1841–1854.

This study evaluates the psychometric properties and factor structure of the Greek FFI (based on the Neo we talked about in this chapter) and provides normative information for its use with Greek populations. It's an interesting application of a test developed in one culture when used within another.

And on the Internet

- The Clifton StrengthsFinder™ at http://education.gallup.com/ content/default.asp?ci=886 is a Web-based assessment tool published by the Gallup organization (yep, the poll people) to help people better understand their talents and strengths by measuring the presence of 34 themes of talent. You might want to take it and explore these themes.

15 Aptitude Tests

What's in Store for Me?

Difficulty Index ☺☺☺☺ (moderately easy)

What's the coolest aptitude test out there? By far, it's the GLAT (the Google Labs Aptitude Test), which you can find (and take) at http://www.google.com/googleblog/2004/09/pencils-down-people.html. Take it and send it on to the Google employment folks—score high enough and they may call you about a job. And, we'll show you an item from this test later in this chapter.

What's an aptitude test? An **aptitude test** evaluates an individual's *potential*—it indicates what someone may be able to do in the future—and does not reflect his or her current level of performance. It's what you may have to take when you apply for a job as a drafting technician or for an advanced degree—aptitude tests attempt to find out how well qualified you are for what might lie ahead. Your past accomplishments may, of course, influence your future ones, but an aptitude test tries to quantify how well prepared you are for that future.

Aptitude tests come in at least two flavors—they assess *cognitive skills*, as on the SAT (which stands for nothing!—see box—and focuses on cognitive skills in areas such as reading and mathematics) taken in the junior or senior year of high school, and they can assess psychomotor performance, such as the Differential Aptitude Test, or DAT (which focuses on psychomotor skills).

> **What's in a Name?**
>
> Yes, believe it or not, the SAT officially, officially, officially stands for nothing. Not Standardized Achievement Test, not Scholastic Aptitude Test, not Silly Accomplishments on Thursday, nothing.

> Why? Well, the publishers at Educational Testing Services in Princeton, New Jersey, didn't have much comment, but perhaps it's because the once-used title of Standardized Achievement Test (30 years ago) is too limiting in what that title says about the test. ETS wants the SAT to be used for many, many different audiences, and leaving the title somewhat ambiguous may allow for that.

Both of these types of aptitude tests are worthy of the title "aptitude test" because they have been shown to have *predictive validity* (see Chapter 4 for more about this kind of validity). Scores on these tests can be used to comfortably and accurately predict a set of future outcomes. In the case of the SAT, the outcome might be performance in college during the first year. In the case of the DAT, it is how well the test taker can perform both simple and complex basic motor skills—both of which are important for success in such jobs as automotive work, engineering skills such as drawing, and the assembly of intricate parts.

So if you can answer this question from the GLAT, you may well be on your way, and here it is:

1
1 1
2 1
1 2 1 1
1 1 1 2 2 1
What is the next line of numbers? _____

Want the answer? Take the test (see the Further Readings section at the end of this chapter for more information).

WHAT APTITUDE TESTS DO

Aptitude tests are used to assess potential or future performance. For example, they might be used to determine how well a person might perform in a particular employment position or profession, and they are very often used by businesses and corporations to better understand the potential of an applicant or employee.

These types of tests tap the ability to use specific job-related skills and to predict subsequent job performance. In our Google example above, this type of item taps thinking and reasoning skills, two skills that the Google guys feel are important and related to the type of work in which they would like new employees to engage.

Aptitude or Achievement: You Be the Judge

It's really easy to confuse aptitude (this chapter), ability (see Chapter 16), and achievement tests (see Chapter 13) because they often overlap in terms of the types of questions being asked as well as their use. For example, an achievement item might very well predict how well someone might do in a particular field (which is kind of an aptitude concern). So, expect to have overlap between test purposes and similarity in test items between these three. What kind of test is it? Usually, the answer lies in what it's being used for.

HOW TO DO IT: THE ABCs OF CREATING AN APTITUDE TEST

Remember that an aptitude test is used mostly to predict performance. As the boss of a company, you might use an aptitude test that looks at the potential of employees to be one of the firm's financial officers. You want to assess the candidate's current knowledge of finance but also his or her potential to fit into a position that has new task demands (like creating and understanding a year-end report).

Another common example is the use of the SAT or the American College Test (ACT), both of which basically consist of achievement-like items, for the prediction of how well a high school student will do during college. As it turns out, these tests do moderately predict performance during that first year, but the predictive validity falls off sharply for the later years. So, although the SAT and ACT are looking at current level of skill (and some people call that ability), these results are also used to point to the future.

THINGS TO REMEMBER

Earlier in this chapter, we pointed out how achievement tests and aptitude tests overlap a great deal. In fact, aptitude tests might include the same kind of material as achievement tests but just be used for a different purpose—and that is, perhaps, the key. For example, at the elementary school level, the Metropolitan Readiness Tests assess the development of math and reading skills. At the secondary school level, the SAT assesses writing, critical reading, and math skills. At the college level, the Graduate Record Exam assesses verbal, quantitative, and analytic skills. Different levels, all used for examining future potential, but all containing many similar, achievement-like items. The key is what aptitude tests are used for—prediction of later outcomes.

You might take the following steps in the creation of an aptitude test. Let's say that this particular test will assess manual dexterity, and it is intended for applicants to culinary school.

1. Define the set of manual dexterity skills that you think are important for success as a chef. This definition probably comes from an empirical examination of graduates and chefs who are established and successful.

2. Now that you know what types of skills distinguish those who are successful from those who are not, create some kind of an instrument that allows you to distinguish between the two groups. Find out which items work (that is, they discriminate between groups or correlate with existing tests) and which do not work.

3. TaDa! You have the beginnings of an aptitude test with a set of tasks that defines and distinguishes between those who do well in culinary school (or at least one set of skills necessary to be successful in culinary school) and those who do not.

4. Now test, test, and test aspiring chefs, working on the reliability and validity of the test, and after lots of hard work, including reliability and validity studies, you might be done.

For example, here's an item from the Law School Admissions Test (or the LSAT, with thanks to the Law School Admission Council). This test consists of five 35-minute sections of multiple-choice questions. One section is on reading comprehension, one focuses on analytical reasoning, and two focus on logical reasoning. A 30-minute writing sample is the last element of the test.

Here's the item from one of the logical reasoning sections.

---

12. Navigation in animals is defined as the animal's ability to find its way from unfamiliar territory to points familiar to the animal but beyond the immediate range of the animal's senses. Some naturalists claim that polar bears can navigate over considerable distances. As evidence, they cite an instance of a polar bear that returned to its home territory after being released over 500 kilometers (300 miles) away.

Which one of the following, if true, casts the most doubt on the validity of the evidence offered in support of the naturalists' claim?

(A) The polar bear stopped and changed course several times as it moved toward its home territory.

(B) The site at which the polar bear was released was on the bear's annual migration route.

(C) The route along which the polar bear traveled consisted primarily of snow and drifting ice.

(D) Polar bears are only one of many species of mammal whose members have been known to find their way home from considerable distances.

(E) Polar bears often rely on their extreme sensitivity to smell in order to scent out familiar territory.

Once this item is given (along with all the others, of course), the test makers take the results and analyze them to find out how effectively they differentiated those who scored high versus those who scored low on the total test. The item may be rewritten, thrown out altogether, revised heavily, and then used again in a subsequent test.

Commercial test publishers like the Law School Admissions Council are constantly revising their tests to be as good and as accurate as possible.

Do aptitude tests sound like "What am I best suited for" tests, like the kind you would take when you visit the career planning center at school? In many ways, they very much are. But because career planning and vocational tests are so important in their own right, we'll leave that discussion for Chapter 17. For now, keep in mind that a vocational test is very much a specialized type of aptitude test.

TYPES OF APTITUDE TESTS

The term *aptitude* encompasses so many different skills and abilities that it is best to break down the term into some of the many different areas on which aptitude tests might focus.

Mechanical Aptitude Tests

Mechanical aptitude tests focus on a variety of abilities that fall into the psychomotor domain, from assembly tests (where the test taker has to actually put something together) to reasoning tests (where the test taker has to use reasoning skills to solve mechanical types of problems). Tests that fall into these categories are the Armed Services Vocational Aptitude Battery Form, the Bennet Mechanical Comprehension Test, and the Differential Aptitude Test.

Artistic Aptitude Tests

How very difficult it is to tell whether one has "promise" (because, after all, that is what aptitude is, right?) in the creative or performing arts. Such tests evaluate artistic talent, be it in music, drawing, or other forms of creative expression. For example, there is the Primary Measures of Music Audition (for Grades K–3) and the Intermediate Measures of Music Audition (for Grades 1–6). Both of these tests require children to listen to music and then answer questions using pictures rather than numbers or words (thereby reducing any confounding that differences in reading ability might introduce). The children must decide whether pairs of tonal or rhythm patterns they hear sound the same or different.

Readiness Aptitude Tests

In the early 20th century, Arnold Gesell started the Child Study Center at Yale University, where he documented the importance of *maturation* as an important process in the growth and development of young children. He not only documented it, he micro-micro studied it, creating extensive film libraries of individual growth and development.

Readiness, Aptitude, and Mental Health

Gesell was interested in how ready children are for school, and the phrase *aptitude test* had not even been coined yet, but nonetheless, that's what his readiness tests assessed. And very interestingly, readiness and well being both fall under the broader umbrella of *hygiene* (another term used then for mental health).

One of his ideas is that children become ready for a particular phase of learning and development at different times, and the introduction and use of readiness tests at all levels of education (but especially the elementary level) serve the purpose of evaluating whether a child is ready for school. For example, the Gesell Child Development Age Scale is designed to determine in which of the 10 Gesell early development periods a child is presently functioning. That information can then be used by early educators and other teachers to decide whether a child is ready for a particular level of activity. And, although we don't call them readiness tests, you can bet that the Graduate Record Exams are used to determine whether students are ready for graduate school.

But at whatever level of education, the intent is the same—to find out if the test taker is ready for what comes next—that's a prediction question, and that's the business of aptitude tests.

Clerical Aptitude Tests

There is an absolutely huge number of people who are employed in clerical positions, including everything from file clerks to cashiers to administrative assistants. These kinds of employment positions require great attention to detail, especially numbers and letters. One of the most famous and often used of these aptitude tests is the Minnesota Clerical Test (or MCT), which measures speed and accuracy in clerical work in high school students and was first used in 1963. This test consists of 200 items, with each item containing a pair of names or numbers. The test taker is simply supposed to indicate whether the pair of names or numbers is the same or different.

Although this may sound like an overly simplified approach, it is a very accurate (and highly predictive) one where the final score is the number of incorrect responses subtracted from the number correct.

SOME OF THE BIG ONES

Table 15.1 shows you some of the most often used aptitude tests and all the information you will ever want to know about them.

SUMMARY

Aptitude tests are very much like achievement tests in that they often test knowledge of a particular topic or subject matter. The big difference is that the results are used for different things than are the results from achievement tests. An aptitude test looks to future potential rather than current levels of performance. In many ways, aptitude and achievement tests are similar—it's just a matter of for what purpose one intends the test to be used and how one interprets the results. Now that you're an expert on achievement, personality, and aptitude tests, it's time to move on to one of the most controversial and interesting types of tests—ability (including IQ) tests.

TABLE 15.1 A List of Some Widely Used Aptitude Tests

Title/Acronym (or What It's Often Called)	Purpose and What It Tests	Grade Levels/Ages Tested	Conceptual Framework	What's Interesting to Note	Publisher (and Where You Can Get More Information If You Want It)
Metropolitan Achievement Tests (METRO-POLITAN8)– Eighth Edition	Assesses achievement in reading, mathematics, language arts, science, and social studies	Grades K–12	The tests were developed (and are revised) based on the curricula that are used in the schools and reflected by popular textbooks in each subject area. Then, items were reviewed by external curriculum specialists. Finally, a committee of professional educators examined the items for bias, and items were revised as needed.	1. One of the easiest aptitude tests published in the 1930s. 2. Scores are used to place students into categories: advanced, proficient, basic, and below basic. 3. Standardization included more than 80,000 students for the 1999-2000 sample. (Yikes!)	Harcourt Assessment, Inc. 19500 Bulverde Road San Antonio, TX 78259 or http://harcourtassessment .com/.
Denver II	Designed to screen for developmental delays. Item scores in four areas (Personal-Social, Fine Motor-Adaptive, Language, Gross Motor) and five test behavior ratings (Typical, Compliance, Interest in Surroundings, Fearfulness, Attention Span)	Birth to age 6	Children's development tends to occur in a predictable pattern, and although there are individual differences across ages, there are enough similarities that a general level of developmental competence can be assessed accurately.	1. Used to be called the Denver Developmental Screening Test 2. Uses a visual form for recording scores that aligns with child's chronological age and accounts for prematurity 3. Easy and quick to use, which appeals to health care providers who are not necessarily trained in the administration of complex tests	Denver Developmental Materials, Inc. PO Box 6919 Denver, CO 80206-0919 or http://www.denverii.com/.

(Continued)

TABLE 15.1 (Continued)

Title/Acronym (or What It's Often Called)	Purpose and What It Tests	Grade Levels/Ages Tested	Conceptual Framework	What's Interesting to Note	Publisher (and Where You Can Get More Information If You Want It)
Differential Aptitude Test (DAT)–Fifth Edition	The DAT measures students' ability to learn or to succeed in a number of different areas. Nine scores in Verbal Reasoning, Numerical Reasoning, Abstract Reasoning, Perceptual Speed and Accuracy, Mechanical Reasoning, Space Relations, Spelling, Language Usage, and Total Scholastic Aptitude	Grades 7–9, Grades 10–12, and adults	Measures broad aptitudes (and has its own kind of "g," or general underlying factor) that have relevance to different educational and occupational domains	1. Used mostly in educational counseling and personnel assessment 2. Often used in career guidance 3. The DAT includes a practice test so students can become familiar with the type of items and time requirements	The Psychological Corporation 555 Academic Court San Antonio, TX 78204-2498 or http://harcourtassessment. com/.
Armed Services Vocational Aptitude Battery (ASVAB)	Intended "for use in educational and vocational counseling and to stimulate interest in job and training opportunities in the Armed Forces."	High school, junior college, and young adult applicants to the Armed Forces		1. Used primarily for testing the potential of armed services enlistees	United States Military Entrance Processing Command 2500 Green Bay Road North Chicago, IL 60064-3094

Title/Acronym (or What It's Often Called)	Purpose and What It Tests	Grade Levels/Ages Tested	Conceptual Framework	What's Interesting to Note	Publisher (and Where You Can Get More Information If You Want It)
	General Science, Arithmetic Reasoning, Word Knowledge, Paragraph Comprehension, Numerical Operations, Coding Speed, Auto-Shop Information, Math Knowledge, Mechanical Comprehension, Electronics Information, Academic Ability, Verbal Ability, Math Ability				The Psychological Corporation 757 Third Avenue New York, NY 10017 or http://harcourt assessment.com/.
Minnesota Clerical Test (MCT)	This tests measures speed and accuracy in clerical work. Variable measures are accuracy of number and name comparison	Grades 8–12 and adults	Designed to assess the accuracy and efficiency of processing numerical and linguistic information	1. Norms are presented for 10 different vocational categories 2. Very easily administered in 15 minutes	

TIME TO PRACTICE

1. Why can the same set of achievement items be used for both an aptitude test and an achievement test?

2. Go to your library and look in the Buros Mental Measurements Yearbook (or go access the Buros Institute online through your library), and summarize one of the reviews of any aptitude test. Be sure to address the conceptual rationale for why the test was created in the first place.

3. Design a 5-item aptitude test (don't worry, you don't have to do any reliability or validity studies) that examines potential in any one of the following professions:
   a. Law
   b. City planner
   c. Medicine
   d. Airline pilot

4. How does an aptitude test differ from an achievement test?

5. Many aptitude tests include the term *readiness* in their title. Why?

ANSWERS TO PRACTICE QUESTIONS

1. Because when it comes to aptitude tests, it is not so much the content (although that is very important as well) as it is the purpose or intent of the test that is important.

2. This one is on your own.

3. One of the first steps is to identify those skills that are important to the selected profession and then create an item. For example, it's very important for airline pilots to be able to read maps. Map-reading skills include being able to decipher symbols and understand directions and map coordinates (among many other skills).

4. The basic difference is the use to which the results are put. Many aptitude tests include items that could appear on an achievement test, but that's not the point or the purpose. Aptitude tests look to future (perhaps) learning ability, whereas achievement tests evaluate current ability.

5. Because one way of defining aptitude is in how ready an individual is for a certain set of next steps, such as moving into a reading curriculum during elementary school.

WANT TO KNOW MORE?

Further Readings

- Hull, C. (1928). *Aptitude testing.* Yonkers-on-Hudson, NY: World Book Company.

This is one of those o-o-o-ld books and one done by a famous experimental psychologist who was interested primarily in learning. Your library has this one, and it can give you great insight into how the history of measuring aptitudes has progressed from what it was more than 80 years ago to the industry it is today.

- Hoffman, E. (2001). *Psychological testing at work: How to use, interpret, and get the most out of the newest tests in personality, learning style, aptitudes, interests, and more!* New York: McGraw-Hill.

Aptitude testing need not be boring. Find out how the leading employers use it to find just who they want. This book talks about employee screening and how to assess job candidates' traits, interests, and skills.

And on the Internet

- Want to cover that big story in your hometown? See if you have what it takes to be a reporter at http://www.richardwarrenfield .com/rpt-ap-t.htm, the home of the Reporter's Aptitude test. (Warning—This is just for fun.)

- You saw it here first—The Google Labs Aptitude Test or GLAT at http://cruftbox.com/blog/archives/001031.html. Print it out and send it in—who knows? Maybe you're what they are looking for.

- Need help with the SAT, GRE, or ACT? Take a look at http://www.number2.com (number 2 pencil, get it?) for free preparation help. Good idea. Good luck.

16 Intelligence Tests

That Rubik's Cube Is Driving Me Nuts

Difficulty Index ☺☺☺ (getting harder)

He said, She said . . .

He: I snuck a look at the school's student records, and Bill's IQ is off the charts. He's a smart one.

She: You mean intelligent, right?

He: Well, he's got a high IQ—if that's not smart or intelligent, what is?

She: If you listened better in our tests and measurement class, you'd know that IQ is a score on a test of intelligence and not necessarily a reflection of how "smart" someone is. In fact, Bill talks a great game (and we know that much of an intelligence test score is based on verbal skills), gets all those As and Bs (he's "book" smart, anyway), and "knows" how to take tests. But intelligent?—the jury may be out on that.

He: Well, what does someone have to be to be smart in your book?

She: I certainly don't know, and much of what we've discussed in class tells us that intelligence is a term mostly reflected by scores on tests that define intelligence in very different ways. How would I know?

He and She are not alone.

F irst, there is as much confusion about what intelligence is and how to measure it as there is about any construct that social and behavioral scientists study. Try to measure it, and there are a whole bunch of new questions to be asked that don't seem to have any easy answers. Is intelligence a universal attribute? Are there different types? Is it a quantifiable entity? If you don't have enough, can you get more?

THE ABCs OF INTELLIGENCE

No physicist has ever seen an atom (just reflections of one), and no social or behavioral scientists has ever "seen" intelligence. Its existence is inferred by the way people behave. And the way they behave, we call tests. And, to finish this little exercise, the way they behave on what we call intelligence tests defines what we call an intelligence score (which most of us know as IQ, or intelligence quotient). But there's much more to the story.

THINGS TO REMEMBER

The definition of intelligence is an elusive task at best, perhaps contributing to why it is so difficult to measure and, even more important, what the outcomes of such tests mean. But when the definition is grounded in thoughtful theory, we have taken an important step in understanding this important source of individual differences.

Intelligence is a construct or a group of related variables (such as verbal skills, memory, mechanical skills, comprehension, and more) and has some theoretical basis to it. And, that's what we're going to talk about here—the different theoretical definitions that people have offered. Because tests of intelligence are so closely tied to the theory on which the tests are based, we have to first talk a bit about these different approaches. That way, when it comes to talk about the development of tests, we can see the logical extension from the idea to its application.

The Big "g"

One of the first conceptualizations of what intelligence is was proposed by Charles Spearman way back in the late 1920s of the previous millennium (around 1927).

Spearman believed that underlying all of intelligent behavior is a general factor that accounts for explaining individual differences in intelligence between people. He named this theory **general-factor theory** and named the actual factor "g" to represent general factor. In other words, there is one type of intelligence that accounts for individual differences between people on this construct, specifically how well one deals with abstract relationships.

However, because not everyone with a high "g" could do everything well (remember, write, do math, assemble a puzzle, etc.), he also recognized that there are a bunch of other factors that are specific in their nature, and he called them the "s" to represent specific types of intelligences. Spearman's theory represents intelligence as this general factor with a bunch of s's floating around inside of it, and these s's are related to one another to varying degrees.

THINGS TO REMEMBER

Today, in the past, and in the future, there have been ongoing debates about whether intelligence is best represented by the big G (for a general underlying ability) or a small s (for more specific and independent abilities). There is no answer, but it's a great question that helps fuel new ideas and approaches to the assessment of intelligence.

For example, the specific type of intelligence associated with one skill (say, assembling blocks in a particular configuration) might be related to basic math skills but unrelated to being able to remember a set of digits.

More Than Just the Big "g": The Multiple Factor Approach

Well, as always with science, Spearman's idea of one, and only one, general factor theory did not exactly fit other models and ideas. In fact, where Spearman thought that there was only one type of intelligence, "g" (although that is a bit nondescript), others such as Louis Thurstone from the University of Chicago (go Maroons) thought that there were different types of intelligence, which he called **primary mental abilities**. Each of these abilities, such as verbal ability, spatial ability, and perceptual speed, is independent of the others.

So, from a very (g)eneral view of intelligence set forth by Spearman, Thurstone put forth a view that relies heavily on the presence of many different types of (primary or basic) intelligences that are, most importantly, *independent* (both conceptually and statistically) of one another. Although it's really tough to find sets of human behaviors or attributes or abilities that are separate from one another, his theory has been the basis for a widely used test of intelligence, the Primary Mental Abilities Test, which has appeared in many different forms since the late 1930s.

TECH TALK

Factors, Factors, and More Factors: Welcome to Factor Analysis

This is kind of neat—new ideas help create methods that are in turn used to look at those ideas. Take intelligence. At one point, the most popular theory of intelligence led us to believe that intelligence was represented by one big superfactor called "g." Then, along came other theorists who believed that intelligence consisted of a bunch of more specific abilities (some related and some not), then a new idea that intelligence is just a collection of *independent* abilities. To verify that last bit of thinking, **factor analysis** was created and refined and has been used ever since. Factor analysis can be used to determine which of a set of variables can be grouped together to form a conceptually sound unit (called a factor, by the way). For example, individual tests that examine one's ability to assemble puzzles and build three-dimensional objects from a model might all fit under a factor called Manipulation Skills. If, indeed, these two tests share something in common across a large number of individuals and, say, do not share something in common with reading skills or other factors we believe are not related to one another—voila! We may have a factor that can stand on its own (is independent), and we may even have an element of our theory of intelligence. Factor analysis is used to validate theories of intelligence as well as study many different phenomena in the social and behavior sciences, and it is well worth knowing about.

The Three-Way Deal

As research on human intelligence continued, theorists came up with theories that reflected new findings. One such theory was contributed by Robert Sternberg and is called the **triarchic theory of intelligence**. The basis for his theory is that intelligence can best be explained through an understanding of how people think about and solve problems—the information-processing approach.

According to Sternberg, in order to understand what we call intelligence and how people differ from one another, we have to look at the interaction between componential intelligence, experiential intelligence, and contextual intelligence.

- **Componential intelligence** focuses on the structures that underlie intelligent behavior, including the acquisition of knowledge. It's what you know.

- **Experiential intelligence** focuses on behavior based on experiences. It's what you did.

- **Contextual intelligence** focuses on behavior within the context in which it occurs and involves adaptation to the environment, selection of better environments, and shaping of the present environment. It's how you behave.

In developing this approach, Sternberg is attempting to ground his theory in the interaction between the individual's skills and abilities and the demands placed on that individual by the environment.

Way More Than One Type of Intelligence: Howard Gardner's Multiple Intelligences

As research on intelligence has become more and more sophisticated and now includes findings from such fields such as neuroscience and developmental psychology, so have these newer theories increased significance for everyday behavior. Such is the case with Howard Gardner's model of **multiple intelligences** (known as MI).

Gardner theorizes that an individual's intelligence is not made up of one general factor, but eight different types of intelligence that work independently of one another, yet in concert with one another. These eight are as follows:

- Musical Intelligence includes the ability to compose and perform music.

- Bodily-Kinesthetic Intelligence includes the ability to control one's bodily movements.

- Logical-Mathematical Intelligence includes the ability to solve problems.

- Linguistic Intelligence includes the ability to use language.

- Spatial Intelligence includes the ability to manipulate and work with objects in three dimensions.

- Interpersonal Intelligence includes the ability to understand others' behavior and interact with other people.

- Intrapersonal Intelligence includes the ability to understand ourselves.

- Naturalist Intelligence includes the ability to identify and understand patterns in nature.

For example, Michael Jordan, the famous former Chicago Bulls basketball player, would excel in kinesthetic intelligence. Yo-Yo Ma, the famous cellist, would excel in musical intelligence, and so on.

Gardner's idea is, indeed, a very interesting one. He assumes that everyone has each of these intelligences to some degree, that all of us are stronger in some intelligences than others, and that some of us (and perhaps most) excel in probably one. You may not be a naturalist and be able to understand patterns of bird flight, or play Mozart's Fifth, but you sure are good at foreign languages and are a real schmoozer (interpersonal intelligence).

Gardner in the Classroom

Last time we looked, this is a book about *tests* and measurement, right? How in the world does one assess such a wide and diverse set of complex intelligences as that proposed by Gardner? Perhaps the traditional paper-and-pencil or performance approach? How about showing a bunch of events and asking the test taker to put them in sequential order? Or remembering a list of words? Those were the more traditional ways that intelligence testing was done and reflects more traditional and historical theories. Also, perhaps the testing room is not the right place to be looking for these skills or abilities or intelligences.

Gardner and his supporters wouldn't think so. Instead, he would suggest that traditional tests of intelligence don't provide the flexibility needed by the test taker to show his or her skills across this very broad range. Interestingly, Gardner emphasizes the importance of individual differences in the assessment of these eight intelligences—shades of what early psychometricians such as Frances Galton talked about almost a century earlier!

For assessment, the development of an *intelligence profile* for each student would be consistent with the model. And, one way to do this might be through student portfolios (see Chapter 11) and the use of independent projects and journals. Also, Linda Campbell suggests five approaches: unique lesson designs where, for example, the use of all or several of the intelligences are emphasized in a lesson; interdisciplinary teaching; student projects; assessments, where students demonstrate their skills and what they have learned; and apprenticeships.

Very different from the same old, same old, and perhaps an indication of where the future of intelligence testing is going.

Emotional Intelligence: A Really Different Idea

Gardner certainly has a new and fresh approach to our understanding and evaluation of intelligence or intelligent behavior. So does Daniel Goleman, who popularized the idea of emotional intelligence.

Emotional intelligence (EI) is the ability to be emotionally sensitive to others and to manage and understand our own emotions and solve problems involving emotional issues. In his 1995 book, *Emotional Intelligence,* Goleman argues that traits and characteristics such as self-awareness and persistence are more important than IQ as we traditionally define intelligence, and that, of course, children should be taught how to identify their own and others' emotions. These are the skills that make real-world people successful, regardless of their native level of intellect.

There are many different tests of emotional intelligence, none of which have really undergone any rigorous psychometric analysis, so they mostly fall under the category of fun but not very useful. And like Gardner's multiple intelligences, perhaps emotional intelligence is not meant to be evaluated in the more traditional way, but instead to depend upon such skill as observation and keeping journals and other, less objective, but surely richer ways of assessing outcomes.

FROM THE BEGINNING: (ALMOST) ALL ABOUT THE STANFORD-BINET INTELLIGENCE SCALE

There's no debate about this: Intelligence is a very complex construct that is difficult to define and difficult to measure. There are differences in intelligence test scores between people with different racial and ethnic backgrounds, differences between males and females, and differences among professions, just to name a few.

However, in spite of these findings, it's very unclear *why* these differences appear. If anything, the best explanation is perhaps that these differences reflect the way the test is constructed and the way items appear on the test. In turn, the content and format reflect the test author's orientation and definition of intelligence. Let's look at one of the most popular tests of intelligence, the Stanford-Binet, to get an overall picture of how such a test was developed and how it is used.

A Bit of History

The Stanford-Binet Intelligence Scale has become one of the most popularly used measures of intelligence.

This is pretty interesting stuff. Around 1905, Parisian Theodore Simon was doing some work in the area of reading. In fact, he had close ties to the famous developmental psychologist Jean Piaget. Piaget's experience with Simon led to Piaget's speculating about the successes and failures of children (who were about elementary school age) which led to Pigaet's famous work on cognitive development.

> **Piaget and Intelligence**
>
> You may remember from your Psych 1 class or introductory child development class that Jean Piaget was one of the foremost and productive cognitive/developmental psychologists. How interesting it is that his definition of intelligence grew from much of his work in France and his later work with his own children (the subjects for many of his early studies). His definition? "Intention"— that those acts showing intention were intelligent acts. Very cool, because it is almost entirely removed from the realm of content, and this focus directly reflects his own theoretical views on development and the development of intelligence.

Well, as Piaget was becoming increasingly intrigued by the nature of the failure to read among normal children, Simon was working with Alfred Binet to develop a test (for the schoolchildren of Paris) to predict and distinguish between those who would do well in school and those who would not. Interestingly, Binet worked with the famous neurologist Jean-Martin Charcot, who also trained Sigmund Freud in the use of hypnotism as a clinical technique. Interesting connections, no?

Anyway, the result of Simon's and Binet's efforts was the first 30-item intelligence scale (in 1905) that was used to identify children who were mentally retarded (or those who were thought not to be able to succeed in school). At first, the items were arranged by difficulty, and, then later, the arrangement was by age level. So, in addition to having a *chronological age* for the child, the test results also yielded a *mental age* (this taking place about 1916).

And, if you're thinking clearly this morning, a ratio of these values gives you a very good idea whether someone is behind, even with, or ahead of his or her chronological age. For example, someone who is chronologically 10 years old, or 120 months, may have a mental age of 10½ years (or 126 months) and therefore be more advanced in his or her mental age for his or her chronological age.

Flash ahead about 100 years, and along the way, the Simon-Binet scale became the Stanford-Binet scale following Lewis Terman's (then at Stanford University) authoring of the authoritative book on the administration and scoring of the test. Also, the IQ score, a ratio of mental to chronological age, was first used. For our 10-year-old, then, the resulting IQ score from a mental age of 10½ years and a chronological age of 10 years is equal to

$$IQ = \frac{MA}{CA} \times 100 = \frac{126}{120} \times 100 = 105$$

As you can see by examining this formula, if one's mental and chronological age are equal, then one's IQ score is 100, just about what we expect if someone is average.

TECH TALK

What Wrong with the IQ Ratio? Lots—Read On . . .

You can imagine how cool it was to have one number, a simple ratio of MA to CA, to express one's theoretical intelligence quotient. But, nope—the reason why this approach was never really embraced was that the upper limit depends upon the upper age limit for the test. For example, if the items go up only to an age level of 21, anyone with a CA of greater than 21 has to have an IQ of less than 100. Not such a good idea and why, today, we don't think of intelligence as IQ, but we use more descriptive and informative terms for describing someone's level of intelligence.

We're now at the fourth edition of the Stanford-Binet, which has undergone many different revisions over this 100-year time span. The test, based on the "g" theory of intelligence we talked about earlier, consists of three different general areas or types of intelligence that are assessed: crystallized intelligence, fluid intelligence, and short-term memory. In theory, these are independent of one another.

Crystallized intelligence reflects knowledge that is acquired, such as the number of elements on the periodical table (105 last we looked) or the author of *Moby Dick* (Herman Melville).

Fluid intelligence is that general ability that Spearman talked about (and we mentioned earlier), including such activities as problem-solving, memory, and learning.

And it is no great surprise that these two different types of intelligence are reflected in the items that are on these intelligence scales. For example, an item on the Stanford-Binet that reflects crystallized intelligence would ask the test taker to identify a common object (which is the result of experience). An example of an item that reflects fluid intelligence might be asking the test taker to copy a pattern that is created by the test administrator (which is more the result of general ability and innate skills and talent than experience).

Today's Stanford-Binet assesses five different factors—fluid reasoning, knowledge, quantitative reasoning, visual-spatial processing, and working memory—these areas being an outgrowth of the fluid, crystallized, and memory focal points mentioned earlier. And, when each of these areas is assessed and scored separately, you have 10 subtests (verbal fluid reasoning, nonverbal fluid reasoning, etc.). In the end, each individual test taker has a score for verbal and nonverbal performance and a full-scale IQ.

The only thing we have left to talk about regarding the Stanford-Binet (in our very brief overview) is how the test is administered. This is interesting because it provides a basis for how many types of intelligence tests are given.

What's the Score? Administering the Stanford-Binet (and Other Tests of Intelligence)

Think about how you might assess someone's level of intelligence, almost regardless of the different models of intelligence that we have discussed so far. One good way would be to find out which test items are the easiest and then begin to look at what the individual could do from that point forward. Then, find out which items become so difficult that it would not be wise to test any further. This range of difficulty helps define the starting and ending points in the scoring of performances on such tests as the Stanford-Binet.

What You See Is Not What You Get

Stephen Gould, the late and great Harvard historian of science and paleontologist, wrote a great book titled *The Mismeasure of Man*. His thesis is that IQ sores are a terrible tool for classifying people. One of his more acute examples is how World War II Eastern European immigrants were given IQ tests as they arrived in this country seeking political asylum. They failed in miserable numbers, and a large proportion were denied their freedom, sent back to their home countries, and died at the hands of brutal bullies. Why did so many fail? This is an easy one—they didn't speak English, the language of the tests! We'll talk much more about this issue in Chapter 19, but, for now, keep in mind that intelligence is as much about the test as it is about everyday human behavior.

The **basal age** is the lowest point on the test where the test taker can pass two consecutive terms that are of equal difficulty. The examiner knows that it is at this point where he or she can feel confident that the test taker is on firm ground and could pass all the items that are less difficult. Then, there's **ceiling age**, and this is the point where at least three out of four items are missed in succession. This is the point at which going any further would probably result in additional incorrect responses; in other words, the test taker's limit, and time to stop.

The number correct on the test is then used to compute a raw score, which is converted to a standardized score and then compared to other scores in the same age group. And because the Stanford-Binet is a standardized test and has had extensive norms established, such comparisons are a cinch to make and very useful.

AND THE FAB FIVE ARE . . .

There are many, many different types of intelligence tests ranging from those that you can find on the Internet and take for fun (no training needed, and you get what you pay for) to those that require years of training to administer and score successfully. In Table 16.1, we show the range of the latter kind—those that take training to learn how to administer and score, and those that have a strong theoretical background and utility in our testing world.

TABLE 16.1   A List of Five Widely Used Intelligence Tests

Title/Acronym (or What It's Often Called)	Purpose and What It Tests	Ages Tested	Conceptual Framework	What's Interesting to Note	Publisher (and Where You Can Get More Information If You Want It)
Wechsler Adult Intelligence Scale (WAIS)	The WAIS is designed to assess intellectual ability by testing verbal skills (vocabulary, similarities, arithmetic, digit span, information, comprehension, and letter-number sequencing) and performance (picture completion, digit symbol coding, block design, matrix reasoning, picture arrangement, symbol search, object assembly, and mazes). There is also a verbal comprehension index, a perceptual organization index, a working memory index, and a processing speed index.	Ages 16 through 89 years	Wechsler viewed intelligence as a merging of the general factor (g) that Spearman identified, coupled with distinct abilities. His practical emphasis was on the ability to act with a purpose in mind and to think in a logical manner.	1. The latest sample used for standardization matches 1995 census data with respect to gender, socioeconomic status, race and ethnicity, educational attainment, and geographical residence. 2. Oldest and most frequently used adult intelligence test. 3. David Wechsler, the author of the original test, studied with Simon (of the Simon-Binet Scale) in Paris, and some 30 years later, Wechsler started the development of his own test. 4. Based on a commonsense view of intelligence, where intelligent behavior is behavior that is adaptive and useful.	The Psychological Corporation 555 Academic Court San Antonio, TX 78204-2498 or http://www.psychcorp .com/.
Stanford-Binet Intelligence Scale (S-B)	The Stanford-Binet Intelligence Scale is designed as "an instrument for measuring cognitive abilities that provides the analysis of the pattern as well as the overall level of	The test is used with ages 2 years through adulthood	This most popular of all intelligence tests focuses on both verbal and nonverbal tests of intelligence.	1. Use of adaptive testing procedure, where test takers answer only those items whose difficulty is appropriate for their performance level. 2. Uses standard age scores for comparison between test takers.	The Riverside Publishing Co. 8420 Bryn Mawr Avenue Chicago, IL 60631 or http://www.riverpub.com/.

(Continued)

TABLE 16.1 (Continued)

Title/Acronym (or What It's Often Called)	Purpose and What It Tests	Ages Tested	Conceptual Framework	What's Interesting to Note	Publisher (and Where You Can Get More Information If You Want It)
	an individual's cognitive development." It provides 20 scores: Verbal Reasoning (Vocabulary, Comprehension, Absurdities, and Verbal Relations); Abstract-Visual Reasoning (Pattern Analysis, Copying, Matrices, and Paper Folding and Cutting); Quantitative Reasoning (Quantitative, Number Series, and Equation Building); Short-Term Memory (Bead Memory, Memory for Sentences, Memory for Digits, and Memory for Objects).			3. The vocabulary subtest is given first to help identify a starting place for other tests.	
Kaufman Assessment Battery for Children (K-ABC)	The K-ABC assesses cognitive development in 16 subtests: Magic Window, Face Recognition, Hand Movements, Gestalt Closure, Number Recall, Triangles, Word Order, Matrix Analogies, Spatial Memory, Photo Series, Expressive Vocabulary, Faces and Places, Arithmetic, Riddles, Reading-Decoding, and Reading Understanding.	Ages 2.5 to 12.5 years	Subtests are grouped into categories that require sequential processing of information and those that require simultaneous processing, with the test taker receiving separate global scores for each. This is basically an information-processing approach.	1. Nonverbal scale available for hearing impaired, speech and language disordered, and non-English speaking children ages 4–12½ years. One of the first tests to provide for these populations of children. 2. Lots of pictures and diagrams among the items. 3. Sociocultural norms for race and parental education were developed and can be used along with other norms. They can also help in scoring and interpretation.	American Guidance Service 4201 Woodland Road Circle Pines, MN 55014 or http://www.ags.com.

Title/Acronym (or What It's Often Called)	Purpose and What It Tests	Ages Tested	Conceptual Framework	What's Interesting to Note	Publisher (and Where You Can Get More Information If You Want It)
Slosson Full-Range Intelligence Test (S-FRIT)	As a quick estimate of general cognitive ability, the Slosson Full-Range Intelligence Test offers verbal, performance, and memory subtests, with the performance subtest divided into abstract and quantitative sections.	Ages 5 to 21 years	Items reflect a concentration on assessment of both crystallized and fluid intelligence.	1. Uses a picture book for some questions 2. Items are arranged in order of difficulty so examiner can get a very quick idea as to test taker's level of intelligence. 3. Often used as a brief intelligence assessment, then followed up by more extensive tests such as the WAIS.	Slosson Educational Publications, Inc. PO Box 280 East Aurora, NY 14052 or http://www.slosson.com/.
McCarthy Scales of Children's Abilities (MSCA)	The McCarthy Scales were developed to "determine . . . general intellectual level as well as strengths and weaknesses in important abilities." Scales tested (using 18 different subtests) are verbal, perceptual-performance, quantitative, composite, general cognitive, memory, and motor.	The test is used with children ages 2 years 4 months to 8 years 7 months.	McCarthy thought it very important to emphasize a test (and the items on it) construction that can identify clinical and educational weaknesses in the child.	1. Test materials include games and toys that help get children's interest and maintain their attention. 2. Good predictor of school achievement. 3. The MSCA is sometimes used as a screening test for readiness to enter a specific school grade.	The Psychological Corporation 555 Academic Court San Antonio, TX 78204-2498 or http://www.psychcorp .com/.

SUMMARY

Guess what? The He said-She said with which we opened the chapter has surely not been resolved; intelligence is still defined within the context of how it is being measured and probably always will be. But the problem there is that tests are defined to assess outcomes, not to define the outcomes themselves. Are we back to the beginning? Not quite. Through extensive research and test development, we know that people who score more highly on tests of intelligence are often more adaptive and generally can figure out how to solve problems and many other challenges that we face each day. That doesn't mean that your basic neighborhood genius can figure out how to start the car or that your basic neighborhood average fellow does not excel in his job. It just means that, in some ways, intelligence is a social construct into which tests provide only some insight.

TIME TO PRACTICE

1. Describe the behaviors of a person whom you think is very intelligent. Now describe the behaviors of a person whom you think is not very intelligent. (Stay away from any kind of physical characteristics such as gender and head size.) Now, how do these two people differ from one another, and is this enough information to start thinking about what you consider to be a definition of intelligence?

2. Given your definition of intelligence from #1 above, design what you think would be a terrific 5-item test of intelligence and provide a rationale for the items that you designed.

3. Using library resources and the Internet, find five different definitions of intelligence. It doesn't matter what the course is. Once you find them, determine what they might have in common with one another. What makes them different? Write one paragraph about how these similarities or differences would lead to different ways to measure intelligence.

4. When Howard Gardner first presented his theory of MI, there were only seven intelligences, and the eighth (natural intelligence) was added later. OK, now it's your turn. See if you can come up with a ninth, and provide a rationale for why it is different from the other eight.

5. Discuss your answer to the following question with your classmates. How has the change in how intelligence has been measured (from Spearman to Gardner) reflect the role we think intelligence plays in our everyday lives?

ANSWERS TO PRACTICE QUESTIONS

Sorry, folks. For this set of five—you're on your own. There are no right or wrong answers, only the fun of thinking about some very interesting topics.

WANT TO KNOW MORE?

Further Readings

- Campbell, L. (1997). Variations on a theme: How teachers interpret MI theory. *Educational Leadership, 55*(1), 14–19.

- Gould, S. J. (1993). *The mismeasure of man.* New York: Norton.

- Herrnstein, R. J., & Murray, C. (1994). The bell curve: Intelligence and class structure in American life. New York: Free Press.

- Lazear, D. (1992). *Teaching for multiple intelligences.* Bloomington, IN: Phi Delta Kappan Educational Foundation. (ERIC Document Reproduction Service No. ED 356 227) (highly recommended)

And on the Internet

- The Consortium for Research on Emotional Intelligence in Organizations shows the application of this model at http://www.eiconsortium.org/.

- Find out just about everything you ever wanted to know (and more) about human intelligence at Human Intelligence: Historical Influences, Current Controversies and Teaching Resources at http://www.indiana.edu/~intell/.

Career Choices

So You Want to Be a What?

Difficulty Index ☺☺☺☺ (moderately easy)

What's the one question that all the adults ask all the high school-age children at almost any family gathering?

So, what do you want to be when you grow up?

Some of these fine young people have some idea, most of them don't, and even those who do will be changing their minds many times before they settle on their first of several jobs or professions. And most interesting, it's not that much different for adults. Although many have positions for which they have trained for years and years (such as a physician or a lawyer), they, too, may change their employment focus and select another vocation depending on a variety of factors, including compensation, benefits, location, and the associated lifestyle that comes with this or that job.

So, any way we look at it from anyone's vantage point, young or old, male or female, white-collar worker or blue-collar worker, many, many more people change jobs throughout their employment career than keep the same one. And, with increased opportunities for technical and higher education, this is happening more than ever before.

This chapter is about how tests of vocational choice or career development can help people make decisions about jobs and job decisions more compatible with their likes and dislikes and their aspirations and goals. The end result may very well be people who are working more in an area they like and enjoy, and therefore are happier. And who could argue with that?

A Rose by Any Other Name

All of the information in this chapter falls under a very general category of vocational testing or assessment, but you might also see it called career development or employment evaluation. Whatever term is used, the theme is the same—help people better understand how their interests and personalities might best be matched up with a vocation or employment.

WHAT CAREER DEVELOPMENT TESTS DO

It's no surprise that career development is as much about what a person is as it is about what that person wants to do. Years of research in this area have verified that one's experience, values, and personality characteristics have a great deal to do with the choices that one makes regarding a career, and those factors have to be taken into account.

In fact, what vocational psychologists or career development psychologists would like to think is that they examine not only what people's interests are but also what it is that would provide individuals with a high level of job and (perhaps) life satisfaction.

So, it is not just that an individual takes the Strong Interest Inventory or the Campbell Interest and Skill Survey, and the test results come back and indicate that person is best suited to be a mechanic, a florist, or a physicist. Rather, the test scores reveal something about that person's interests and where he or she might best fit. But in conjunction with those test scores, there's another very important set of factors—including personality, values, and desires—that enters into the equation, and that's where a terrific career counselor can help. To quote a well-known career counselor and a leading vocational psychologist, Dr. Tom Kreishok, "The last thing about career counseling is the career—it's all about the person." Well said.

LET'S GET STARTED: THE STRONG INTEREST INVENTORY

One of the best examples of a vocational interest or career planning test is the Strong Interest Inventory (or SII), which is a direct outgrowth of the Strong Vocational Interest Blank (or SVIB).

Edward Strong was very clever in his design and development of the original SVIB in 1928, and it all started with his work in trying to place military people in suitable jobs. He thought that in order to get a good reflection of one's vocational interests, questions should be asked about how much the test taker likes or dislikes various occupations, areas of study, personality types, and leisure time activities. Then, he found out how people who are *currently* in certain occupational positions would have answered these very same questions. By empirically keying those answers (from folks already working) with the responses of the test takers, he could pretty well look for a fit between people and occupations. Is it perfect? No. Does it work pretty well? Yes.

Strong's early work is based on the assumption that the most successful people in an occupation have a certain profile of characteristics that reflects what it takes to be successful. If a test taker identifies with that profile, the likelihood is better than average that he or she will succeed in that profession as well.

The current edition of the SII consists of 317 items that are organized into seven different sections. The first five sections of the test ask test takers to indicate whether they like, dislike, or are indifferent to certain topics, occupations, or people characteristics. So, this part of the test might look something like this.

	Like	Dislike	Indifferent
Assertive people	—	—	—
Mathematics	—	—	—
Athletes	—	—	—
Psychology	—	—	—
Shy people	—	—	—
Fixing things	—	—	—

Once the test is scored (and this has to be done by the publisher), a long and detailed printout of the test taker's score and profile are available. Scores are assigned to each of six General Occupational Themes as follows:

- *Realistic.* These people prefer activities that are practical and hands-on and that result in tangible results, such as building, repairing, or fixing. Example vocations could be carpenter, roofer, builder, and carpet installer.

- *Investigative.* These people prefer to solve problems that involve science and engineering, and they enjoy challenging situations that demand intellectual activity. Example vocations could be chemist, biologist, engineer, and forensic scientist.

- *Artistic.* These people prefer activities that include the self-expression of ideas. Examples could include a musician or a film maker and activities such as creating or enjoying art.

- *Social.* These people like to help others and find themselves attracted to situations where social causes are important. Example vocations could include teachers, social workers, and psychologists.

- *Enterprising.* These people prefer activities that include self-management and leadership in addition to selling. Example vocations could be sales, management, and advertising.

- *Conventional.* These people like activities where structure and order are a part of the work world. Example vocations could include data analysis, secretaries, and accountants.

The results of the test identify the most prominent of the six different areas, some of the suggested professions in that area, and the knowledge and skills that are required as well as the tasks that are relevant to the occupations.

For example, partial report output would contain something like this:

Occupation	Knowledge or Skills	Tasks
Teacher	Child development for both normal and abnormal children, planning activities, methods of designing curricula, empathy	Teaching students, communicating with parents, working collaboratively with other teachers

And there would be several occupations listed for which one might be qualified and well worth considering.

It is these themes for which scores are assigned, and the profile of these scores reflect both the environment in which a person might work as well as a specific type of person. Then, it's just a matter of the scoring system matching up the test taker's profile with the extensive database of profiles for different occupations that the publisher has on hand.

JOHN HOLLAND AND THE SELF-DIRECTED SEARCH (SDS)

John Holland's six occupational themes turn up again and again in the literature on vocational testing, and for good reason. It is a very clearly thought-out, empirically validated foundation for assessing important clues to career development preferences. The Self-Directed Search (the popular test based on Holland's theory and framework) shows effectively how Holland's RIASEC model (for the first letter of each theme as you saw above in our discussion of Strong's test) can be incorporated. The test consists of 228 items.

What is perhaps most notable about this particular vocational interest test is that it was designed to be self-administered, self-scored, and self-interpreted—really taking this important area of assessment directly to the test taker.

In Figure 17.1, you can see how the different vocational themes can be organized to form a hexagon. These themes (also called *work personalities*) are not arranged in a willy-nilly fashion with any theme going anywhere. Rather, they are organized so that adjacent themes are similar to one another and opposite themes are dissimilar to one another. For example, in Holland's model, social and artistic occupations seem to have several things in common—that's why they are adjacent to one another. People who select a particular vocational track within either of those themes (such as a film maker—the artistic theme) might be comfortable in a vocation pointing toward another as well (such as a teacher—the social theme).

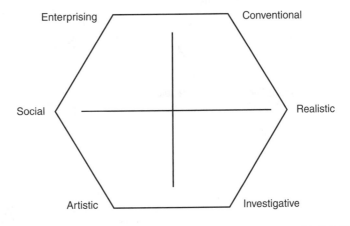

Figure 17.1 Holland's Six Vocational Themes and How They Work Together

Opposites Don't Attract

A good way to test Holland's model would be to see what the correlations (see Section 3 of Appendix A) are between adjacent and opposite occupational themes, right? Consider it done. Lenore Harmon and her colleagues did such and found that, indeed, the data support the theory. For example, there is a correlation between the adjacent Social and Enterprising occupation themes (r = .42), and the adjacent themes of Realistic and Investigative (r = .52), but none between the opposite occupational themes of Artistic and Conventional (r = −.04) or the themes of Realistic and Social (r = .06). It's very nice when ideas, such as Holland's model, are supported by real data!

Well, once Holland developed these themes, he could look at individuals in particular vocations, administer his test, and find out the pattern of themes for that vocation. And, the result is that individuals can be assigned a three-character code (called a Holland Code) that characterizes an individual's strengths relative to the descriptions within Holland's six different themes. For example, with a code of RES, you would most resemble the *Realistic* type, less resemble the *Enterprising* type, and even less resemble the *Social* type. If your code does not include a particular type, then it means that you resemble this type of person (who would be happy in a particular profession) least of all.

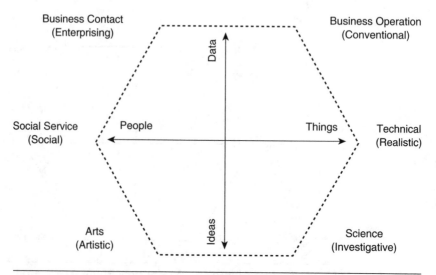

Figure 17.2 Holland Code Career Model

Holland (and his coauthors) have compiled a dictionary of these codes, the *Dictionary of Occupational Codes,* with more than 1,300 occupations from helicopter pilots (an RIS) to blood donor recruiters (an ESC) represented. Here's just a sample of the selection of codes and the accompanying and suggested occupations.

Occupation	First Theme	Second Theme	Third Theme
Director of a day care center (ESC)	Enterprising	Social	Conventional
Medical assistant (SCR)	Social	Conventional	Realistic
Director of nursing (SCE)	Social	Conventional	Enterprising
Tax preparer (CES)	Conventional	Enterprising	Social

Jobs, Jobs, and More Jobs

Want to find out all there is to know about jobs, what they pay, who's needed, and more? Visit the Department of Labor's Web site at http://www.dol.gov/ and visit the *Occupational Outlook Handbook,* where you can find out such neat things as the prospects for welders being very good with the salary at about $30,000 per year. If you're interested in being a physician, your salary can be tops (about $150,000 per year for a family practice physician), but the demand is just about average and the working conditions are very often much longer than that of other jobs. There is also an extensive research library at this site, as well as links to state and other federal agencies that deal with labor and work issues.

SOME MAJOR CAVEATS: CAREER COUNSELING 101

Here comes the buyer-beware commercial.

Richard Nelson Boles wrote the universe's best guide to career choices, how to make them, and so on. It's called *What Color is Your Parachute* (published by Ten Speed Press), and it is in its b-zillionth edition and you should get a copy right away—no matter where you are in your career path. This fellow is the guru of vocational counseling and has five interesting and important rules about taking any vocational tests.

First, not all tests are right for all people. Some people, in fact, hate tests altogether. So, the test itself has to be the kind in which the test taker is willing to invest the time and energy in order for the results to be useful.

THINGS TO REMEMBER

Just the thought of what profession is right for you probably creates some excitement, but some anxiety as well. Putting your trust in a test to help you determine that might be hard to do, but remember, as Boles says, that a test score is only one of many data points. Use all your resources to help you investigate and explore career opportunities.

Second, no test is *the* test for everyone. Some tests, because the format is better liked, perhaps, may provide different results from other tests (even when the same person takes both tests). It's a matter of everything from the type of test, the items, the format, and more. Career development isn't so finite a process that one test, not matter how good it is, will provide all the answers. So, should you take more than one vocational test? Sure—if you have the time and money, what could hurt?

Third, Boles believes what the great psychoanalyst Sigmund Freud said as well—when it comes to important decisions, trust your emotions. In Boles's case, he says to trust your intuition. No test will provide a definitive direction in which to go—only suggestions that you need to incorporate into your own wishes, desires, and life circumstances.

Fourth, you're the one, and there's no one like you. Even if you are an identical twin, your fingerprints are different (bet you didn't know that). So, when it comes to test scores, you may not be the only one to get that same score, but that's the only score you get—treat your unique qualities as important factors in consideration of the test profile that results from the testing.

Finally, test-schmest—it's only a score. There's a lot more to deciding on a career path or choosing one track over another than one score. The more you know about yourself, the more useful the test outcomes will be.

FIVE CAREER TESTS

Career and vocational tests really can help people identify themes in their work aspirations. These tests are not magic—they cannot identify exactly what it is people want to do professionally, but they can help. Look at the five tests in Table 17.1 and see how inclusive they are of so many different work themes and ideas that may be related to vocations. And, look at how different the audience is and the purpose of the test, from the very often-used Strong to the less often used, but interesting (often given to high school students), Armed Services-Civilian Vocational Interest Survey.

SUMMARY

If you think that human behavior is complicated, you're right. Just try to figure out what the different factors are that steer one person onto one career path and another person onto a completely different one. It's tough at best, but very clever vocational psychologists and career counselors recognize that career directions depend upon personality, values, interests, and other factors all working in tandem. And, these same people have developed a darn good set of tools that provides a reliable and valid assessment—a terrific starting point—of the possibilities that one should consider.

TIME TO PRACTICE

1. *This is gonna cost you.* Instead of that double latte cappuccino two times this week, take the $9.95 that you will save and go to http://www.self-directed-search.com/ and take the Self-Directed Search. It takes only 15 minutes, and you'll quickly get back an extensive report.

2. What is the general rationale that a developer of a vocational assessment tool might use, and why do you think it would work?

TABLE 17.1 A List of Five Widely Used Career Development Tests

Title/Acronym (or What It's Often Called)	Purpose and What It Tests	Grade Levels/ Ages Tested	Conceptual Framework	What's Interesting to Note	Publisher (and Where You Can Get More Information If You Want It)
Strong Interest Inventory (Strong or SII)	The Strong's purpose is to "identify general areas of interest as well as specific activities and occupations," and it provides scores on six general occupational themes—Realistic, Investigative, Artistic, Social, Enterprising, Conventional—plus Interest, Occupational, and Personal Style Scales.	Ages 16 through adult	Based on Holland's Occupational Themes	1. Men's form published and used since 1927; a women's form followed in 1933. 2. Uses a Personal Style Scale to get some indication of leadership style and ability to work with people.	Consulting Psychologists Press, Inc. 3803 E. Bayshore Rd. PO Box 10096 Palo Alto, CA 94303 or http://www.cpp.com/.
Self-Directed Search (SDS)	The SDS is a vocational inventory designed to identify "a person's particular activities, competencies, and self-estimates compared with various occupational groups."	Ages 12 through adult	The SDS is based on Holland's personality typology as it applies to vocational preferences. Here, people's vocational interests can be classified into the six categories of Realistic, Investigative, Artistic, Social, Enterprising, and Conventional.	1. Considers personality traits in decisions about how vocational choices are made. 2. Loads of foreign translations, including Chinese, Finnish, French, and Greek. 3. Braille editions available.	Psychological Assessment Resources, Inc. PO Box 998 Odessa, FL 33556 or http://www.parinc.com

Title/Acronym (or What It's Often Called)	Purpose and What It Tests	Grade Levels/ Ages Tested	Conceptual Framework	What's Interesting to Note	Publisher (and Where You Can Get More Information If You Want It)
Kuder Occupational Interest Survey (KOIS)	The KOIS assesses "promising occupations and college majors in rank order, based on examinee's interest pattern" and yields information on four scales—Dependability, Vocational Interest Estimates, Occupations, and College Majors.	Grade 10 through adult	The KOIS measures interest in careers that require advanced technical or college training and is based on Holland's model of six personality factors. The belief is that personality factors are related to job interest.	1. Test takers are presented with 100 triads of activities and asked to select the activity they like the most and the activity they like the least. 2. An audiotape is available to help users interpret results of the KOIS. 3. There are (yikes) 119 occupational scales, 48 college major scales, plus the 10 traditional Kuder generic interest scales.	National Career Assessment Services, Inc. 601 Visions Parkway PO Box 277 Adel, IA 50003 or http://www.ncasi.com/.
Armed Services-Civilian Vocational Interest Survey (ASVIS)	The test taker organizes interests and makes career decisions about military and civilian jobs in the following eight occupational groups: administrative-clerical personnel, communications, computer and data-processing, construction-engineering-craft, mechanical-repairer-machining, service and transportation, health and health care, scientific-technical-electronic.	High school through adult	The rationale for the test design is that the objectives are based on the predictive validity of interests in future job satisfaction in those jobs.	1. Self-administering, self-assessing, and self-scoring. 2. Used to help explore the overlap between civilian and military jobs.	CFKR Career Materials Inc. PO Box 437 Meadow Vista, CA 95722

(Continued)

TABLE 17.1 (Continued)

Title/Acronym (or What It's Often Called)	Purpose and What It Tests	Grade Levels/ Ages Tested	Conceptual Framework	What's Interesting to Note	Publisher (and Where You Can Get More Information If You Want It)
Campbell Interest and Skill Survey (CISS)	The CISS "measures self-reported interests and skills" yielding 99 scores in the categories of orientation (such as organizing and helping), basic (such as leadership and sales), occupational (such as hotel manager and ski instructor), and special and procedural scales.	Ages 15 years through adult	Primarily, the CISS focuses on the importance of self-reported interests and self-reported skills, both thought to be important to an individual's career planning.	1. Contains 200 interest items (test takers rate their interest) and 120 skill items (test takers rate their skill). 2. CISS Special Scales include interest and skill scores for academic focus, extraversion, and the variety of the test taker's interests and skills. 3. Test results make up a CISS Profile, a comprehensive, computer-generated report.	Pearson Assessments 5601 Green Valley Drive Bloomington, MN 55437 or http://www.pearson assessments.com/.

3. Check off which of the six Holland occupation themes characterizes each of these occupations. You may want to go back and look at their descriptions, which were presented earlier in the chapter.

Occupation ↓	Check Off the Occupational Theme					
	Realistic	Investigative	Artistic	Social	Enterprising	Conventional
Educational programming director	____	____	____	____	____	____
Golf club manager	____	____	____	____	____	____
Paralegal	____	____	____	____	____	____
Lathe operator	____	____	____	____	____	____
Airplane flight attendant	____	____	____	____	____	____

4. Now that you have done #3 above and know the correct answers, write a one- or two-sentence description as to why a lathe operator should be an RCE and a paralegal an SEC.

5. Identify 10 people you know pretty well, be they friends, parents, or other relatives, and identify what they do for a living (try to select someone other than fellow students). How well do you think that their professional activity reflects their personal characteristics? In other words, intuitively, how well do you think Holland's system works?

ANSWERS TO PRACTICE QUESTIONS

1. Hope you had fun. Now be sure to review the five caveats we mentioned by Richard Boles at the end of this chapter when you read the SDS report and think about the results.

2. Here's the idea. There are people who have been in occupations who have certain traits and characteristics and also like a particular environment in which to work (at home, on the road, etc.). If one could find out what those characteristics and preferences are within each occupation, then one may be able to match those characteristics in other people who are not yet employed, but show an interest, in a particular area or activity.

3. Here are the Holland Codes.

Occupation ↓	Check Off the Occupational Theme					
	Realistic	Investigative	Artistic	Social	Enterprising	Conventional
Educational programming director	___	___	___	2	1	3
Golf club manager	___	___	___	3	1	2
Paralegal	___	___	___	1	2	3
Lathe operator	1	___	___	___	3	2
Airplane flight attendant	___	___	3	2	1	___

4. Be sure to consider the type of person who might take such a job and why. For example, it should not be any surprise that the first occupational theme for a golf club manager is enterprising—that's his or her job—to generate business and manage others.

5. On your own, and this question is easiest to answer if you select from a wide group of people you know who participate in a diverse group of professional activities.

WANT TO KNOW MORE?

Further Readings

- Gottfredson, G. D., & Holland, J. L. (1996). *Dictionary of Holland occupational codes* (3rd ed.). Lutz, FL: Psychological Assessment Resources.

- Harmon, L. W., Hanson, J. C., Borgen, F. H., & Hammer, A. L. (1994). Strong Interest Inventory: Applications and technical guide. Stanford, CA: Stanford University Press.

And on the Internet

- The National Career Development Association at http://www.ncda.org/ promotes career development across the life span and does this by providing lots of professional materials, information, and assistance to career development professionals.

- The Job Hunter's Bible at http://www.jobhuntersbible.com/counseling/ctests.shtml offers some great advice (see the box in this chapter) and also some links to online vocational interest tests that are free or darn cheap, such as the Princeton Review Career Quiz (at http://www.princetonreview.com/cte/quiz/default.asp?menuID=0&careers=6) or the Holland Self-Directed Search (at http://www.self-directed-search.com).

PART V

It's Not Always As You Think: Issues in Tests and Measurement

Snapshots

O K—here come the big ones. This part is full of ideas that are controversial, are discussed endlessly, and suggest questions that have no easy answers. Think that we can just give a test and leave it at that? Sure, if the test (and even this is big, perhaps) is a 7th-grade spelling test. Once we get into personality and intelligence assessments, and even vocational and career development tests, we're in new territory because there are so many implications for even the *act* of assessment, let alone what the scores mean. Test bias and test fairness (the focus of Chapter 18) rear their ugly heads, and we can be in trouble if we're not careful with the way we design and use these powerful tools.

The test bias and fairness questions are multidimensional and full of everything from parental concerns to politics. But politics becomes even a more essential consideration when we talk about policies and laws that govern testing practices such as the **No Child Left Behind Act.** Passed in 2002, this federal law requires that all children make progress in every grade. Read about it and other legal topics related to testing in Chapter 19, and know about it, because it is surely going to have an impact on whatever you do.

18 Test Bias

Fair for Everyone?

Difficulty Index ☺☺ (something to think hard about)

Here's what we know—tests are not uniformly fair and just, and, in many cases, they are downright unfair. Here's what we don't know—how to make them better (or more fair). You know a good deal about tests and measurement (see the past 17 chapters), and you now need to learn a bit more about how a test can be biased (and how that differs from being unfair) and what you can do to reduce bias and make the test as fair as possible. Read on.

THE $64,000 QUESTION: WHAT IS TEST BIAS?

This is the $64,000 question, because the definition of test bias gives us a clue as to how it might be remedied. Unfortunately, the definitions are complex and introduce factors that are often very difficult to deal with in a complex society such as ours.

TECH TALK

Adapting Testing

There's something relatively new on the scene called Adaptive Testing or Computer Adaptive Testing (or CAT). This technique uses computers (duh) and adjusts the difficulty of items based on the test taker's ongoing performance. In other words, based on the previous items that the test taker has gotten right or wrong, the CAT program will choose subsequent items to maximize efficiency and get closer to (guess what?) the test taker's true score (the goal of all tests, right?).

This fits very closely with the idea of item response theory and most closely reveals the test taker's true ability. Here's how it works according to Lawrence Rudner and his terrific CAT tutorial at http://edres.org/scripts/cat/catdemo.htm.

First, all the test items are evaluated to determine which one is the best "next" one given the test taker's performance up to that point.

Second, the best next item is administered.

Third, the computer program estimates a new ability level based on the test taker's responses to all of the administered items.

The goal—to get as close as possible to the test taker's true score, thereby producing more reliable (and more valid) assessments.

Let's look at a combination of many different definitions to give us a flavor for what we are dealing with. In the most simple form, **test bias** occurs when test scores vary across different groups because of factors that are unrelated to the purpose of the test. For example, if we are administering an intelligence test to both males and females and there is a systematic difference in test scores as a function of gender, the test could very well be biased.

Another way to say the same thing is that if one predicts test score based on group membership, then the observed score will either over- or underestimate the test taker's true score (remember that from Chapter 3?). If this happens consistently for members of a given group, this is evidence of test bias.

But in our example, why isn't the difference in scores just a "true" function of gender? That is, males and females really do differ. Well, then, the underlying theory and construct of intelligence on which the test is based would state explicitly that the gender difference is expected. It's either the test is really biased, or the test detects real differences between groups. Which explanation is true (bias or true differences) is a really tough call to make and requires lots and lots of empirical investigation.

Test Bias or Test Fairness?

So far, we've talked a bit about test bias and how it is present when a test differentially favors one group over another. But test fairness is another story, one that we should introduce to you as well.

Test fairness touches on the very sensitive issue of the use of tests and the social values that underlie such usage. Whereas test bias is the result of an analysis that any of us can learn to apply, fairness is a question of values and judgment—both topics that most of us have to think long and hard about until we think we are doing the right thing. In other words, just because you can distinguish between adults who are "smart" and those who are "not so smart" (and do it in an unbiased manner) does not mean that the judgments made based on these results provide a valid basis for placing people in different social categories or imposing interventions and all the implications that result, such as employment and social opportunities and so on.

THINGS TO REMEMBER

Both test bias and test fairness stand as important issues, but they are closely related as well. Tests need to be unbiased in that they validly assess some outcome, but they have to be fair as well in their use, and the interpretation of their results should further society's goals.

For example, let's say that you are the admissions officer for a college and you use a set of selection criteria such as SAT scores, the number of hours of extracurricular activities in which applicants have participated, or even if applicants can afford to pay school costs. You want to be darn sure that there is some philosophy or set of value-based rules that underlies your model of how this admissions information will be used. And, this philosophy should be written down and explicit so anyone can read and understand it. For example, you may deem that SAT scores are important but will count for only 25% of the weight in determining if someone is admitted. Or, you may deem that ability to pay is irrelevant or that cumulative high school GPA is important. And, of course, you have to state why. Why should SAT scores count for only 25%? Why not more? Why not less?

We studied validity in many different places so far throughout this book, and you can always think of a valid test (and the many ideas that are conveyed) as the gold standard—the goal we seek in our development and use of tests.

Indeed, a valid test should be both unbiased and fair. And Samuel Messick takes our conventional definitions of validity and extends them one step further to what he calls consequential validity. **Consequential validity** is a simple and elegant idea. We need to be concerned about how tests are used and how their results are interpreted. We worry about construct validity and whether a test does what it is supposed to, but we often forget about why we are using a test in the first place, the importance of how we interpret scores, and the consequences of this or that interpretation.

Don't ever take any of this test fairness stuff lightly. Whether you're a teacher, administrator, public health official, or law enforcement officer, you administer the test and are in control of how the results are used and interpreted.

Proceed with caution.

MOVING TOWARD FAIR TESTS: THE FAIRTEST MOVEMENT

Plenty of people are dissatisfied with the "business" of test administration and want the way tests are designed and administered, and the way test scores are interpreted, to change radically—all in an effort to reduce bias due to gender, class, culture, or any other factor that results in invalid test scores and in the inappropriate use of them as well.

One group, the National Center for Fair and Open Testing (FairTest), is an organization that "works to end the misuses and flaws of standardized testing and to insure that evaluation of students, teachers and schools is fair, open, valid and educationally beneficial." Who could argue with that?

But, indeed, there have been plenty of arguments, even with the basic principles that FairTest espouses (and these are their exact words):

1. *Assessments should be fair and valid.* They should provide equal opportunity to measure what students know and can do, without bias against individuals on the bases of race, ethnicity, gender, income level, learning style, disability, or limited English proficiency status.

2. *Assessments should be open.* The public should have greater access to tests and testing data, including evidence of validity

and reliability. Where assessments have significant consequences, tests and test results should be open to parents, educators, and students.

3. *Tests should be used appropriately.* Safeguards must be established to ensure that standardized test scores are not the sole criterion by which major educational decisions are made and that curricula are not driven by standardized testing.

4. *Evaluation of students and schools should consist of multiple types of assessment conducted over time.* No one measure can or should define a person's knowledge, worth, or academic achievement, nor can it provide for an adequate evaluation of an institution.

5. *Alternative assessments should be used.* Methods of evaluation that fairly and accurately diagnose the strengths and weaknesses of students and programs need to be designed and implemented with sufficient professional development for educators to use them well.

These are lofty goals, and even if, at times, they are very difficult to reach, they are well worth striving for.

MODELS OF TEST BIAS

Now that we have a working definition of test bias, let's extend that discussion a bit and examine what models or frameworks have been presented that elaborate on this basic definition.

The Difference-Difference Bias

Well, this is surely the most obvious one, but one most fraught with some very basic problems. This model says that if two groups differ on some factor obviously unrelated to the test, such as race, gender, racial or ethnic group membership, or political affiliation (you get the idea), then the test is biased.

Now, what's good about this model is that the assumption might be correct, and it is surely a simple way to look at things. For example, scores on a particular intelligence test may indeed reveal a difference between males and females, and maybe that is a result of test bias. But, here's the problem with this line of thinking—maybe the difference it reflects is *real,* and there's no bias whatsoever. Wow—so much for test bias, right?

Let's take another example—a difference in achievement test scores between two different racial groups. Now, maybe these two groups got different training, their teachers had different expectations, and so on. So, the differences do not reflect a bias in the test or the trait or characteristics of ability being measured, but, rather, they reflect the circumstances under which these children were educated or raised, or a set of different expectations.

So differences in performance are useful to note, and it's even more useful to find out the source of these differences. But claiming that a difference in performance is the result of a test's bias (not knowing that the test is biased) has no more basis in fact than claiming that the groups were differentially prepared to take the test. This is not easy stuff, especially when we recognize that testing and assessment are a multibillion-dollar industry that affects almost everyone in one way or another.

Item by Item

Here's a step in the right direction given what we just said above about differences in group scores.

Instead of looking at overall group performance, perhaps an analysis should be done on an item-by-item basis where group performance is examined for each item and any discrepancies studied further. If students from different groups, say, males and females, perform differently on an item that requires thinking at the synthesis level (remember Bloom's taxonomy from Chapter 13?), then perhaps that item is biased. But do keep in mind the same caveat as for the difference idea above—different performances on any one item can be due to differences in true ability or a host of other factors.

On the Face of Things

Remember content or face validity, which was discussed in Chapter 4? This type of validity judges the face value of particular items and usually uses an expert judge to make a determination.

It can be the same with test items where biased items misrepresent ethnic groups, age groups, and gender characteristics. For example, what about a set of pictorial items that shows only white people as examples? That has nothing to do with the test items per se, but it sure sends a message that nonwhite test takers don't exactly identify with the folks in the illustration. Or, what about the use of stereotyped language, such as reading comprehension passages that characterize men in certain occupations and women in others? Not good.

The Cleary Model

Here's an alternative model that makes a bunch more sense than the previous ones we discussed.

Way back in 1968, T. Anne Cleary defined test bias as a test that measures different things for different people. She devised a somewhat elaborate regression model to show this, but the fundamental assumption is that people with the same test scores (such as on the SAT) should do equally well when related to some external criterion (such as first-year scores in college). So, if a test is not biased, then, for example, both black and white students' SAT scores should predict equally well their first-year college scores. This is a regression model (a more advanced form of correlations), and it's a pretty cool way to examine test bias.

The key here is to look at what predicts test outcomes and make sure that the prediction holds true under different circumstances.

Having Fun Yet?

Here's an attempt to highlight the issue of test bias and to point out how challenging it actually is to complete test items when they are drawn from another culture. The *Chitling Test of Intelligence* uses black-ghetto experiences as the basis for a test and tries to show the cultural bias found in many IQ tests. This test was designed by Adrian Dove, a black sociologist and shows exactly how dangerous it is to assume that the majority culture has ownership of what is "intelligent." Take a look at five of the 30 items, shown here:

1. A "handkerchief head" is:

   (a) a cool cat, (b) a porter, (c) an Uncle Tom, (d) a hoddi, (e) a preacher.

2. "Hully Gully" came from:

   (a) East Oakland, (b) Fillmore, (c) Watts, (d) Harlem, (e) Motor City.

3. If you throw the dice and 7 is showing on the top, what is facing down?

   (a) 7, (b) snake eyes, (c) boxcars, (d) little Joes, (e) 11.

4. Hattie Mae Johnson is on the County. She has four children and her husband is now in jail for non-support, as he was unemployed and was not able to give her any money. Her welfare check is now $286 per month. Last night she went out with the highest player in town. If she got pregnant, then nine months from now how much more will her welfare check be?

   (a) $80, (b) $2, (c) $35, (d) $150, (e) $100.

5. Many people say that "Juneteenth" (June 19) should be made a legal holiday because this was the day when:

   (a) the slaves were freed in the USA, (b) the slaves were freed in Texas, (c) the slaves were freed in Jamaica, (d) the slaves were freed in California, (e) Martin Luther King was born, (f) Booker T. Washington died.

And the answers are 1(c), 2(c), 3(a), 4(a), and 5(b). How'd you do? Want to see how well you would do on the entire 30-item test? Go to http://www.wilderdom.com/personality/intelligenceChitling TestShort.html and have some fun, but, beware, this sociologist is making a very important point: What's intelligent for you might not be for others.

Playing Fair

It's really not hard to inadvertently create items or tests that are biased. In fact, because we all have our own stereotypes, they can sneak pretty easily into any test that we devise or prevent us from seeing clearly how another test might be biased.

So, here's our handy-dandy four-step procedure to ensure that the test you create and the test that you use as created by others are not biased.

1. First, in the development phase, *try to be clear as possible in recognizing your own biases or stereotypes* when it comes to different groups of people (be they different because of race, gender, ability, rival high school—whatever). Know the sample of test takers with which you are going to be working, and make every effort to eliminate your own biases from the design of items and tests.

THINGS TO REMEMBER

 Recall that quote about throwing stones and living in a glass house? As a test designer, giver, or scorer, the more you know about your own biases and prejudices (and yes, we all have them), the more fair you can be and the more aware you are of the impact your own beliefs have on your evaluations and assessments.

2. If in doubt (and we should all have doubt about test bias to some extent), *show it to a buddy who may belong to the very group you feel might be slighted.* Don't think that the description of women is fair on the aptitude test you are about to administer? Ask a female colleague for her judgment.

3. *If, at any time, you find your own test development efforts to be short on being unbiased, stop and start over, asking for help from someone more experienced than you.* If you find that you are using a commercial or standardized test, write to the publisher. Any good publisher welcomes such feedback because their primary aim is to please their consumers (you) and to develop a test that is as unbiased as possible.

4. *Test takers are different from one another, not only in their ability or personality, but in the way they learn* and what form of assessment is most accurate for any one individual. Is a written test unfair to a learner whose strength is in aural learning? We would not expect a blind student to read items, right? Any test that would demand such would be biased

and unfair, and you would be particular insensitive to administer such. But there would probably not be any problem presenting the test orally and allowing the student to type or use some type of assistive device.

Where It All Started: Test Differences Between Black and White American Children

Everything about the American system of justice and politics screams for the equal treatment of people, right? It's codified in our laws and even in the ethics we espouse. So, we expect that, given no other circumstances to the contrary, people are equal—in their value, performance, potential, and unique contributions.

Imagine the controversy that evolved when, during the 1960s and 1970s, it was reported that black children scored about 15 points lower than white children on standardized tests for intelligence. When such important factors as social class and social status are factored in, then the difference is reduced to about 5 to 7 points. All of this has been documented over and over again, so most believe that the data are trustworthy and accurate—although that says nothing about whether the difference is as trustworthy and accurate, and what that difference might mean.

And, is it possible to separate the biology of race from the conditions of culture and such—a very difficult question to frame correctly, let alone answer? This question is the big Kahuna—and there's no getting around it being in the face of every test company that proposes to measure something that has even the slightest relationship to social class, economics, or group membership—any source of bias. Although we are doing better as test designers, test givers, and test scorers—we are still stuck, giving tests that are biased and that treat people from different groups differently. And, there may well be no solution in the design and administration of the test but only in our awareness of how to analyze and interpret the test score (and pay attention to consequential validity).

Explanations? There are plenty, including test bias (of course), although many studies have not satisfactorily proved this to be the case; genetic differences (very, very complicated and complex to study); and environmental factors—just about every factor and combination of factors you can imagine.

One interesting hypothesis has been put forth by George Farkas from Penn State University—he calls it *talk deficit*. He summarizes research that shows that parents' verbal interactions with their preschool children account for much of the early test score differences between children of different social class and racial backgrounds. He contends that to reduce this gap, increased verbal interaction between parents and children has to begin very early and be addressed consistently. He bases his thesis on the premise that higher test scores are associated with greater verbal skills, and that the more parents verbally interact with their children, the better the children's verbal skills and the higher their test scores.

Our advice? Strive to create tests that are as unbiased and fair as possible—it's unlikely that a test of anything is fair to all cultures under all circumstances. But, if nothing else, test bias and test fairness have to be part of every test-related discussion.

This is a huge topic and one that exemplifies almost all of the issues in dealing with questions of bias and fairness.

SUMMARY

Test bias and test fairness are surely not easy topics to deal with, but they have to be confronted if our practice of testing (on the increase, for sure) is going to mean anything and be used for the common good. As a practitioner or researcher, you're on the front lines of this discussion and really have to think about and take all that we have said into account.

TIME TO PRACTICE

1. Along with three of your classmates or colleagues, create a five-question test that is as biased as you can possibly make it. Be sure that you ask another four members of your class to do the same, or perhaps the entire class can be divided into such groups. Once you are done, trade questions with another group and answer the following questions:
   a. Most important, what personal stereotypes or personal biases may have been operating when the questions were constructed?
   b. Why are the test questions you are examining biased?
   c. Is it possible to change them to be less biased or unbiased?

2. What is the difference between test bias and test fairness?

3. What's the difference model of test bias, and what's wrong with it?

4. List five social implications for the use of biased tests.

5. Is a culturally fair or unbiased test of *anything* possible?

ANSWERS TO PRACTICE QUESTIONS

1. You're on your own for these, but try to examine the questions that are created very carefully, and, in doing so, learn how to avoid as much bias in item construction and administration as possible.

2. Test bias has to do with the differential performance of groups on a test as a function of characteristics unrelated to the concepts or ideas being tested, such as race, gender, and social class. Test fairness has to do with the utility and application of testing and test results—a question of values.

3. The difference model of test bias says that when there is a difference between groups in their scores on a test, it is a function of group differences based on some characteristic, such as gender. The problem with this model is that the group membership variable may very well be the reason for the difference!

4. Here are five starters:
   a. Unfair hiring practices
   b. Inaccurate test results
   c. Inaccurate placement of individuals in groups
   d. Inadequate screening
   e. Inappropriate diagnoses

5. We'll leave this tough one to you and your teacher and classmates. Our answer could be "Yes, but . . ."

WANT TO KNOW MORE?

Further Readings

- Herrnstein, R., & Murray, C. (1994). *The bell curve: Intelligence and class structure in American life.* New York: Free Press.

  This is one of the books that started the heated discussion that still continues about race and intelligence. This is a hornet's nest of a book that has stimulated countless useful, and useless, discussions.

- Gould, S. J. (1996). *The mismeasure of man* (rev. ed.). New York: Norton.

  A cogent, well-written, and engaging response to *The Bell Curve* (see above).

And on the Internet

- The Chitling Test too easy (or too hard) for you? Try the 10-item Original Australian Intelligence Test, which is based on the culture of the Edward River Australian Aboriginal community in North Queensland. You can find it at http://www.wilderdom .com/personality/intelligenceOriginalAustralian.html. Have fun!

- The National Center for Fair and Open Testing (or FairTest) at http://www.fairtest.org/index.htm contains oodles of information about testing bias and the many different projects in which FairTest is currently involved, including misuse of the SAT and ACT tests and the improvement of student assessment.

19

The Law, Testing, and Ethics

No Child (Should Be) Left Behind and Other Concerns

Difficulty Index ☺☺☺ (moderately easy and provocative as well)

I f you create, administer, or score tests; or you interpret test scores; or you are a butcher, a baker, or a candlestick maker; or a doctor, a police officer, or a teacher—you need to know about the legal aspects of testing and assessment.

This chapter will introduce you to major legislation and policies that affect the use of tests in our society. Any one of these topics deserves hundreds of pages of detailed examination and lots of discussion. We don't have the room here for the detailed examination, but it's critical for you to at least know what these laws are and what policies they include.

NO CHILD LEFT BEHIND OR NCLB: WHAT IT IS AND HOW IT WORKS

The purpose of the **No Child Left Behind Act** of 2001 (also called NCLB, which is based on the Elementary and Secondary Education Act of 1965) is "to close the achievement gap with accountability, flexibility, and choice, so that no child is left behind." Sounds good, and no one would object to this end, but, as always, the devil is in the details. And, there are tons of details.

You can get some idea of how extensive and ambitious this 600+-page bill is (as is almost any legislation at the federal level) by looking at the names of the ten "titles," all of which deal with some aspect of education as follows:

- Title I deals with improving the academic achievement of the disadvantaged.

- Title II deals with preparing, training, and recruiting high-quality teachers and principals.

- Title III focuses on language instruction for limited English proficient and immigrant students.

- Title IV focuses on 21st-century schools (dealing with everything from guns to parental consent).

- Title V promotes parental choice and innovative programs.

- Title VI discusses flexibility and accountability.

- Title VII focuses on Indian, Native Hawaiian, and Alaska Native education.

- Title VIII deals with aid programs.

- Title IX deals with general provisions.

- Title X (finally) deals with amendments to other statutes.

No Child Left Unrecruited

Want to know, in part, why NCLB is such a controversial law? It contains a provision that requires public secondary schools to provide military recruiters with contact information for every student as well as access to the school. Parents of individual students can choose not to participate. If the school, however, does not comply, it faces having its federal aid eliminated. All laws contain sections that may seem unrelated to the title and primary intent of the law itself—one of the reasons why legislation is often so hotly contested every step of the way.

How Testing Fits in

NCLB has as a primary mission the assurance that all children (and it really is all) will meet or exceed their state's level of academic achievement on the state assessments. So, in order to meet this requirement (and to not meet it in theory can lead to losing federal funds), there has to be a huge amount of testing that occurs on a regular basis—just think of every student in every public school in the United States being tested across math and reading (and other subjects in the future), which began in the 2005–2006 school year. It's staggering. And, these subjects must be taught by "highly qualified" teachers who must be "certified" by the state. Also sounds good, but what's "highly" mean? And, how are teachers certified?

Here's the schedule of some other NCLB events or milestones:

- The math and reading assessment starts in the 2005–2006 academic year for Grades 3–8, but students in Grades 10–12 have to be tested as well, as part of an earlier law.

- By the 2007–2008 school year, assessment of science is to begin for Grades 3–5, 6–9, and 10–12.

- All students, and that means all students, must participate, including students with disabilities and those who have limited English proficiency. Test scores have to be reported and broken down by race and income to measure progress and gaps among certain groups.

- And, the way that schools will be judged successful is based on the results of these testings.

The final goal? All students are at academic proficiency by the end of the 2013–2014 school year.

As you might expect, the major problem with these requirements is that they are very expensive to implement. Testing is very expensive (the State of Kansas spends well over $5 million each year), as is the training and hiring of only "highly qualified" teachers. The testing that is done, also, is not diagnostic in nature, leading to remedial actions, but rather solely a summative assessment indicating a child's position relative to his or her peers. The price tag for this and many more provisions is so staggeringly high that state legislators complained to the federal government, and several requirements of the law have been relaxed. For example, rural school districts need not meet the "highly qualified" teacher requirement in every room until 2007.

What's Assessed and How

All this talk about assessment is fine but of not much value unless we have some standards to use to assess outcomes. Even if children are tested in math and reading each year, it's pretty important to know what a state department of education means when its representatives say that a child or a class or a school system has met the "standards." So, each state must do the following:

- Show that it has adopted academic standards that will be used by the state, local educational agencies, and schools to gauge student achievement.

- Apply the same standards to all schools and children in the state.

- Set these academic standards for all subjects as identified by the state. The standards have to include mathematics, reading or language arts, and science (later on).

NCLB: Want to See Something Dramatic?

The feds aren't messing around with the NCLB bill. States really are supposed to identify which schools are meeting standards and which are not, and many of the states publicize which schools do and don't make it. Take Connecticut, for example. They published (for the 2001 school year) their list of the 149 schools that need to make more progress (and you can find it at http://www.cbia.com/ed/NCLB/zpdf/schoolstoimprove.pdf). You can imagine how difficult it is for teachers, students, and their families to be singled out. But it is the law.

What's the Big Deal About NCLB?

Here's the big deal. For all kinds of reasons, the NCLB law is proving very difficult to adhere to and maybe even impossible to manage. Here are some (and there are plenty) of the objections:

1. The bill calls for all students to be tested, meaning that children even of low proficiency in English and with significant disabilities are expected to perform at grade level. Their scores, like everyone's, are averaged to produce an indicator of how well the school system has done. Comparing schools and, of course, school districts becomes untenable because of the lack of comparability of the school populations. The "one-size-fits-all" notion is not reasonable.

2. Only public schools are expected to meet these standards. Both private schools and charter schools are not, leading advocates for other than private schools to gain some political advantage over those public schools who don't make the grade.

3. The bill has never been funded at the levels proposed by the federal government, leading to shortages in teachers and training to make those who are not highly qualified, as dictated by the law. Lack of funds also prevents the use of standardized tests (which are very expensive) to chart progress.

4. There are no rewards for doing well, only sanctions for not.

5. What constitutes a "highly qualified" teacher is open to discussion. And, even if the school districts know, such teachers are very expensive (they are usually senior faculty). Training good teachers to be better is also expensive.

THE EDUCATION FOR ALL HANDICAPPED CHILDREN ACT AND THE INDIVIDUALS WITH DISABILITIES EDUCATION ACT: WHAT THEY ARE AND HOW THEY WORK

In 1975, President Gerald Ford signed into law Public Law 94-142, known as the **Education of Handicapped Children Act**. The law is a statement of affirmation that special needs children have the right to a free and appropriate public education in the **least restrictive environment** (often referred to as LRE). In many ways, it was as much a move toward the civil rights of children with special needs as the passage of the Civil Rights Act some 10 years earlier.

The four purposes of PL 94-142 were as follows (straight from the *Education for All Handicapped Children's Act of 1975*):

- "Assure that all children with disabilities have available to them . . . a free appropriate public education which emphasizes special education and related services designed to meet their unique needs"

- "assure that the rights of children with disabilities and their parents . . . are protected"

- "to assist States and localities to provide for the education of all children with disabilities," and

- "to assess and assure the effectiveness of efforts to educate all children with disabilities"

The law was amended in 1997 and is known as the **Individuals With Disabilities Education Act** or IDEA.

Why such a law? To begin with, more than 10 million children in the United States today have a variety of special needs—from mildly to severely handicapped—and traditional special education programs were not meeting their needs. In many cases, these programs were not providing *any* educational experience. And as you might expect, in order for us to evaluate whether these children are receiving the services they need, a great deal of assessment needs to be undertaken—hence, the importance of knowing about these laws for those of us who study tests and measurement.

And has it worked? You bet. Almost 200,000 infants and toddlers and their families, and nearly 6 million children and youth, receive special education and related services to meet their individual needs; these numbers were very low prior to the enactment of PL 94-142. Also, more children attend school in their neighborhood rather than in special schools or institutions (both of which are very expensive propositions), and high school graduation rates and post-secondary school enrollment are up as well. In other words, people who might not have had a chance at a fully integrated public life now have the opportunity.

What IDEA Does

IDEA has six principles, each of which is codified as law, and school districts are required to attend to them in the administration of educational programs.

First, all children are entitled to a free and appropriate public education. This means that special education and related services will be provided without any charge to the parents at public expense, and these services will meet standards set by the state and suit the individual needs of the child.

Second, evaluations and assessments will take place only to the extent that they help place the child in the correct program and measure his or her progress. The people doing the evaluations must be knowledgeable and trained, procedures for assessment must be consistent with the child's levels of skill (remember our discussion about bias), and tests must be as nondiscriminatory and unbiased as possible. In other words, visually impaired children should not be required to read, and children with physical handicaps should not be required to manipulate objects if they cannot. The message? Find another way.

Third, an **Individualized Education Program** (IEP) will be developed and adhered to for each child. These written plans for children will be revised regularly and include input from parents, students, teachers, and other important interested parties.

Fourth, children with disabilities will be educated in what is called a least restrictive environment. This means they take classes with their nondisabled peers, and only those children who cannot be educated in regular education in a satisfactory fashion should be removed.

Fifth, both students and parents play a prominent role in the decision-making process. The more involved both parties are, usually, the better the decisions. Both should have input into the creation of the IEP, the parents should help educate the school personnel about their child, and the child can help express his or her needs.

Finally, there should be a variety of mechanisms to ensure that these previous five principles are adhered to and, if not, how any disagreements between students, teachers, parents, and school can be resolved constructively. Those mechanisms for resolution have to be in place *before* students begin programs, not after. Some of the mechanisms include parental consent, mediation, parental notification, and parental access to records.

THE TRUTH IN TESTING LAW: HIGH-STAKES TESTING

Testing is very high stakes. Just ask a high school senior who is taking the SAT, a college premed major trying to get into medical school, or a mechanic trying to pass national standards for advanced engine repair. And as the stakes get higher, the public becomes more wary of the process used to develop, administer, and score tests. And, of course, people always want to know what part a test or score or item plays in the admission process, be it to college or to the Peace Corps.

The Goldilocks Problem: It's the Standards, Dummy!

A few years ago, there was a controversy over testing that is emblematic of testing practices all over the country—just what settles for a pass? New York State requires that all students pass a math test (among others) before being given a diploma, and those who receive a high-enough score receive a Regent's Diploma (kind of like graduating with honors). Anyway, the math test was given; a huge proportion of students failed; and there was, of course, an uproar from teachers, parents, and students. The basic claim was that the items were just too hard, students could not use scratch paper, the instructions were confusing, and on and on. Whether those criticisms are accurate or not, the test was redesigned and readministered, and a huge number passed—far more than—you guessed it—teachers, parents, or students would have thought. The result is, as Susan Ohanian (at http://www.susanohanian.org) calls it, a Goldilocks problem—too hard, then too soft, but never just right.

What this exemplifies is that as testing continues to be a high-stakes activity, there needs to be more accountability than ever on the part of the test givers because the implications for scores that are too high (too few students graduate) or too low (too many unqualified students graduate) are far reaching and very serious.

Almost 30 years ago (1979), New York State Senator Ken LaValle helped ensure that a Truth in Testing law was passed that kind of turned the testing industry upside down. Up until this time, most of the huge test publishers created their tests in a vacuum with very little regulation or scrutiny from the outside. Their efforts were not subject to examination of any kind, and if a test question was lousy or a test lacked content or criterion validity, that was the publisher's business and no one else's. **Truth in Testing** requires that admissions tests given in New York State (such as the SAT test) be available for review of their content and scoring procedures, that the test items be released to the public, and that there be due process for any student accused of cheating.

Well, you can imagine the response of the test publishing companies (and some of it justified). For example, if the test items were made public, that test item would no longer be available to the pool of items from which the test is constructed. Also, the publishers' copyright would be violated—after all, they "own" the items. And, as you know by now, it takes a great deal of effort to create even one item that really works well—both in its power to test the topic as well to assess accurately and fairly the content being sampled. The law would incur a gigantic expense. In the end, although it means a more open approach to testing, it also means a more expensive one for students, because someone has to pay for the extra development time for new items and such, and it also means that each item might never be used again.

The outcome? Well, the past 30 years have found admissions tests still being administered in New York State (and there being no gigantic and unsolvable problems), and the State Board of Education in New York State recently called for all tests to be administered in an open and transparent manner.

FAMILY EDUCATIONAL RIGHTS AND PRIVACY ACT, OR FERPA: WHAT IT IS AND HOW IT WORKS

You know that there is more recorded information that you can shake a stick at on just about every American citizen. And, although much of this is public, much of it is private and open only to the individual or his or her parents or caretakers.

That's the case with school information, and that's the reason for the **Family Educational Rights and Privacy Act** (FERPA; also known as the Buckley Amendment), passed in 1974. The law applies to any public or private elementary, secondary, or postsecondary school and any state or local education agency that receives federal funds. Because almost all public schools and virtually all private schools receive some sort of federal funding, the law applies. It basically says that parents have certain rights to their student's education records, and that these rights transfer to the student when he or she becomes 18 or begins educational programs beyond high school. And, as you might suspect, most of this information has to do with test scores and other assessment outcomes.

In sum, here's what the law says:

1. Parents or students can inspect the student's education records, but schools are not required to provide copies of records unless it is impossible for parents or eligible students to review the records (such as if they had to travel a long distance, which may be the case if rural records are centralized).

2. Parents or eligible students can request that their school correct records that the parents or students think are inaccurate. And, if the school decides not to change a record, a formal hearing could be the next step. If the school still decides not to change the record, then a statement about the discrepancy must be placed in the student's permanent record.

3. Schools must have written permission from the parent or eligible student in order to release any information from a student's education record. But, schools can share records with the following, and for the following reasons:
   a. School officials with legitimate educational interest, such as colleges
   b. Other schools to which a student is transferring
   c. Specified officials for audit or evaluation purposes
   d. Appropriate parties in connection with financial aid to a student
   e. Organizations conducting certain studies for or on behalf of the school
   f. Accrediting organizations
   g. Appropriate parties in compliance with a judicial order or lawfully issued subpoena
   h. Appropriate officials in cases of health and safety emergencies
   i. State and local authorities within a juvenile justice system, pursuant to specific state law

Good idea? Seems like it. No one wants their private information shared with commercial interests, which had been happening. But, there are some not-so-savory aspects to the law as well. First, there's a huge amount of paperwork generated by the implementation of the law. Second, lots of questions were left unanswered by the original law, such as secondary school students' access to college letters of recommendation (the law has since been amended to prohibit this), and concerns were voiced earlier about the Selective Service having access to student records (to be used for recruitment—see the note earlier in this chapter). Even though this is a more than 30-year-old law, it's still in play and still needs to be fine tuned.

ETHICS AND ASSESSMENT: 10 THINGS TO REMEMBER

Almost every professional group that deals with human behavior in any form has a code of ethics to which it suggests its members seriously consider adhering in their everyday work. Whether it be the Society for Research in Child Development, the American Psychological Association, the National Association for the Education of Young Children, or the American Educational Research Association—all of their codes of ethics tend to have the same themes in common.

Almost every institution has a board (called the Human Subjects Committee or HRC at the University of Kansas) whose sole purpose is to review research plans and proposals in order to ensure that the possibility of any ethical violations is minimized. Usually, external funding agencies require a review and a pass from the board in order for the funding to occur. And, many universities also require all research (student, faculty, and other) to be submitted for review. There's a board wherever you go to school or teach—take advantage of it. And, by the way, all of these boards, regardless of their name, fall under the general and generic heading of Institutional Review Boards, or IRBs.

Rather than review each for each organization, we've put together an amalgam of the different points so that we capture the similarities and help provide you with the most important of the rules you need. Even if you never give a test, you'll surely be taking them and need to know this information.

So, here's a nice summary. Note that some of these deal much more directly with assessment, but, because assessment is so often a part of the entire research effort, some of the points deal with the research process as well.

1. Nothing should be done that harms the participants physically, emotionally, or psychologically. All tesing formats and content should be carefully screened to be sure that such threats are eliminated or, if that's not possible, minimized. For example, if you need to ask difficult questions about child abuse or money problems or bad adult relationships, do so with great care and consideration.

2. When behavior is assessed, especially in a research setting, then the test takers should provide their consent. And when children or adults who are incapable of providing such consent are used, then someone who cares for them (a parent, a relative of record, and so forth) should provide that consent. For example, if you are assessing the effectiveness of certain experimental designs on the behavior of adults who are low functioning, you have to get permission from the people who care for these adults or who are legally responsible for their well being.

3. If incentives are used (such as paying people to complete a survey or an interview), the incentives should be reasonable and appropriate. For example, paying an adolescent $100 for 5 minutes of his or her time to talk about drug use is surely not appropriate.

4. Without reservation, test takers' responses should be anonymous. Your research methods instructor can talk with you more about this, but it should be impossible for any outside party to identify a name associated with any of the responses collected.

5. Not only should the research materials be anonymous, but, as the researcher in your testing and assessment activity, you must ensure that the records will be kept in strictest confidentiality.

6. If the collection of assessment information is for research purposes, then the people who are participating should be given an opportunity to know the results of the research and, in some cases, have their individual results explained to them. This is not as important in a school setting because the achievement test scores speak for themselves, but, for standardized and other kinds of tests, this can make a significant difference.

7. But, although you want to share things with participants, you have to be judicious in your reporting. If you are a licensed school psychologist and you are administering a personality test, you want to be careful how much information you share with the child versus how much you share with the parents. You want to be informative and helpful but not provide more information than the child needs to know, because the information may end up being hurtful.

8. Assessment techniques should be used that are appropriate to the purpose of the testing and appropriate to the audience being tested. What this means is that if you can't find the right tool to use, then don't use any.

9. Tests that are constructed under your watch need to have all the qualities of any assessment tool that we recognize to be most important, including reliability, validity, appropriate norms, and the elimination of bias.

10. Finally, what you are doing needs to make sense. Frivolous testing is exploitive and unfair.

SUMMARY

At absolute best, all of the legal issues that surround testing are a challenge. And, in the wisdom of our governance system, there are laws that some of us feel are right on target in terms of being fair, whereas others believe that they are too encroaching upon individual freedoms or even commercial interests. The answers? There are none. Surprised? Don't be—in these complex times, such complex matters need to be addressed by all parties, including test makers, test takers, and those who make the laws, to help ensure that questions of fairness and equity are raised and at least addressed, if not fully answered.

TIME TO PRACTICE

1. Contact a local, state, or federal representative (be it a senator, member of Congress, legislative aide) and ask that person how he or she thinks NCLB has benefited children in the United States. This should take about 4 weeks from the time of inquiry to an answer. Once that amount of time has passed, compare your answers with your classmates.

2. Using the (real bricks and mortar) library or the Internet, find a highly opinionated article in favor of NCLB, and then find one that expresses strong opposition. Compare the two on the major points.

3. What are some of the advantages of IDEA? What does the law have to do with inclusion?

4. What are the relative merits (and demerits) of Truth in Testing laws like the one in New York State?

5. If you were the Director of Testing for the Universe J, what would be five principles on which you would operate to ensure that testing procedures were fair? Don't be afraid to use what you have learned in other chapters, and think broadly.

ANSWERS TO PRACTICE QUESTIONS

1. This one is on your own, and you can e-mail. Call or write a snail mail letter, but be persistent until you get some kind of answer.

2. Another on your own. You should not have to look far to find partisan views.

3. IDEA, foremost, ensures a fair, free, and appropriate education for all students, regardless of their level of disability. There are many other advantages (and some important costs, such as $$$!). Inclusion is an important philosophical principle that no children should be left out of educational opportunities, and IDEA helps ensure that.

4. Among the merits are full disclosure so that the public can see how tests are developed and validated, and what the correct answers are to test items, among others. Some of demerits are that Truth in Testing increases the costs of the test to test takers and, if items are not used again, can threaten the validity of the test.

5. Here are just a few:
   a. Tests should be unbiased.
   b. Test scores should reflect performance accurately.
   c. Tests should be used for placement in such a fashion that it ensures an individual's well being.
   d. Tests should never be used to punish the test taker.
   e. Tests should be used only by qualified personnel.

WANT TO KNOW MORE?

Further Readings

• Aldersley, S. (2002). Least restrictive environment and the courts. *Journal of Deaf Studies and Deaf Education, 7,* 189–199.

Want more history? This paper provides a description and an analysis of how the federal courts in the United States have interpreted the least restrictive environment clause in the Individuals With Disabilities Education Act. It focuses on deaf children and traces the legislation and its impact.

- Crocker, L. (2003). Teaching for the test: Validity, fairness, and moral action. *Educational Measurement: Issues and Practice, 22,* 5–11.

Measurement professionals need to focus their attention on four fundamental areas of measurement research and practice as they relate to NCLB, including improving the methods used to validate test content, expanding the definition of fairness, developing guidelines for the consequences of test use, and preparing teachers for new roles as competent in the assessment area.

- Gallagher, J. J. (2004). No Child Left Behind and gifted education. *Roeper Review, 26,* 121–123.

One of the foremost names in gifted education, Gallagher argues that the increased attention in education demanded by the No Child Left Behind Act can help make the case for differentiated curricula for gifted students, properly trained teachers, and better evaluation tools to be able to measure their advanced skills and learning.

And on the Internet

- Take a look at The National Center for Fair and Open Testing at http://www.fairtest.org/. This site is full of information about standardized testing and is very opinionated in its presentation, but you will certainly learn to identify the important issues surrounding testing.

- Right from the federal government, a summary of the No Child Left Behind law at http://www.ed.gov/nclb/landing .jhtml?src=pb. Like it or not, here's where you need to go to get an accurate accounting of what's involved.

- You have to subscribe for this one and pay, but, at Questia, you can find thousands of articles on thousands of topics, including these on NCLB (at http://www.questia.com/Index.jsp?CRID= no_child_left_behind_ act&OFFID=se1&KEY=nclb).

Appendixes

Snapshots

Appendix A

Your Tests and Measurement Toolkit

Y ou may know all about the information in this appendix, especially if you already have had an introductory statistics course. On the other hand, maybe all of this is new to you, and you need to come up to speed with the rest of your classmates, or you just need a short refresher.

That's what Appendix A is all about. We'll go through an introduction to basic descriptive statistics in Section 1, and then in Section 2 comes an introduction to the normal curve and what distributions of test scores look like. In Section 3, we'll review correlations, which are measures of the relationship between two variables (such as the number of hours studying and test scores).

This appendix is just the facts—very much to the point and less fun than usual (but still fun enough not to bore you to death) ☺.

So, you can read this appendix before you start the course or refer to this appendix as needed. If you need even more basic stat help, you might want to take a look at *Statistics for People Who (Think They) Hate Statistics*, also published by Sage. A significant amount of this appendix is adopted from that book.

SECTION 1: THE BASIC STATS YOU NEED: MEASURES OF AVERAGE AND VARIABILITY

When we have lots of data, such as personality test scores for a group of adults, we need some way to organize and represent them. That's what averages and measures of variability allow us to do.

An **average** is the one value that best represents an entire group of scores. It doesn't matter whether the group of scores is the number correct on a spelling test for 30 fifth graders, the batting percentage of each of the New York Yankees, or the number of people who registered as Democrats or Republicans in the previous election. In all of these examples, groups of data can be summarized using an average. Averages, also called **measures of central tendency**, come in three flavors: the mean, the median, and the mode.

Computing the Mean

The **mean** is the most common type of average. It is the sum of all the values in a group, divided by the number of values in that group. So if you had the spelling scores for 30 fifth graders, you would add up all the scores and get a total, and then divide by the number of students, which is 30.

The formula for computing the mean is shown here

$$\overline{X} = \frac{\Sigma X}{n}$$

where

$\overline{X}$ (called "X bar") is the mean value of the group of scores or the mean.

Σ or the Greek capital letter sigma, is the summation sign, which tells you to add together whatever follows it.

X is each individual score in the group of scores.

n is the size of the sample from which you are computing the mean.

To compute the mean, follow these steps:

1. List the entire set of values in one or more columns. These are all the Xs.

2. Compute the sum or total of all the values.

3. Divide the total or sum by the number of values.

For example, if you needed to compute the average score for 10 students on a spelling test, you would compute a mean for that value. Here is a set of 10 such scores (a perfect score is 20).

Spelling Test Score
15
12
20
18
17
16
18
16
11
7

The mean or average number of correctly spelled words is 15. And, here are the above numbers plugged into the formula.

$$\overline{X} = \frac{\Sigma X}{n} = \frac{15 + 12 + 20 + 18 + 17 + 16 + 18 + 16 + 11 + 7}{10} = \frac{150}{10} = 15$$

Some Things to Remember About the Mean

- The mean is sometimes represented by the letter M and is also called the typical, average, or most central score.

- In the formula, a small n represents the sample size for which the mean is being computed. A large N (like this) would represent the population size.

- The sample mean is the measure of central tendency that most accurately reflects the population mean.

- The mean is like the fulcrum on a seesaw. It's the centermost point where all the values on one side of the mean are equal in weight to all the values on the other side of the mean.

- Finally, the mean is very sensitive to extreme scores. An extreme score can pull the mean in one direction or another and make it less representative of the set of scores and less useful as a measure of central tendency.

Computing the Median

The median is also an average but of a very different kind. The **median** is the midpoint in a set of scores. It's the point at which one half, or 50%, of the scores fall above and one half, or 50%, fall below. It's got some special qualities that we will talk about later in this section, but, for now, let's concentrate on how it is computed. There's no standard formula for computing the median.

To compute the median, follow these steps:

1. List the values in order, either from highest to lowest or lowest to highest.

2. Find the middle-most score. That's the median.

For example, here are 5 SAT verbal scores ordered from highest to lowest.

740

560

550

490

480

There are five values. The middle-most value is 550, and that's the median.

Now, what if the number of values is even? Let's add a value (540) to the list so there are six scores. When there is an even number of values, the median is simply the average between the two middle values. In this case, the middle two cases are 540 and 550. The average of those two values is 545. That's the median for that set of six values.

What if the two middle-most values are the same, such as in the following set of data?

600

550

550

480

Then the median is the same as both of those middle-most values. In this case, it's 550.

Why use the median instead of the mean? For one very good reason. The median is insensitive to extreme scores, whereas the mean is not.

What do we mean by extreme? It's probably easiest to think of an extreme score as one that is very different from the group to which it belongs. For example, in our original list of five scores, shown again here,

740

560

550

490

480

the value 740 is more different from the other five than any other value in the set, and we would consider that an extreme score.

The average or mean of the set of five scores you see above is the sum of the set of five divided by five, which turns out to be 564. On the other hand, the median for this set of five scores is 550.

Given all five values, which is more representative of the group? The value 550, because it clearly lies more in the "middle" of the group, and we like to think about the average as being representative or assuming a central position.

Computing the Mode

The mode is the third and last measure of central tendency we'll cover. It is the most general and least precise measure of central tendency. The **mode** is the value that occurs most frequently, and there is no formula for computing the mode.

To compute the mode, follow these steps:

1. List all the values in a distribution, but list each only once.

2. Tally the number of times that each value occurs.

3. The value that occurs most often is the mode.

For example, here is a set of categories and test score ranges.

Category	Number of Students
Pass High	90
Pass	170
Fail	40

The mode is the value that occurs most frequently, which in the above example is Pass. That's the mode for this distribution.

Understanding Variability

You just learned about different types of averages, what they mean, how they are computed, and when to use them. But when it comes to descriptive statistics and describing the characteristics of a distribution, averages are only half the story. The other half is measures of variability.

In the most simple of terms, **variability** reflects how scores differ from one another. For example, the following set of test scores shows some variability:

98, 86, 84, 88, 94

The following set of scores has the same mean (90) and has less variability than the previous set:

92, 89, 91, 90, 88

And, the next set has no variability at all—the scores do not differ from one another—but it also has the same mean as the other two sets we just showed you.

90, 90, 90, 90, 90

Variability (also called spread or dispersion) can be thought of as a measure of how different scores are from one another. It's even more accurate (and maybe even easier) to think of variability as how different scores are from one particular score. And which score do you think that might be? Well, instead of comparing each score to every other score in a distribution, the one score that could be used as a comparison is—that's right—the mean. So variability becomes a measure of how much each score in a group of scores differs from the mean.

Remember what you already know about computing averages—that an average is a representative score in a set of scores. Now, add your new knowledge about variability—that it reflects how different scores are from one another. Each is an important descriptive statistic. Together, these two (average and variability) can be used to describe the characteristics of a distribution and show how distributions differ from one another.

The range, the standard deviation, and the variance are the most commonly used measures of variability.

Computing the Range

The **range** gives you an idea of how far apart scores are from one another and is computed simply by subtracting the lowest score in a distribution from the highest score in the distribution.

In general, the formula for the range is

$$r = h - l$$

where

r = the range

h = is the highest score in the data set

l = is the lowest score in the data set

Take the following set of scores, for example (shown here in descending order):

$$98, 86, 77, 56, 48$$

In this example, $98 - 48 = 50$. The range is 50.

Computing the Standard Deviation

Now we get to the most frequently used measure of variability, the **standard deviation**, representing the average amount of variability in a set of scores. In practical terms, it's the average distance from the mean. The larger the standard deviation, the larger the average distance each data point is from the mean of the distribution.

Here's the formula for computing the standard deviation.

$$s = \sqrt{\frac{\sum(X - \overline{X})^2}{n-1}}$$

where

s = the standard deviation

$\sum$ = is sigma, which tells you to find the sum of what follows

$\overline{X}$ = is the mean of all the scores

n = is the sample size

This formula finds the difference between each individual score and the mean $(X - \overline{X})$, squares each difference, and sums them all together. Then it divides the sum by the size of the sample (minus 1) and takes the square root of the result. As you can see, and as we mentioned earlier, the standard deviation is an average deviation from the mean.

Here are the data we'll use (with achievement test scores ranging from 50–100) in the following step-by-step explanation of how to compute the standard deviation.

Student	Math Test Score
1	67
2	65
3	78
4	80
5	82
6	67
7	91
8	89
9	77
10	84

1. List each score. It doesn't matter whether the scores are in any particular order.

2. Compute the mean of the group.

3. Subtract the mean from each score as you can see here.

Student	Math Test Score	$\bar{X}$	$X-\bar{X}$
1	67	78	−11
2	65	78	−13
3	78	78	0
4	80	78	2
5	82	78	4
6	67	78	−11
7	91	78	13
8	89	78	11
9	77	78	−1
10	84	78	6

4. Square each individual difference. The result is the column marked $(X - \bar{X})^2$:

Student	Math Test Score	$\bar{X}$	$X-\bar{X}$	$(X-\bar{X})^2$
1	67	78	−11	121
2	65	78	−13	169
3	78	78	0	0
4	80	78	2	4
5	82	78	4	16
6	67	78	−11	121
7	91	78	13	169
8	89	78	11	121
9	77	78	−1	1
10	84	78	6	36
			Sum = 0	Sum = 758

5. Sum all the squared deviations about the mean. As you can see above, the total is 758.

6. Divide the sum by $n-1$, or $10-1 = 9$, so then $758/9 = 84.22$.

7. Compute the square root of 84.22, which is 9.18. That is the standard deviation for this set of 10 scores.

What we now know from these results is that each score in this distribution differs from the mean by an average of 9.18 points.

Computing the Variance

Here comes another measure of variability and a nice surprise. If you know the standard deviation of a set of scores and you can square a number, you can easily compute the variance of that same set of scores. This third measure of variability, the **variance**, is simply the standard deviation squared.

In other words, it's the same formula you saw earlier, without the square root bracket as follows:

$$s^2 = \frac{\sum(X-\overline{X})^2}{n-1}$$

If you take the standard deviation and never complete the last step (taking the square root), you have the variance. In other words, $s^2 = s \times s$, or the variance equals the standard deviation times itself (or squared). In our earlier example, where the standard deviation was equal to 9.18, the variance is equal to 9.18^2 or 84.22.

Some Things to Remember About
the Standard Deviation and Variance

• The standard deviation is computed as the average distance from the mean. So, you will need to first compute the mean as a measure of central tendency. Don't fool around with the median or the mode in trying to compute the standard deviation.

• The larger the standard deviation, the more spread out the values are, and the more different they are from one another.

• Just like the mean, the standard deviation is sensitive to extreme scores. When you are computing the standard deviation of a sample and you have extreme scores, note that somewhere in your written report.

- If s = 0, there is absolutely no variability in the set of scores, and they are essentially identical in value. This will rarely happen.

SECTION 2: THE NORMAL CURVE (A.K.A. THE BELL-SHAPED CURVE)

What is a normal curve? The **normal curve** (also called a **bell-shaped curve**, or bell curve) is a visual representation of a distribution of scores that has three characteristics as shown in Figure A.1.

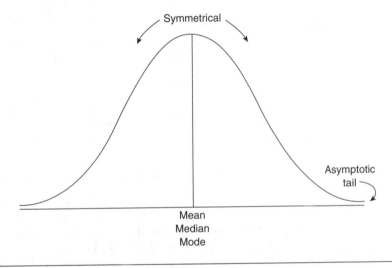

Figure A.1   The Normal, or Bell-Shaped, Curve

Some things to note about the normal curve.

First, the normal curve represents a distribution of values where the mean, median, and mode are equal to one another. If the median and the mean are different, then the distribution is skewed in one direction or the other. The normal curve is not skewed. It's got a nice hump (only one), and that hump is right in the middle.

Second, the normal curve is perfectly symmetrical about the mean. If you fold one half of the curve along its center line, the two halves would fit perfectly on each other. They are identical. One-half of the curve is a mirror image of the other.

Finally (and get ready for a mouthful), the tails of the normal curve are **asymptotic**—a big word. What it means is that they come closer and closer to the horizontal axis, but never touch.

More Normal Curve 101

You already know the three main characteristics that make a curve normal or make it appear bell shaped, but there's more to it than that. Take a look at the curve in Figure A.2.

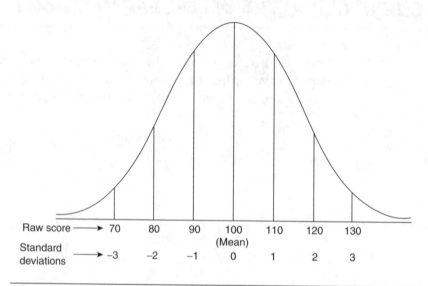

Figure A.2   A Normal Curve Divided Into Different Sections

The distribution represented here has a mean of 100 and a standard deviation of 10. We've added numbers across the x-axis that represent the distance in standard deviations from the mean for this distribution. You can see that the x-axis (representing the scores in the distribution) is marked from 70 through 130 in increments of 10 (which is the standard deviation for the distribution), the value of 1 standard deviation.

A quick review tells us that this distribution has a mean of 100 and a standard deviation of 10. Each vertical line within the curve separates the curve into a section, and each section is bound by particular scores. For example, the first section to the right of the mean of 100 is bound by the scores 100 and 110, representing 1 standard deviation from the mean (which is 100).

And below each raw score (70, 80, 90, 100, 110, 120, and 130), you'll find a corresponding standard deviation (–3, –2, –1, 0, +1, +2, and +3). As you may have figured out already, each standard deviation in our example is 10 points. So 1 standard deviation from the mean (which is 100) is the mean plus 10 points, or 110.

If we extend this argument further, then you should be able to see how the range of scores represented by a normal distribution with a mean of 100 and a standard deviation of 10 is 70 through 130 (which includes −3 to +3 standard deviations).

Now here's a big fact that is always true about normal distributions, means, and standard deviations: For any distribution of scores (regardless of the value of the mean and standard deviation), if the scores are distributed normally, almost 100% of the scores will fit between −3 and +3 standard deviations from the mean. This is very important, because it applies to all normal distributions. Because the rule does apply (once again, regardless of the value of the mean or standard deviation), distributions can be compared with one another.

With that said, we'll extend our argument a bit more. If the distribution of scores is normal, we can also say that between different points along the x-axis (such as between the mean and 1 standard deviation), a certain percentage of cases will fall. In fact, between the mean and 1 standard deviation above the mean (which is 110), about 34% (actually 34.13%) of all cases in the distribution of scores will fall.

Want to go further? Take a look at Figure A.3. Here you can see the same normal curve in all its glory (the mean equals 100 and the standard deviation equals 10)—and the percentage of cases that we would expect to fall within the boundaries defined by the mean and standard deviation.

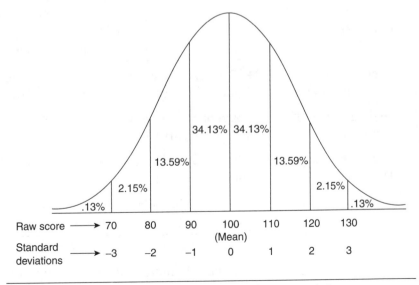

Figure A.3   Distribution of Cases Under the Normal Curve

Here's what we can conclude.

The distance between ...	Includes	And the scores that are included (if the mean = 100 and the standard deviation = 10) are from
The mean and 1 standard deviation	34.13% of all the cases under the curve	100 to 110
1 and 2 standard deviations	13.59% of all the cases under the curve	110 to 120
2 and 3 standard deviations	2.15% of all the cases under the curve	120 to 130
3 standard deviations beyond and above	0.13% of all the cases under the curve	Above 130

If you add up all the values in either half of the normal curve, guess what you get? That's right, 50%. Why? The distance between the mean and all the scores to the right of the mean underneath the normal curve includes 50% of all the scores.

And because the curve is symmetrical about its central axis (each half is a mirror image of the other), the two halves together represent 100% of all the scores.

Now let's extend the same logic to the scores to the left of the mean of 100.

The distance between ...	Includes	And the scores that are included (if the mean = 100 and the standard deviation = 10) are from
The mean and −1 standard deviation	34.13% of all the cases under the curve	90 to 100
−1 and −2 standard deviations	13.59% of all the cases under the curve	80 to 90
−2 and −3 standard deviations	2.15% of all the cases under the curve	70 to 80
−3 standard deviations and below	0.13% of all the cases under the curve	Below 70

Now, be sure to keep in mind that we are using a mean of 100 and a standard deviation of 10 only as sample figures for a particular example. Obviously, not all distributions have a mean of 100 and a standard deviation of 10.

All of this is pretty neat, especially when you consider that the values of 34.13% and 13.59% and so on are absolutely independent of the actual values of the mean and the standard deviation. The value is 34% because of the shape of the curve, not because of the value of any of the scores in the distribution or the value of the mean or standard deviation.

In our example, this means that (roughly) 68% (34.13% doubled) of the scores fall between the raw score values of 90 and 110. What about the other 32%? Good question. One half (16%, or 13.59% + 2.15% + 0.13%) falls above (to the right of) 1 standard deviation above the mean, and one half falls below (to the left of) 1 standard deviation below the mean.

And because the curve slopes, and the amount of area decreases as you move farther away from the mean, it is no surprise that the likelihood that a score will fall more toward the extremes of the distribution is less than the likelihood that it will fall toward the middle. That's why the curve has a bump in the middle and is not skewed in either direction.

The value of all this? Simple. In any set of test scores that is normally distributed, we can assume that there are probabilities of occurring associated with specific scores. For example, the probability of any one student getting a 110 or below is about 84% or 34.13% + 13.59%. And, these probabilities can be used as benchmarks to help us understand how likely (or unlikely) it is that a particular outcome will occur.

SECTION 3: WHAT ARE CORRELATIONS ALL ABOUT?

Measures of central tendency and measures of variability are not the only descriptive statistics that we are interested in using to get a picture of what a set of scores looks like. You have already learned that knowing the values of the one most representative score (central tendency) and a measure of spread or dispersion (variability) is critical for describing the characteristics of a distribution.

However, sometimes we are just as interested in the relationship between variables—or to be more precise, how the value of one variable changes when the value of another variable changes. The way we express this interest is through the computation of a simple correlation coefficient—very important in the calculation of reliability coefficients of all sorts (test-retest, etc.). And, an important part of test development and use, as you learned about in Chapter 4, is validity, and validity coefficients are almost always expressed as correlations.

A **correlation coefficient** is a numerical index that reflects the relationship between two variables. The value of this descriptive statistic ranges between –1 and +1. A correlation between two variables is sometimes referred to as a bivariate (for two variables) correlation, also called the Pearson product-moment correlation.

Types of Correlation Coefficients: Flavor 1 and Flavor 2

A correlation reflects the dynamic quality of the relationship between variables. In doing so, it allows us to understand whether variables tend to move in the same or opposite directions when they change. If variables change in the same direction, the correlation is called a **direct correlation** or a **positive correlation**. If variables change in opposite directions, the correlation is called an **indirect correlation** or a **negative correlation**. Table A.1 shows a summary of these relationships.

TABLE A.1	**Types of Correlations and the Corresponding Relationship Between Variables**			
What Happens to Variable X	*What Happens to Variable Y*	*Type of Correlation*	*Value*	*Example*
X increases in value	Y increases in value	Direct or positive	Positive, ranging from .00 to +1.00	The more time you spend studying, the higher your test score will be.
X decreases in value	Y decreases in value	Direct or positive	Positive, ranging from .00 to +1.00	The less money you put in the bank, the less interest you will earn.
X increases in value	Y decreases in value	Indirect or Negative	Negative, ranging from –1.00 to .00	The more you exercise, the less you will weigh.
X decreases in value	Y increases in value	Indirect or Negative	Negative, ranging from –1.00 to .00	The less time you take to complete a test, the fewer you'll get right.

Now, keep in mind that the examples in the table reflect generalities. For example, regarding time to completion and the number of items correct on a test: In general, the less time that is taken on a test, the lower the score.

Things to Remember About Correlations

- A correlation can range in value from −1 to +1.

- The absolute value of the coefficient reflects the strength of the correlation. So a correlation of −.70 is stronger than a correlation of +.50. One of the mistakes frequently made regarding correlation coefficients is when students assume that a direct or positive correlation is always stronger (i.e., "better") than an indirect or negative correlation because of the sign and nothing else.

- A correlation always reflects the situation where there are at least two data points (or variables) per case.

- Another easy mistake is to assign a value judgment to the sign of the correlation. Many students assume that a negative relationship is not good and a positive one is good. That's why, instead of using the terms *negative* and *positive*, the terms *indirect* and *direct* communicate meaning more clearly.

The Pearson product-moment correlation coefficient is represented by the small letter *r*, with a subscript representing the variables that are being correlated. For example,

r_{xy} = the correlation between variable X and variable Y

$r_{weight \cdot height}$ = is the correlation between weight and height

$r_{SAT \cdot GPA}$ = is the correlation between SAT score and grade point average (GPA)

Computing a Simple Correlation Coefficient

The computational formula for the simple Pearson product-moment correlation coefficient between a variable labeled X and a variable labeled Y is shown here:

$$r_{xy} = \frac{n\Sigma XY - \Sigma X \Sigma Y}{\sqrt{[n\Sigma X^2 - (\Sigma X)^2][n\Sigma Y^2 - (\Sigma Y)^2]}}$$

where

r_{xy} = the correlation coefficient between X and Y

n = is the size of the sample

X = is the individual's score on the X variable

Y = is the individual's score on the Y variable

XY = is the product of each X score times its corresponding Y score

X^2 = is the individual X score, squared

Y^2 = is the individual Y score, squared

Here are some test scores (a screening test for language skills in young children is the X variable and a screening test for physical skills in young children is the Y variable) we will use in this example.

	Language Skills (X)	Physical Skills (Y)	X^2	Y^2	XY
	2	3	4	9	6
	4	2	16	4	8
	5	6	25	36	30
	6	5	36	25	30
	4	3	16	9	12
	7	6	49	36	42
	8	5	64	25	40
	5	4	25	16	20
	6	4	36	16	24
	7	5	49	25	35
Sum or Σ	54	43	320	201	247

Before we plug the numbers in, let's make sure you understand what each one represents.

ΣX, or the sum of all the X values, is 54

ΣY, or the sum of all the Y values, is 43

ΣX^2, or the sum of each X value squared, is 320

ΣY^2, or the sum of each Y value squared, is 201

ΣXY, or the sum of the products of X and Y, is 247

Here are the steps in computing the **correlation coefficient**.

1. List the two values for each participant. You should do this in a column format so as not to get confused.

2. Compute the sum of all the X values, and compute the sum of all the Y values.

3. Square each of the X values, and square each of the Y values.

4. Find the sum of the XY products.

You can see the answer here:

$$r_{xy} = \frac{(10 \times 247) - (54 \times 43)}{\sqrt{[(10 \times 320) - 54^2][(10 \times 201) - 43^2]}}$$

$$r_{xy} = \frac{148}{213.83} = .692$$

The correlation between scores on the language screening test and scores on the physical skills screening test is .692.

Bunches of Correlations: The Correlation Matrix

What happens if you have more than two variables, such as three measures of overall school performance? How are the correlations illustrated? Use a correlation matrix like the one shown below—a simple and elegant solution.

	Math Score	Participation in Extracurricular Activities	SAT Scores
Math Score	1.00	.71	.84
Participation in Extracurricular Activities	.71	1.00	.59
SAT Scores	.84	.59	1.00

As you can see, there are three variables in the matrix: math score, participation in extracurricular activities (on a scale from 1 through 10), and SAT scores.

For each pair of variables, there is a correlation coefficient. For example, the correlation between math scores and SAT score is .84.

In such a matrix (with three variables), there are always $3!/(3–2)!2!$, or three things taken two at a time for a total of three correlation coefficients. Variables correlate perfectly with themselves (those are the 1.00 values down the diagonal), and because the correlation between math score and SAT scores is the same as the correlation between SAT scores and math score, the matrix creates a mirror image of itself.

You will see such matrices (the plural of matrix) when you read journal articles that use correlations to describe the relationship between several variables, such as tests taken on separate occasions.

Understanding What the Correlation Coefficient Means

Well, we have this numerical index of the relationship between two variables, and we know that the higher the value of the correlation (regardless of its sign), the stronger the relationship is. But because the correlation coefficient is a value that is not directly tied to the value of an outcome, just how can we interpret it and make it a more meaningful indicator of a relationship?

Here are different ways to look at the interpretation of that simple r_{xy}.

Using Your Rule-of-Thumb Rule

Perhaps the easiest (but not the most informative) way to interpret the value of a correlation coefficient is by eyeballing it and using the information here to make a decision.

Size of the Correlation Coefficient	General Interpretation
8 to 1.0	Very strong relationship
.6 to .8	Strong relationship
.4 to .6	Moderate relationship
.2 to .4	Weak relationship
0 to .2	Weak or no relationship

So if the correlation between two variables is .5, you could safely conclude that the relationship is a moderate one—not strong, but certainly not weak enough to say that the variables in question don't share anything in common.

This eyeball method is perfectly acceptable for a quick assessment of the strength of the relationship between variables, such as a description in a research report. But since this rule of thumb does depend on a subjective judgment (of what's "strong" or "weak"), we would like a more precise method. That's what we'll look at now.

A Determined Effort: Squaring the Correlation Coefficient

Here's the much more precise way to interpret the correlation coefficient: computing the coefficient of determination. The coefficient of determination is the percentage of variance in one variable that is accounted for by the variance in the other variable.

We already pointed out how variables that share something in common tend to be correlated with one another. If we correlated math and English grades for 100 fifth-grade students, we would find the correlation to be moderately strong because many of the reasons why children do well (or don't do well) in math tend to be the same reasons why they do well (or don't do well) in English. The number of hours they study, how bright they are, how interested their parents are in their schoolwork, the number of books they have at home, and more are all related to both math and English performance and account for differences between children (and that's where the variability comes in).

The more these two variables share in common, the more they will be related. These two variables share variability—or the reason why children differ from one another. And on the whole, the brighter child who studies more will do better.

To determine exactly how much of the variance in one variable can be accounted for by the variance in another variable, the **coefficient of determination** is computed by squaring the correlation coefficient.

For example, if the correlation between GPA and number of hours of study time is .70 (or $r_{GPA \bullet time} = .70$), then the coefficient of determination, represented by $r^2_{GPA \bullet time}$, is $.7^2$, or .49. This means that 49% of the variance in GPA can be explained by the variance in studying time. And the stronger the correlation, the more variance can be explained (which only makes good sense). The more two variables share in common (such as good study habits, knowledge of what's expected in class, and lack of fatigue), the more information about performance on one score can be explained by the other score.

However, if 49% of the variance can be explained, this means that 51% cannot—so even for a strong correlation of .70, many of the reasons why scores on these variables tend to be different from one another goes unexplained. This amount of unexplained variance is called the **coefficient of alienation.**

Appendix B

The Guide to (Almost) Every Test in the Universe

O K, not every test, but just about every one that you will need.

There are several places where you can find information about the tests mentioned in this book and the thousands of other tests that are available.

First, there are always the volumes and volumes of information available in the library, including professional journals and books.

For example, here's an article about the MMPI:

Barthlow, D. L., Graham, J. R., Ben-Porath, Y. S., Tellegen, A., & McNulty, J. L. (2002). The appropriateness of the MMPI-2 K correction. *Assessment, 9,* 219–229.

and here's an online article from the *Wall Street Journal* Web site about the Graduate Record Exams:

http://www.collegejournal.com/exams/gre_about.html

I'm sure you know how to use a basic search engine to search the Internet for what you might need.

And, if you enjoy big, thick, expensive books, you might try

Plake, B. S., Impara, J. C., & Spies, R. A. (2003). *The fifteenth mental measurements yearbook.* Lincoln, NE: Buros Institute for Mental Measurements.

It's also called the MMY, is about 1,000 pages, and costs about $200.

But, you know where else you can find this and more information? That's right, the online site for the MMY. In fact, this most useful of all sources, the MMY is available online through the Buros Center for Mental Measurements at the University of Nebraska, which you can find at

http://www.unl.edu/buros/

shown in Figure B.1.

This site can be used to get all kinds of information about tests, including helping you find a particular test for a particular purpose, find test reviews, and, of course, find out how you can purchase a test when the time comes.

The Buros Institute covers 18 categories of testing with hundreds of tests in each category:

- Achievement
- Behavior Assessment
- Developmental
- Education
- English and Language
- Fine Arts
- Foreign Languages
- Intelligence and General Aptitude
- Mathematics
- Miscellaneous
- Neuropsychological
- Personality
- Reading
- Science
- Sensory-Motor
- Social Studies
- Speech and Hearing
- Vocations

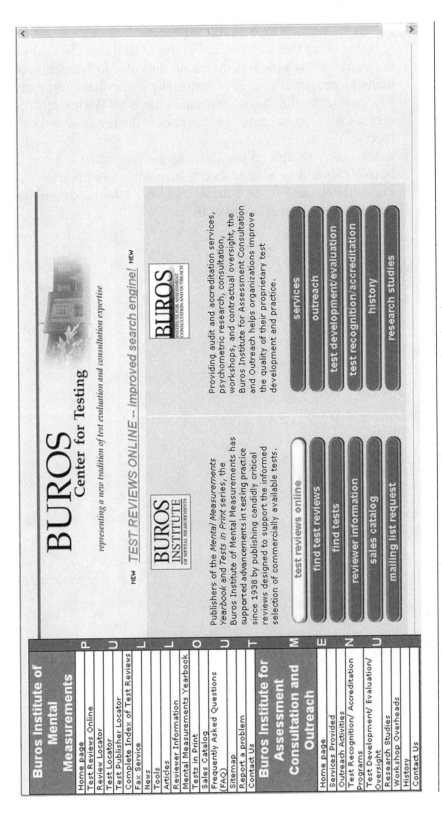

Figure B.1 Buros Center for Mental Measurements at the University of Nebraska

343

How's that for a nice bunch of choices?

If you go to this site, you are going to find that the cost of each online review is $15, and there's no discount for students. But for many of you, your college or university subscribes to this site, and you can get to the Buros Institute's online MMY through the university's library system so you can review the tests you want for free (sort of).

You won't be able to use the URL or Web address given above, but you should be able to find it on your main library's Web site under databases, or, of course, call and ask the original search engine—your reference librarian.

GLOSSARY

Achievement Test

A test that assesses knowledge in a particular content area.

Alternative

The part of a multiple-choice question that can be used to complete the stem or answer the question.

Aptitude Test

A test that evaluates an individual's potential.

Asymptotic

The quality of the normal curve such that the tails never touch.

Average

The most representative score in a set of scores.

Basal Age

The lowest point on an intelligence test where the test taker can pass two consecutive terms that are of equal difficulty.

Bell-Shaped Curve

A distribution of scores that is symmetrical about the mean, median, and mode and has asymptotic tails.

Ceiling Age

The point on an intelligence test where at least three out of four items are missed in succession.

Closed Interview

An interview consisting of predefined questions that are highly structured (*see* Fixed Response Interview).

Coefficient of Alienation

The proportion of variance unaccounted for in the relationship between two variables.

Coefficient of Determination

The proportion of variance accounted for in the relationship between two variables.

Componential Intelligence

A type of intelligence that focuses on the structures that underlie intelligent behavior including the acquisition of knowledge.

Concurrent Validity

A type of validity that examines how well a test outcome is consistent with a criterion that occurs in the present.

Consequential Validity

How tests are used and how their results are interpreted.

Construct Validity

A type of validity that examines how well a test score reflects an underlying construct.

Content Validity

A type of validity where the test items sample the universe of items for which the test is designed.

Content-Referenced Test

A test that focuses on the mastery of a particular content.

Contextual Intelligence

A type of intelligence that focuses on behavior within the context which it occurs and involves adaptation to the environment.

Conversational Interview

See Unstructured Interview

Correct Alternative

The alternative in a multiple-choice question that is correct.

Correlation Coefficient

A numerical index that reflects the relationship between two variables.

Correlation Matrix

A set of correlation coefficients.

Criterion Based or Criterion-Referenced Test

One where there is a predefined level of performance used for evaluation.

Criterion Contamination

When a criterion variable is related to what is being measured.

Criterion Validity

The property of a test hat reflects a set of abilities in a current or future setting.

Criterion-Referenced Test

The use of a specific criterion or level of performance to evaluate an individual's performance.

Cronbach's Alpha or Coefficient Alpha

A measure on internal consistency.

Crystallized Intelligence

The type of intelligence which involves the acquisition of information.

Decile

The first 10 percentile ranks.

Difficulty Index

A measure of difficult a test item is.

Direct Correlation

A positive correlation where the values of both variables change in the same direction.

Discrimination Index

A measure of how well an individual test item discriminates between those who scored high on a test and those who scored low.

Distracters

Alternatives in a multiple-choice question that are not correct.

Education of Handicapped Children Act

A law signed in 1975 by Gerald Ford that guarantees that all children, regardless of disability, have the right to a free and appropriate public education. Now known as the Individuals With Disabilities Education Act or IDEA.

Error Score

The difference between a true score and the observed score.

Essay Items

Items where the test taker writes a multi-sentence response to the question.

Experiential Intelligence

A type of intelligence that focuses on behavior based on experiences.

Factor

A collection of variables that are related to one another.

Factor Analysis

A statistical technique that examines at the relationship between a group of variables.

Family Educational Rights and Privacy Act (FERPA)

A federal law which protects the privacy of students and their test results.

Fixed Response Interview

Another term for a closed interview.

Fluid Intelligence

The type of intelligence that reflects problem-solving ability.

General Interview

An interview that is restricted to a certain type and content of questions but not asked in any particular order.

General-Factor Theory

A theory about intelligence that proposes a single factor is responsible for individual differences in intelligence.

Guided Interview

An interview where the interviewer guides the interviewee in a particular direction.

Highly Structured Interview

An interview where the questions (and the directions) are predefined.

Indirect Correlation

A negative correlation where the values of variables move in opposite directions.

Individualized Education Program

A component of public law 94-152A; written plan of educational goals and strategies for children who are referred for special programs.

Individuals With Disabilities Education Act (IDEA)

A federal law that guarantees a free and appropriate education for all children regardless of level of disability.

Intelligence Test

A test that measures intelligence (a very broadly defined construct).

Internal Consistency Reliability

A type of reliability that examines the one-dimensional nature of an assessment tool.

Interrater Reliability

A type of reliability that examines the consistency of raters.

Interval Level of Measurement

A measurement system that assigns a value to an outcome that is based on some underlying continuum and has equal intervals.

Interview

A set of questions that elicits answers about material that is not accessible though more traditional assessment techniques.

Item Analysis

A method for analyzing the characteristics of a test item.

Item Response Theory (IRT)

A method that is used to examine test responses by examining patterns of responses, rather than partial or total scores.

Key

The correct answer to a test question.

Least Restrictive Environment (LRE)

An environment that places the least restrictions on a child with disabilities.

Level of Measurement

The amount of information provided by the outcome measure.

Matching Items

Items where premises are matched with the correct option.

Mean

A type of average where scores are summed and divided by the number of scores.

Measurement

The assignment of labels to outcomes.

Measures of Central Tendency

The mean, median, and mode.

Median

The point at which 50% of the cases in a distribution fall below and 50% fall above.

Method Error

Error due to differences in test administration.

Mode

The most frequently occurring score in a distribution.

Multilevel Survey Batteries

Achievement tests that test material at more than one level and in several different topic areas at once.

Multiple Choice

Items where there are several alternatives from which to choose.

Multiple Intelligences (MI)

A viewpoint that intelligence consists of independent types of intelligence such as kinesthetic and musical.

Multitrait-Multimethod Matrix

A method of determining construct validity that uses multiple traits and multiple methods.

Negative Correlation

A value that ranges from 0 to –1 and reflects the indirect relationship between two variables.

No Child Left Behind Act (NCLB)

A federal law that focuses on academic achievement in the elementary grades.

Nominal Level of Measurement

A measurement system where there are differences in quality rather than quantity.

Nondirective Interview

An interview where there are few prewritten questions; also called an unguided interview.

Normal Curve

Bell-shaped curve.

Normalized Standard Score

A score that belongs to a normal distribution.

Norms

A set of scores that represent a collection of individual performances.

Norm-Referenced Scores

Scores which have meaning when compared to each other.

Norm-Referenced Test

A test where an individual's test performance is compared to the test performance of other individuals.

Objective Personality Test

A test that has very clear and unambiguous questions, stimuli, or techniques for measuring personality traits.

Observed Score

The score that is recorded or observed.

Open-Ended Essay Question

An item where there are no restrictions on the response, including the amount of time allowed to finish.

Open-Ended Response

A response which allows the individual to elaborate upon his or her response.

Options

The item in a matching item that is matched with a premise.

Ordinal Level of Measurement

A measurement system that describes how variables can be ordered along some type of continuum.

Parallel Forms Reliability

A type of reliability that examines the consistency across different forms of the same test.

Pearson Product-Moment Correlation

See Correlation Coefficient

Percentile

The point in a distribution below which a percentage of scores fall; also called a percentile score.

Personality Test

A test that measures enduring traits and characteristics of an individual.

Personality Trait

An enduing quality like being shy or outgoing.

Personality Type

A constellation of traits and characteristics.

Portfolio

A collection of work that shows efforts, progress, and accomplishment in one or more areas.

Positive Correlation

A value that ranges from 0 to 1 and reflects the direct relationship between two variables.

Predictive Coefficient

The correlation of a test with a criterion in the future.

Predictive Validity

A type of validity that examines how well a test outcome is consistent with a criterion that occurs in the future.

Premise

The term in a matching item that is matched with options.

Primary Mental Abilities Test

A test of intelligence that focuses on a set of primary abilities that reflect a general notion of intelligence.

Projective Personality Test

Test that has ambiguous or unclear stimuli.

Q1

The 25th percentile; also called the first quartile.

Q2

The median; also called the 50th percentile.

Q3

The 75th percentile; also called the third quartile.

Range

The highest minus the lowest score and a gross measure of variability.

Ratio Level of Measurement

A measurement system is that includes an absolute zero corresponding to an absence of the trait or characteristic being measured.

Raw Score

The observed or initial score that results from an assessment.

Reliability

The quality of a test such that it produces consistent scores.

Scales of Measurement

Different ways of categorizing measurement outcomes.

Short Answer and Completion Items

Items that are short in structure and require a short answer as well.

Spearman-Brown Formula

A measure of reliability used to correct for the computation of split-half reliability coefficient.

Split-Half Reliability Coefficient

A measure of internal consistency.

Standard Deviation

The average deviation from the mean.

Standard Error of Measurement (SEM)

A simple measure of how much observed scores vary from a true score.

Standard Score

A type of score that uses a common metric.

Standardized Test

A test that has undergone extensive test development including the writing and rewriting of items, hundreds of administrations, the development of reliability and validity data, and the development of norms.

Stanines

One of nine equal segments in a normal distribution.

Stem

The part of a multiple-choice question that sets the premise for the question.

Supply Item

A short answer item in the form of a question.

T score

A standard score that has a mean of 50 and a standard deviation of 10.

Table of Specifications

A grid (with either one or two dimensions) that serves as a guide to the construction of an achievement test.

Teacher-Made Test

A test constructed by a teacher (Duh!).

Test

A tool that assesses an outcome.

Test Bias

When test scores vary across different groups because of factors that are unrelated to the purpose of the test.

Test Fairness

The degree to which a test fairly assess an outcome independent of traits and characteristics of the test taker unrelated to the focus of the test.

Test-Retest Reliability

Reliability that examines consistency over time.

Trait Error

Error due to differences in an individual.

Triarchic Theory of Intelligence

A theory of intelligence that consists of componential intelligence, experiential intelligence, and contextual intelligence.

True Score

A theoretical score which represents an individual's typical level of performance.

True-False Items

An item with two possible answers, one of which is correct.

Truth in Testing

A law first passed in New York State that guarantees access to tests and their results.

Unguided Interview

See Nondirective Interview

Unstructured Interview

The type of interview where specific questions are not predetermined, but the interviewee is allowed to generate the direction in which the interview goes, with guidance from the interviewer; also called a conversational interview.

Validity

The quality of a test such that it measures what it is supposed to do.

Variability

The amount of spread or dispersion in a set of scores.

Variable

Anything that can take on more than one value.

Variance

The square of the standard deviation, and another measure of a distribution's spread or dispersion.

Vocational or Career Test

A test that assesses interest in particular vocations or careers.

z score

The number of standard deviations between a raw score and the mean.

REFERENCES

Bloom, B. S. (Ed.) (1956). *Taxonomy of educational objectives: The classification of educational goals: Handbook I: Cognitive domain.* New York: Longmans, Green.

Burkhardt, K., Loxton, H., & Muris, P. (2003). Fears and fearfulness in South African children. *Behaviour Change, 20*(2), 94–102.

Hill, J., Brooks Gunn, J., & Waldfogel, J. (2003). Sustained effects of high participation in an early intervention for low-birth-weight premature infants. *Developmental Psychology, 39*(4), 730–744.

McCarney, S. B., & Arthaud, T. J. (1998). *Emotional or Behavior Disorder Scale–Revised.* Columbia, MO: Hawthorne Educational Services.

Robertson, G. J. (1990). A practical model for test development. In C. R. Reynolds & R. W. Kamphaus (Eds.), *Handbook of psychological and educational assessment of children: Intelligence and achievement* (pp. 62–85). New York: Guilford.

Verhaeghe, R., Mak, R., VanMaele, G., Kornitzer, M., & De Backer, G. (2003). Job stress among middle aged health care workers and its relation to sickness absence. *Stress and Health: Journal of the International Society for the Investigation of Stress, 19*(5), 265–274.

INDEX

ABOUT THE AUTHOR

Neil J. Salkind has been teaching at the University of Kansas for 30 years in the Department of Psychology and Research in Education with a courtesy appointment in the Department of Human Development and Family Life. He regularly teaches courses in developmental theories, life-span development, statistics, and research methods. He received his PhD in human development from the University of Maryland. He has published more than 80 professional papers and is the author of several college-level textbooks, including *Child Development, Exploring Research,* and *Introduction to Theories of Human Development* (Sage, 2004). He was editor of *Child Development Abstracts and Bibliography* from 1989 through 2002. He is active in the Society for Research in Child Development and is an active writer in the trade area. He lives in Lawrence, Kansas, in a big old house that always needs attention. His hobbies include cooking, masters swimming, restoring an ancient Volvo P1800, and collecting books and reading them.